Bridging the Gap Between Asset/Capacity Building and Needs Assessment

To my beloved sister, June Altschuld (1927–2013), and her courageous battle against the insidious nature of Parkinson's disease.

Bridging the Gap Between Asset/Capacity Building and Needs Assessment

Concepts and Practical Applications

James W. Altschuld

The Ohio State University

Los Angeles | London | New Delhi
Singapore | Washington DC

Los Angeles | London | New Delhi
Singapore | Washington DC

FOR INFORMATION:

SAGE Publications, Inc.
2455 Teller Road
Thousand Oaks, California 91320
E-mail: order@sagepub.com

SAGE Publications Ltd.
1 Oliver's Yard
55 City Road
London EC1Y 1SP
United Kingdom

SAGE Publications India Pvt. Ltd.
B 1/I 1 Mohan Cooperative Industrial Area
Mathura Road, New Delhi 110 044
India

SAGE Publications Asia-Pacific Pte. Ltd.
3 Church Street
#10-04 Samsung Hub
Singapore 049483

Printed in the United States of America

Library of Congress Cataloging-in-Publication Data

Altschuld, James W.

Bridging the gap between asset/capacity building and needs assessment : concepts and practical applications / James W. Altschuld, The Ohio State University.

pages cm
Includes bibliographical references and index.

ISBN 978-1-4522-2019-2 (pbk.)
ISBN 978-1-4833-1113-5 (web pdf)

1. Evaluation research (Social action programs)
2. Needs assessment. 3. Strategic planning. 4. Social planning. 5. Institution building. I. Title.

H62.A4595 2014
658.4′012—dc23   2013031694

This book is printed on acid-free paper.

Acquisitions Editor: Vicki Knight
Associate Editor: Kalie Koscielak
Assistant Editor: Katie Guarino
Editorial Assistant: Jessica Miller
Production Editor: Libby Larson
Copy Editor: Melinda Masson
Typesetter: C&M Digitals (P) Ltd.
Proofreader: Susan Schon
Indexer: Terri Corry
Cover Designer: Candice Harman
Marketing Manager: Nicole Elliott

MIX
Paper from
responsible sources
FSC
www.fsc.org   FSC® C014174

14 15 16 17 18 10 9 8 7 6 5 4 3 2 1

Brief Contents

Detailed Contents

Preface

The author has been aware of criticisms of needs assessments for a long time. He had so much to write about needs and their determination that there was no inclination to go into the negatives and what might be done because of them. Many of the ideas in this text were on the back burner, tepid, warm, not piping hot. Periodically he returned to them with the thought maybe there is another book that would be useful and could span the gap between the needs assessment school and its opposite counterpart, asset/capacity building.

As time passed and with additional reading, the recognition came that these opposing camps might be more alike than originally envisioned. Were they really that different, and what did they look like in practice? Was there a hybrid, and did the two supposedly antithetical positions have more in common than original impressions led us to believe? Getting beyond the passion on each side, what did the literature have to say about this?

Based on what was found, there is a middle ground, and a synthesis between the two positions could be formulated. This became apparent when a set of studies was reviewed that, although they began from more of an asset/capacity-building premise, included almost seamlessly a major needs component. It seemed to be a natural combination, and when that was noted the book went from vision to reality. It should span the gap across needs assessment and asset/capacity building—attempting to meld the two into a meaningful process.

POINT OF VIEW

It cannot be denied that the author staked his reputation on writing about aspects of needs assessment: theoretical bases; value of the activity; a model for its conduct; methods that fit its various phases; analysis and synthesis of needs data; and reporting and utilizing results to guide organizational change, development, and improvement. He and colleagues have conducted research studies on needs assessment processes and methods. Yes, he is wedded to that type of thinking, and it remains consistent and prominent in his perceptions and the text.

Needs might represent opportunities to some, but to others they are not the way to go. They are discrepancies saying that something is wrong and has to be corrected. They reinforce a deficit, dependent mind-set, and for asset/capacity builders they raise a question: Should we ever be planning and moving from this "down" type of scenario? That stance of opposition to needs assessment is acceptable, appropriate, and valid. So is the choice of one or the other, but can we operate from a balance where the two are in joint, complementary operation? That is the governing mantra of the text. Hopefully it will straddle and do justice to both approaches.

The goal is to come up with a happy medium for a combined form of needs- and asset-based development. Reasoned compromises with respect to each must be made to reach that point. A hybrid model, guide, or framework will be created for accomplishing this by addressing the following topics:

First, the conflict between needs assessment and asset/capacity building will be examined historically and philosophically. (Chapter 1)

Second, the two ways will be contrasted pursuant to posing an integrated unified framework across them. (Chapter 2)

Third, the framework will be enhanced by adding procedures and methods for implementing each of its steps. (Chapters 3, 4, and 5)

Fourth, from there it should be straightforward to generate a checklist for rating any improvement or change effort on the extent to which it reflects a blend of looking at needs and assets. (Chapter 6)

Fifth, current needs assessments and asset/capacity-building projects will be analyzed in relation to a key section of the checklist for the degree to which they exhibit properties within it. (Chapters 7–8)

Sixth, across the chapters what are lingering concerns, what research questions and studies might be posed that push thinking and the discussion further along, and what about the bottom line—utilization? (Chapter 9)

IS THE TEXT THEORETICAL OR HANDS-ON?

The answer is neither and both. Without some historical grounding on a focused argument between two sharply held sets of values it would not be possible to write this book. They must be analyzed and considered.

Some theory as to the basic premises of the camps and contrasts between them is necessary. That provides the foundation for the synthesis. Chapter 1 is about that with Chapter 2 making comparisons that guide us into the new hybrid framework. To some degree these chapters are a bit more about the past and theory.

The third chapter consists of practical procedures for how the framework could be implemented with emphasis on its first three steps. Chapter 4 then takes us through the critical fourth step. Collectively these activities deal with a number of important questions. How do we organize and proceed? What are insights into the process? What are possible methods and processes? When would it be best to use them? Now the book has gone from establishing the underpinnings for a combined approach into what it would mean in real-world terms. This is hands-on. Chapter 5 completes the procedures in the framework.

The checklist in Chapter 6 helps us to plan and think through what we are doing and to evaluate what others have done. It should be useful for evaluators, planners, policy makers, needs assessors, and asset/capacity builders in judging their efforts and in reviewing existent studies.

The last three chapters include the examination of actual, fairly current mixed needs assessments—asset/capacity-building endeavors (7 and 8) and potential research questions and utilization (9). What methods have been employed, what hasn't been used, and what might we want to learn about the hybrid? Thus the book will have gone from the theoretical grounding for a synthesized approach to concrete illustrations of procedures and processes, and finally to investigations that will enhance understandings.

An overall outcome of the text would be to open up avenues for delving into and probing how to work in situations of organizational, institutional, and community change. The word *framework* is more appropriate than *model* for the synthesis in Chapter 2 and the steps in Chapters 3, 4, and 5 that make it come alive. A model is more rigid, and what is offered is not a finished product but a proposal in progress that others will alter, modify, disagree with, and even reject. That is OK since the hope is that it will engender discussion about how we can better conduct needs assessment and asset/capacity-building projects. Indeed, it is anticipated that the framework will mutate in regard to many of its features and steps.

Chapters 7 and 8 capture a snapshot of where the current practice across needs assessment and asset/capacity building is and offer glimpses into where it could be. That is the rationale behind the final chapter (9).

It is to pose questions that might advance the art and implementation underlying what we do.

Does it make sense?

Will its results improve communities and organizations?

Is it realistic to try to combine two seemingly different approaches?

What might be shorter ways to accomplish its steps?

To what kinds of contexts might it best be applied?

Where would it not work, and why?

What might be the cost implications of its use?

Does its premise of the external consultant as a catalyst resonate, and can it resonate?

What does it mean if one is internal or external to the organization or community in terms of operation?

Are there times when roles in the process have to become directive in order to get activities completed?

What are the desirable characteristics for the facilitator?

What are common problems in implementation?

What are likely or optimum time periods for implementation, and what are the limitations depending on the scope of the endeavor?

This is a short sampling of concerns. The needs assessment and asset/capacity-building journey is not easily undertaken. It can and most probably will be filled with pitfalls and difficulties, but should be worthwhile. If the text provides insights to just a few new portals, the author will be pleased. If it challenges conventional wisdom and leads to new questions and directions, then it will have achieved its purpose. If in the process you enhance and improve it, so much the better. Go forth and enjoy the journey.

Supplemental readings and exercises are available online at www .sagepub.com/altschuld

Acknowledgments

O ver the years I have worked with many individuals (and former students) who have contributed to my books and articles on needs assessment. Before going to specifics, a hearty thank-you is extended to them. You have challenged me, and made for much better products on my part; I am in your debt, and always will be.

As for this book, I must first note the contributions of Hsin-Ling Hung at the University of North Dakota and her students who diligently found references when I requested them. This was helpful, and I am very grateful for the thoughtfulness. This book would not be what it is without your input and sources. All of you were a godsend.

In the same vein, I thank Traci L. Lepicki of The Ohio State University for her willingness to show me how to do things when I got stuck and for always making time in the confines of a very busy professional and personal (family) schedule. I know that it pushed her to extremes, but rest assured it was deeply appreciated.

Gratitude is expressed to Teresa Spaeth, Nan Larson, and Jennifer Wagner-Lahr of Minnesota's Agricultural Utilization Research Institute for their openness and helpfulness in gaining access to that case. Richard Jurin of the University of Northern Colorado, an old friend, I appreciate you for directing my attention to a critical set of resources. Jennifer Wene, Kathy Rowe, Arnie Skidmore, Ron Porta, and Kevin Johnson currently or formerly with the Worthington (Ohio) Public Schools gave of their precious time to locate historically relevant materials. Yi-Fang Lee of National Taiwan Normal University has been along for the ride for more than 12 years since we first met in Taipei. She has been a part of numerous needs assessment studies and research endeavors. I am so pleased that you were there. The assistance of Ana Veronica Neves of Portugal and Steven Altschuld who guided his father through some technical issues is gratefully noted.

To Barbara E. Heinlein of The Ohio State University, what can I say?! For close to a quarter of a century you have performed alchemy on crude word-processed documents, transforming them to a precious metal. My work looks so much better due to your involvement and suggestions. In all honesty you have been a miracle worker in your own special way.

As for my SAGE kinfolk, what should be mentioned other than high fives? Vicki Knight (managing editor), you were wonderful in guiding me on prior endeavors and providing advice from the prospectus for this book to the final product. I know that this took extra time on your part, and I am in your debt. You stand out for your willingness to be involved in this manner. Jessica Miller (Vicki's assistant), thanks for jumping into this effort.

To those in the production, editing, and marketing functions at SAGE (Nicole Elliott, executive marketing manager; Libby Larson, production editor; Melinda Masson, copy editor; and Candice Harman, cover designer) who like Barbara above were instrumental in the development of a high-quality effort, you make a big difference, you should know that, and you are to be commended for it.

What would a book be without the commentary of reviewers who spot strengths, areas needing improvement, and weaknesses? The time you put into doing this task comes at an expense to you, but it led to insightful, harder-hitting, and more meaningful material. Respectfully, you are:

Judith Birgen, *Chicago State University*

Kenneth Goldberg, *National University*

Paul Komarek, *Cincinnati State Technical and Community College*

Brian P. Leung, *Loyola Marymount University*

David P. Moxley, *University of Oklahoma, Anne and Henry Zarrow School of Social Work*

Barbara Soniat, *National Catholic School of Social Service at Catholic University of America in Washington, DC*

Lastly is my family. To Ruth and our sons, Steven (Karen, Andrew, and Lindsay) and David (Gina Signoracci and Ms. Princess), I express my love for who you are, what you do, and your support.

About the Author

 **James W. Altschuld, PhD**, received his bachelor's and master's degrees in chemistry from Case Western Reserve University and The Ohio State University (OSU), respectively. His doctorate is from the latter institution with emphases in educational research and development and sociological methods. He is now Professor Emeritus in the College of Education and Human Ecology at OSU after 27 years of teaching research techniques and program evaluation. For the latter he developed and taught a sequence of courses on theory, needs assessment, and design. He has authored or coauthored seven previous books. Six were on needs assessment (four in the Needs Assessment Kit of 2010 for which he also served as editor for a fifth one), and one was on the evaluation of science and technology education.

In addition he has written numerous articles and chapters on how to assess needs as well as on evaluation research, practice, training, and credentialing/certification. He has been presenting nationally and internationally for over 40 years, has given many workshops, and has been the recipient of local, state, and national honors including the Alva and Gunnar Myrdal Practice Award from the American Evaluation Association for contributions to the field of evaluation.

1

Beginnings

A DIALOGUE

Here is a conversation that might have taken place at the author's academic institution. Participants are the author (**TA**) and a person who is a composite of former students (**FS**) who took his needs assessment courses during the 24 years he taught them.

TA Hey FS, it's great to see you after so many years. What have you been doing since you graduated?

FS It's nice to see you. I went into program planning and development after finishing and have been able to use some of the needs assessment concepts and methods you taught in my work. You will recall I was not too sure if they all fit into my thinking. What have you been doing?

TA It's good as a teacher to know that things were useful and I certainly hope meaningful, but I did sense you were somewhat skeptical in the course. As for me I have continued to write and conduct NA research since I left the university.

A couple of years ago I was involved with producing a new NA kit, and recently I am into another book about comparing asset/capacity building to needs assessment to see if it is possible to bridge the gap between the two, to create some sort of synthesis.

FS I'm surprised to hear this. In class and I understand even professionally you were almost always thought of as proselytizing for needs assessment. What happened? Why did your thinking change?

TA You are correct. Yes, I was out there hawking about needs and indeed built my reputation on the topic. It took me all over the U.S. and to other countries and led to many opportunities on projects that came from teaching about needs and how we learn about them.

At the same time I encountered another approach, one in opposition to NA. Frankly, I paid lip service to it, and as time passed I incorporated some of it into the classes but admittedly with very limited coverage and little discussion.

FS That's kind of vague. Could you be more concrete about what you did?

TA After about 10 years of the courses I added a reference about assessing the needs of the rural elderly by Iutcovich (1993).

It seemed to be a mixture of assessment and asset/capacity building with regard to senior citizens. This was about the mid-'90s.

Then later, I also brought into key tables the concept of looking at assets and resources in communities and how they could be utilized for improvement and growth. Along the way I was coming to the recognition that I ought to not only broaden my thinking but even reevaluate it.

FS As you were talking I was reflecting on the classes, and I can't seem to dredge up anything about what you've just said. Am I forgetting something, did I not attend in class, or am I simply getting older?

TA The answer to all three of your questions is yes, and the blame lies entirely with you. Only kidding! One other possibility is that you participated before some of this thinking was embedded in my approach to NA.

I guess that the fault is mine. Although the Iutcovich article was in the handout materials for courses, it was not reviewed even once in all the years of NA at the university. Sorry about that.

As far as the table entries, at best they were highlighted for something like 10 minutes, and that was it. That was the total extent of coverage.

FS This seems to be a big departure for you, so what exactly are you planning to do in this new book?

TA I'm shifting from a previous stance of focusing on discrepancies as the sole starting point for planning and development. I still consider that idea to be important but recognize that individuals might shy away or feel uncomfortable with what a need means or denotes. It is seen as a problem, a discrepancy, or an indication of something being amiss or wrong.

The critics are right: That is a negative kind of thinking that could certainly get us off on the wrong foot. Don't misunderstand me—needs are integral to where I am and to how I view planning and improving what we do as institutions, agencies, and societies. On the other hand, being positive is valuable, and we should not lose sight of assets and strengths that we, as communities, as individuals, and through our organizations, bring to the table. Our skills, motivation, organizations (governmental and otherwise), commitment, and fiscal resources are part of the foundation that enables us to advance and that must be in the focal lens.

This is a radical change and will be difficult for me to do. Here's the way I am going to accomplish it. My thoughts are to give a brief background and history of the two competing viewpoints and then to compare and contrast them, sort of a philosophical bases examination.

That could be done by dispelling what I see as misperceptions about them and finally proceed to their unique and in-common features and methods followed by real-world examples, ones that are bridging the gap between needs assessment and asset/capacity building. I want to dissect these works and probe into how they accommodated the two opposite sides of the thought process. I have been finding reports in the literature that are going in this direction.

FS What I am understanding is that there is a "positive thesis" as to how we make progress emanating from strengths and assets and an "antithesis" that looks at weaknesses or needs as the fundamental thing, and you want to see if you can meld them together, the "synthesis." (See Figure 1.1.) If that is correct and it appears fairly straightforward, why is this book necessary?

TA That is the underlying premise of the book. Why it is necessary gets to the heart of the matter. One answer is that there is not a large literature base that deals with the blending of the perspectives, and it will help to reduce the gap between the two sides. Excuse the pun, my slipping into needs jargon—I just could not avoid it. Going further, it will describe an emerging set of needs assessment/asset/capacity-building efforts now accessible.

One other thing that it could do is to relieve some tension that may be there for some adherents to one or the other camp. It could be that the synthesis will lead into more meaningful efforts in our communities and organizations than either side could produce by itself.

FS As you described that, I perceived that there is some beneath-the-surface friction that might arise from this effort. Since I have to go in a few minutes, give me the long story short. Is that a delicate spot in this?

TA It is, and some prior criticisms of NA have valid points, and for that matter the same applies to asset/capacity building. The idea is not to brush these away; instead, it is to see them as related to extremes in usage, which may not be so common. I think that there is a middle ground in most situations, and so I will put forward the idea that more will be achieved by bringing disparate positions together than by rigid ties to either one. *Delicate* is very relevant to what is being attempted.

I too have to go. It was delightful seeing you again, and best wishes.

FS Same here, and you definitely have your work cut out for you. Good luck on this newest venture.

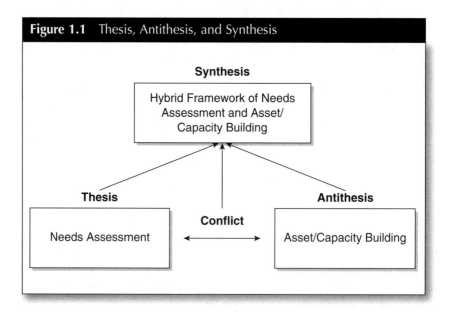

Figure 1.1 Thesis, Antithesis, and Synthesis

Synthesis

Hybrid Framework of Needs Assessment and Asset/ Capacity Building

Thesis

Needs Assessment

Conflict

Antithesis

Asset/Capacity Building

EARLY CRITICISM AND DEFENSE—1970S AND 1980S

Some history about how the dialectic came about and evolved to the point where a synthesis might be appropriate is helpful. As the author began to read about needs assessment early in his career, he found an article by Kamis titled "A Witness for the Defense of Need Assessment" (1979). What an odd title because an approach to planning is just that, something that is useful but would be adapted and tailored to a context—that is nothing unusual or unexpected. There are advantages and disadvantages to using it, and assessors must understand concepts and techniques, but why would it have to be defended? It seems that any issues associated with conducting a needs assessment are obvious and anticipated—what's the big deal? What is there to be defensive about and to warrant the article?

Recognize that from the 1970s to the mid-1980s much was happening in needs assessment—a sampling follows. Warheit, Bell, and Schwab (1979) were writing about the topic from a federal perspective. Neuber and Associates (1980) were doing similar work as was Lauffer (1982). Kaufman (1987) was in the process of developing and publicizing his systems-oriented model (Organizational Elements Model—OEM) for identifying and then resolving needs. Some of that effort has been continued up to the present by Kaufman (1992; Kaufman & Guerra-Lopez, 2013) and students he trained.

At the same time, Witkin conducted a major research study in the late 1970s about needs assessment strategies used by school districts to comply with federal funding and its requirements that programs be based upon identified needs. She surveyed districts in the United States and collected information and materials from them. From a detailed, extensive examination of what came from that effort her first book was published in 1984.

It contained a rationale for assessing needs, a theoretical framework, and a solid overview of methods. Additionally, although not in depth, a three-phase process model for needs assessment was proposed. To this day, the book is a seminal contribution to the field.

In 1987, McKillip followed with his text on needs analysis. It was oriented toward social services rather than education, business, or communities. It is important to note that he did cover the assessment of resources or strengths but not in a manner that would be viewed as asset/capacity building (see Kretzmann & McKnight, 1993). Resources in his case were to resolve needs that were determined mostly by quantitative assessments of discrepancies, in other words after needs had been identified, analyzed, and prioritized, were they to enter the picture, but certainly not as a starting point.

That is contrary to what asset/capacity building is even while the act of finding and cataloging resources might be similar to or overlap with it. The intentionality is quite different, and McKillip would not be considered an asset/capacity builder.

There were more writings about needs assessment in this period, but enough is here to give a sense of the interest in the topic and discrepancy-based planning. Against that backdrop, the title of Kamis's article was striking and implied that there were negative feelings about such activities for changing communities, organizations, and agencies. Kamis presaged literature that would appear later. What are her main points and the reasoning underlying them?

First, Kamis noted that needs assessment, or NA, was really in its infancy (remember it was 1979 although criticisms persist to the present). Standards for the "what should be" condition of needs assessment were hard to come by or were value positions in areas such as education and recreation, and assessing needs in community programs and health had changed from doing social good to being predicated on shortages (needs) and as concrete justifications for expenditures. The foundation had to be driven by data that clearly depict needs (problems) as a guide for agencies and institutions. Solutions for problems must flow out of data that assessors generate and that directly attend to the causes of discrepancies. Second, Kamis went on to acknowledge some criticisms, among other concerns:

- Needs assessment activities cost precious resources.
- Most results do not address the funding for solutions related to underlying problems.
- Hard-core empirical data are based on social indicators and don't fully reflect human situations (hence the later emphasis on multiple sources of data including qualitative ones).
- The data collected may lead to inferring needs rather than observing or measuring them.
- Perceptive data should be used and are a valuable source of data (an outgrowth of previous entries).
- Poor payoffs from identifying discrepancies and gaps have been realized to date, calling into question whether the expenditures for assessment are worth it.

- There is a lack of conceptual frameworks underlying the endeavor.
- Assessments might be done retrospectively rather than prospectively.
- Different needs might not be treated in detail; that is, there is not a fine enough sifting of what was found.
- There is a lack of good methods for pulling data together.
- There is a tendency to stop at the identification of needs, without probing what is causing them.
- Assessors might not understand factors that lead to the utilization of findings.
- Needs assessments are fads, ego trips for those who advocate their use.
- Need represents a negative, a problem, not an uplifting concept.
- The evaluation of the costs versus benefits of completed assessments is not evident in the literature or in reports.

For the defense of the enterprise, Kamis emphasized that assessment provided useful information and social indicators and quantitative measures help in identifying and understanding gaps. They are not the entirety of what might be delved into, but they are important for decision making and should not be disregarded. She went on to observe that many quantitative variables and/or social indicators from databases have been reasonably chosen and are reliable, valid, and defensible. There are values inherent in their selection and use, but they just cannot be easily dismissed, and, as she put it,

Knowledge influences policies. It is a slow but worthwhile process. (Kamis, 1979, p. 9)

NA was beginning to be viewed as having merit when Kamis made her comments, and from the current vantage point she predicted, ahead of the curve, that it would grow and evolve in line with the criticisms. As we learned how to perform assessments, they would improve and be of more value. They would become accepted as part of the planning environment for new programs for social improvement. They would be another resource in the tool kit of those working on dimensions of positive change.

She went further by noting that many assessments done prior to her article were based not on a single method but on multiple ones. They were not as narrow as critics had suggested. Sometimes they collected information about perceived need from interviews, focus group interviews, and observations in conjunction with quantitative methods. She felt that such information was good for understanding and we should not shy away from it.

Kamis was open-minded in her rejoinder to the critics and agreed with what they offered, especially in regard to refining and improving methods, data analysis, and how information from different sources can be amalgamated into a meaningful summary with well-formed conclusions and recommendations. The instruments and procedures were also of concern as to the truthfulness of information for decisions. Were they trustworthy for making changes in services for program recipients?

Her discussion took on issues forthrightly, not defensively as in her title but from the stance of doing a more sophisticated job of identifying and working with needs. Thus she made suggestions for enhancing NA practice, some of which have been discussed.

CONTINUED DEVELOPMENT AND CRITICISM—1980S AND 1990S

Despite advancements in assessments and even with more theoretical foundations being provided (Witkin, 1984), by the late 1980s a negative theme was still there as was the sharp attack on needs assessment, especially its linkage to positivism and quantification. Weintraub (1988, 1989) posited that it was a cold, numbers type of thing and not very meaningful in promoting positive growth. It was not getting to the personal level, tapping into what people and groups actually do or could do and what would energize them for improvement. Exhibit 1.1 contains the gist of her position.

Exhibit 1.1 Main Points in Weintraub's Critique of Needs Assessment

Needs assessment and program planning has a technocratic flavor and feel to it. It does not include the voice of those for whom the effort is supposedly done.

It is not value free but value laden, and positions and ideas embedded in it should be fully acknowledged, not camouflaged.

In the extreme it could be compared to what occurs in highly regulated police states although the author noted that she was not seeing assessors or planners like those in control.

There was an undue focus on positivism in many needs assessments. She underscored that there are alternative routes to knowledge and obtaining insights into human conditions and problems.

Needs assessment comes from a cult of efficiency, and there are a lot of concerns about whose needs are being determined by whom and according to what approach for assessing them.

She points to a lack of humanistic dimensions inherent in the procedures and in the philosophical stance.

This led to a rebuttal by Witkin (1988, 1992), who by then was a stalwart voice for needs assessment. She had worked in and written about the field for more than a decade and felt she had to rise to the challenge (B. R. Witkin, personal communication to J. W. Altschuld, 1992, 1993). Her comments are in Exhibit 1.2.

Exhibit 1.2   Some of Witkin's Counterpoints to Weintraub

Acknowledged the comments in Exhibit 1.1 and resonated with most of them especially the values woven into an assessment and the "what is" and "what should be" conditions.

Saw needs assessment as inherently democratic since it incorporated many views into identifying discrepancies and gaps.

Needs were to be the determiners of direction in contrast to what was earlier, for programs and projects, administrative fiat. This was an improvement over other ways of thinking.

Needs assessment could be hierarchical as the criticisms implied but if done properly could lead to open discussions about changes in how we move forward.

Needs assessment is based on locally determined goals/objectives and should be a result of shared decision making and leadership as much as possible. Partnership is to be encouraged.

If assessment is incorrectly implemented or implemented in a highly shortened fashion, it could be technocratic and top-down.

It should include an assortment of data and concerns, issues, and input from many different voices. It all depends on how it is carried out.

(Continued)

(Continued)

Positivism is there, but so is interpretation of qualitative data. Results come from both approaches.

Needs assessments and what they produce aren't to be foisted on service recipients and service deliverers. Instead they arise from multiple stakeholders and involved constituencies.

From Witkin's (1998/1992) perspective part of the problem resided in how assessments were conducted, not so much in their philosophical underpinnings. Yet the argument persisted and intensified with the publication of "Building Communities From the Inside Out" by Kretzmann and McKnight in 1993. It focused on the value of asset and capacity building for improvement with needs assessment being perceived as the wrong path to follow. Its critique of NA was harsh, and the battle lines were explicitly drawn with a cease-fire nowhere on the horizon.

The main emphasis was that when needs are identified the concern is on what's wrong with communities and organizations. Deficiencies, and things that are amiss, dominate thinking and are not uplifting or morale boosting, with stress on the negative, and that is depressing. That becomes the reality governing thought, programming, and outlook. When you start this way, it is difficult to move forward—it's a turnoff.

Kretzmann and McKnight (1993) suggested that in low-income urban areas, while problems are definitely there and known, doing needs assessments does not empower a community but instills a client or recipient-of-service mentality with no incentives for its assets and strengths to be the change agent. In this scenario the community isn't proactive, initiative doesn't take place, and a needs-based approach does not lead to change and will ultimately fail.

(Interestingly this same idea was raised by a nationally known political commentator about the presidential election in 2012. David Brooks (Brooks, 2012) noted that the intense negative campaigning might not be the best way to make a case to the public. He suggested decreasing the negatives about an opponent and focusing more on what people can do in policies and action—that is, relying more on positive psychology for a small number of fundamental changes.)

What Kretzmann and McKnight posit is that communities become involved in assessing their strengths and capacities and adapt a more "can do" attitude and stance.

- What are our churches and religious institutions, community organizations, schools, and so forth able to do and provide?
- What can businesses, health providers, cultural groups, libraries, and similar entities offer, and what do they currently offer?
- What synergies could they develop across strengths if they began to think about doing so?
- How could the assets and capabilities be leveraged, ramped up for the greater good?
- What's positive about what we have and our capacity to use it to grow?
- Surely the creativity and ability are there to do this if we concentrate on strengths to solve problems. We have assets, and we should take advantage of them.
- What about the talents, skills, and accomplishments of individual citizens (for they are many and should not be overlooked)?
- How could they be incorporated into and helpful for movement forward and change?
- How could they be linked together in a synergy for the future?

We can build our communities from within. We have faith in ourselves as people to affect the current status. Should we not be able to take the reins? It is our domain and destiny. If we assume leadership, the situation is empowered, invigorated, and meaningful. The straitjacket of dependency must be broken, and that happens by being involved in and committed to the process. This is the avenue through which progress will be achieved. This position does not eschew external help and funds, but the parameters of development are internal and not other directed. Rather than needs being the game plan, look at the assets and capacity that can be tapped into with the right catalyst. The various components of the community are the key ingredients for building a better environment.

A group would begin by cataloging and collecting information about the vast array of resources it has. They are found in organizations and individuals and are abundant in every community. Sure, there are negatives and problems, but this view is diametrically opposite to a needs-based one, and procedures for obtaining data are predicated on assets. Identifying assets would be heavily internal, driven and guided by the community, as contrasted to a more external, technocrat-led approach.

Therefore one distinction is that needs assessment would be more an external, expert-led, stark scientific process, and asset/capacity building would be noticeably more locally controlled. After all, consultants are involved in endeavors for a short span of time. They will disappear from the scene, but the community or organization remains. It becomes stronger and more able to proceed, if it relies on itself, its own energy, and its own ideas. It is capacitated, and this is healthy.

Kretzmann and McKnight's position, like Witkin's, was seminal for its philosophy and methodological uniqueness. Their efforts had proponents, as did hers. There are examples of both in the literature. What is the right way to go, what is the wrong way, what works, and what are the choices? Is one best in certain contexts and the reverse in others? Could it even be that neither is wrong or right? There is logic in both camps, so what should we do in a change-oriented situation? What are the advantages of each, and could they be used in a complementary manner? Would a synthesis be a step forward and lead to more beneficial and satisfying outcomes for communities and organizations?

HISTORICAL VIEWS LEANING TOWARD SYNTHESIS—1990S TO 2000S AND BEYOND

Figure 1.2 is a snapshot of the history leading to the synthesis that will be proposed. From where does it come, is there a foundation, and are there examples of its use?

Evidence in support of blending the two approaches comes from the mid- to late '90s up to the present. In the figure, an inverted pyramid contains the evolution in thinking with the current combined usage of needs assessment and asset/capacity building at the top. The bottom is a narrow base starting with Kamis's article and some criticism. (If this was a full history, it might have gone back to the Egyptian Book of the Dead [see British Museum, 2011], but the goal is to set the stage for bridging the gap, not a complete timeline.) In the '80s, Witkin's (1984) standout work, McKillip's (1987) text, and others appear as well as an escalating attack on needs assessment culminating in 1993 with the Kretzmann and McKnight groundbreaking effort.

What has taken place since is important and explains how needs assessment and asset/capacity building can be unified to improve communities and organizations. Where are they complementary, and can the advantages of each blend into a meaningful structure and platform?

Figure 1.2 Some Historical Events in Needs Assessment and Asset/Capacity Building Up to the Present

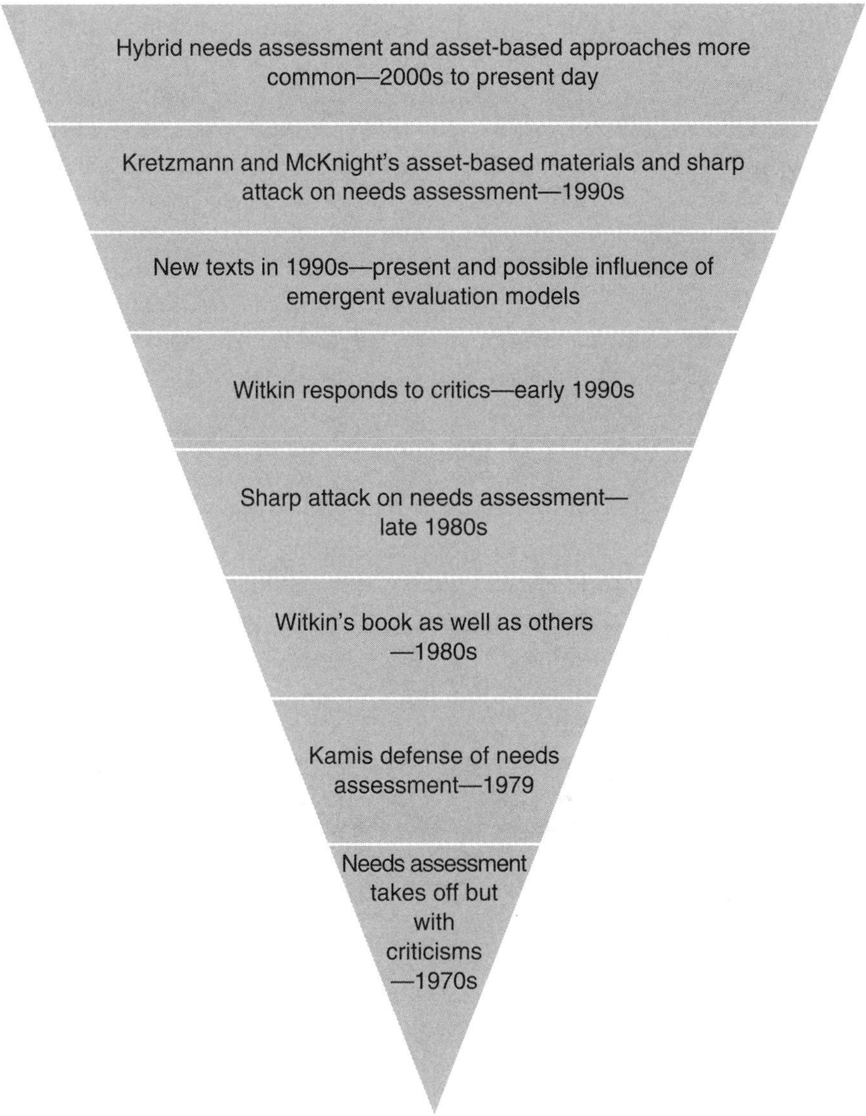

Hybrid needs assessment and asset-based approaches more common—2000s to present day

Kretzmann and McKnight's asset-based materials and sharp attack on needs assessment—1990s

New texts in 1990s—present and possible influence of emergent evaluation models

Witkin responds to critics—early 1990s

Sharp attack on needs assessment—late 1980s

Witkin's book as well as others—1980s

Kamis defense of needs assessment—1979

Needs assessment takes off but with criticisms—1970s

Besides what is in the figure, another event that may have had a profound influence should be discussed. It was mostly informal, and just about all of the prime players are no longer professionally active (the author may be the last). When the Evaluation Network and the Evaluation Research Society were merging into the American Evaluation Association (1985–86), there was a small group of needs assessors (mainly in health or mental health) searching for an organizational home. By default and mutual interest they had with evaluation, they joined AEA, eventually becoming a Topical Interest Group (TIG) in the association. It has been small but continuously active since then as an important force for keeping needs assessment alive and promoting research about its practice.

AEA is perceived as affecting thinking about needs assessment and how it is conducted. Emerging conceptualizations of evaluation included empowerment evaluation and greater concerns for the roles of recipients of service, not seeing them as targets or "subjects" for programs in accord with the guiding principles for evaluators. Evaluation capacity building also entered the mind-set of evaluators and hence that of the needs assessors who were now part of the evaluation scene.

Empowerment evaluation embraces the principle that the self-determination of people and groups for their own improvement is a key to progress. Capacity building as portrayed through the evaluation lens refers to developing within organizations the ongoing practice of evaluation as integral to the organization's functioning and learning. These movements and their relationships to needs assessment and asset/capacity building are in Tables 1.1 and 1.2.

Table 1.1 Aspects of Empowerment Evaluation and Relationship to Needs Assessment and Asset/Capacity Building	
Aspect of Empowerment Evaluation	*Relationship to Needs Assessment and Asset/Capacity Building*
Defining/describing the mission of the organization.	Pertinent to many things in NA and A/CB. A normal first step.
Taking stock of activities currently done. Open discussion of how well the activities are carried out.	Ties in well with the identification of present status that occurs early in NA. Certainly how well something has worked is congruent with the idea of assets and capacity building.

Aspect of Empowerment Evaluation	Relationship to Needs Assessment and Asset/Capacity Building
Planning for moving into the future.	This is a generic activity that links to both entities in this column heading. NA and A/CB are about the future, change, and development. NA may have more of a short-term outlook whereas A/CB may be longer term.
Specifics for moving into the future: • Goals • Developing strategies • Documenting progress	The steps apply to assessing needs and leveraging assets and capacity. There is much overlap between the two sides of the table.

Source: Based on Fetterman (2005).

Table 1.2 Aspects of Capacity Building for Evaluation Purposes and Relationship to Needs Assessment and Asset/Capacity Building

Aspect of Capacity Building	Relationship to Needs Assessment and Asset/Capacity Building
Referred to as evaluation capacity building (ECB). This is about enhancing evaluation capacity internal to an organization.	By using the abbreviation ECB, confusion is avoided. NA and A/CB resonate with ECB in regard to improving by means of information.
Creating a culture for maintaining an evaluation presence in an organization, doing quality evaluation studies, and using results for change and development.	Similar idea but with the intent of ascertaining needs or assets that can be focused or turned into change. Not dealing with evaluation as on the left but on establishing a culture for improvement via both NA and A/CB.
Strong connection to an organizational learning perspective.	Ideas overlap, but the emphasis on evaluation sustainability inside an organization in the other column is a bit different. NA and A/CB are similar yet unique.

(Continued)

Table 1.2 (Continued)	
Aspect of Capacity Building	*Relationship to Needs Assessment and Asset/Capacity Building*
Going toward staff commitment and an infrastructure for sustaining evaluation and its usage.	The needs assessors or asset capacity builders want to foster an environment that facilitates the organization or community in a growth type of mode.

Source: Based on Baizerman, Compton, & Stockdill (2005).

It would be hard to imagine that a portion of the ideas in the tables in small, subtle ways or overtly did not impact needs assessors participating in AEA meetings, events, and discussions. Moreover, such evaluation ideas are related to the tenets of asset/capacity-building efforts in community development and in health promotion efforts. It is reasonable to assume that evaluation movements did affect NA and A/CB and vice versa. In Figure 1.3 they are shown along with other factors that point toward the emergence of the hybrid framework.

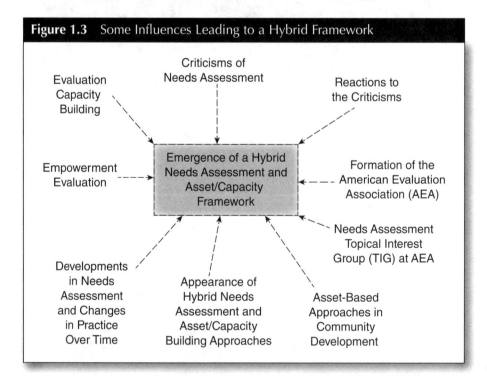

Figure 1.3 Some Influences Leading to a Hybrid Framework

Continuing with the historical journey, in 1995, Witkin and Altschuld's text considerably expanded the three-phase model (pre-assessment, assessment, post-assessment). This was followed by another book by Altschuld and Witkin (2000) with the phases now having 14–15 major steps with additional emphasis being devoted to why the assessment was being done, who should be involved in it, needs-based decision making, and how needs are translated into programs and actions for organizations, institutions, schools, and others. The acceptance of results would be enhanced through greater involvement of various stakeholders.

NA maintained its technical side with quantitative information still important, but it was mutating in relation to how to get the assessment off the ground, what methods or mix of methods should be employed, what solution strategies might be best for identified needs, and how to implement them. Illustrations of these changes are below.

- Who, what persons or groups, should lead the assessment and be fully incorporated in determining needs and solutions from Phase 1 (Pre-assessment) to the end of the process, Phase 3 (Post-assessment)?
- Who makes the decisions, and what are the roles of various players in decision making?
- How should the assessment be focused? What are the salient issues to those potentially affected by them, not driven by external needs assessors? (Phase 1)
- What are appropriate methods for examining issues? (Phase 2, Assessment)
- Should there be a mix of qualitative and quantitative procedures with concerns about how to put results together for a comprehensive and deep understanding of problems? (Phase 2)
- How valid will the summary be in the eyes of a large and involved constituency? Does it coincide with what they view as important? (Phases 1 and 2)
- How do we prioritize, and who sets the priorities for action? (Phases 2 and 3)
- What are the criteria for priorities?
- What are potential solution strategies, and how well do they mesh with the local situation? How do we choose them, and will they work within the setting? (Phase 3)
- With whom does the responsibility for the implementation of a solution reside, and what is the role of an external needs assessor as NA goes through the three phases?

- Have we evaluated the process of needs assessment and whether initiated changes have worked? Have individuals and groups benefited from what has been done and, if so, how? (Phase 3)

The evolving three-phase model doesn't yet tie into asset/capacity building, but the two positions are getting noticeably closer than before! A shifting perception of the circumstances surrounding change and growth is there. It is not the needs assessment of yore. Awareness of complexity is being embedded in a pronounced fashion in the gestalt of needs assessment. (The writers did not consciously deal with criticisms of needs assessments, but their thinking was beginning to alter and move in a somewhat new direction.)

Roughly from 2000 to the current time, other things were happening that propel synthesis. Altschuld (Witkin sadly passed away in the late 1990s, but the guess is that she would have agreed) had begun to analyze his views and in 2004 wrote a paper about needs assessment as a way for organizations to learn about what they were doing wrong and transforming themselves accordingly. It was becoming a mechanism for organizations to grow and introspect.

Personnel were going to have to be intimate with all facets of the assessment and thereby come to deeper understandings about the organization, what its current status was, and what it might do in the future. Needs assessment was under the aegis of the organization or community and individuals within it and less externally led. The experience was not an isolated act but one that should include all parts of the organization from top to bottom.

Other needs assessment books were also coming out in the period such as Gupta, Sleezer, and Russ-Eft's work (2007, currently being updated), which was oriented toward business organizations. In 2009–2010, Altschuld and a group of colleagues produced a five-volume Needs Assessment Kit (Altschuld, 2010b) with some books breaking new ground.

One was devoted to how the process of needs assessment might start—which often had been treated as a short or very small part of one chapter. Who should be initiating the activity, what should the agency be undertaking to better understand itself, and what kinds of information might be collected? Even the use of micro-ethnology was considered for initial efforts.

Not capacity building, this had more similarity with some of the ideas suggested by Kretzmann and McKnight (1993). NA was becoming part of a richer landscape.

And that pattern continued in the methods book in the kit with treatment of only five methods that were most commonly seen in assessments. Several of them were qualitative and coming from almost a community perspective (an organization in this context might be viewed as a community) although not totally. Another book dealt with taking information from multiple procedures and sources and assembling it into a coherent summary of results—what do they say individually about needs, and do they agree or conflict in their findings? The final volume in the kit examined how decisions for action are made and interpersonal factors that shape them, focusing less on technical concerns and more on the complex milieu of intraorganizational relations. This was not capacity building, but indeed different from earlier views.

Along similar lines, Watkins, West Meiers, and Visser (2012) were dealing with NA in their book written for the World Bank. From the viewpoint of developing nations, the concern for community involvement and direction is clear as a critical element in shaping how a society, or groups in sectors within it, improve. The book has an extensive compendium of methods. Also Kaufman and Guerra-Lopez in 2013 reentered the expanded listing of library resources on assessment.

Overall, NA was more respectful of the rights of individuals and groups and that their input was vital in processes, procedures, and direction setting, and a driving force in assessing needs and utilizing resources to resolve them. Still the critics would be right in saying that it was based on discrepancies but softer in this regard. Is it old wine in new bottles? It was insufficient for a synthesis, but the terrain had shifted and was more amenable to compromise.

HISTORY CONTINUED—EMERGENT ASSET/CAPACITY-BUILDING VIEWS LEANING TOWARD SYNTHESIS

Concurrent with what was happening in needs assessment, there was a noticeable trend in publications from the asset/capacity-building side of the ledger in fields such as public health, health, social programming, and crime prevention. For the latter, Neves (2011) proposed tweaking available assets to crime prevention through environmental design, CPTED. One example was simply moving a park bench so that people would have a better view of potential threatening situations. In an e-mail survey she conducted (Neves, 2013) about interrelated principles of CPTED (natural surveillance and access control, territorial reinforcement, and maintenance and management), a prominent feature was the idea of leveraging existing aspects and resources available in locations. So assessing assets to reduce crime is important.

Additionally, asset/capacity-building studies often used methods (photovoice, community determination of information to be collected, cataloging of resources, rapid appraisal, and others) not commonly seen in needs assessment. These were implemented under the umbrella that strengths, not "what's amiss," are foremost. What do we have, and how can it be utilized for a higher level of community or organizational performance? Many of the articles and reports reviewed indicated that communities looked at needs in accord with resources by means of "hard" data, surveys, or the outcomes of database analyses with such information entering significantly into deliberations. In practice, the two camps were drifting toward a middle ground and had undergone a practical synthesis. A very natural and seamless blending was making sense.

For those conducting these projects there was a strong commitment to the asset/capacity-building philosophy but without much hesitation at looking at needs and quantifiable data. There was concern about toward what goals and problems we should be applying what had been learned about strengths. Gaps were helpful in setting the direction, governing not the process but just a part of it. This evolution was striking and helped needs assessors deal with an obvious criticism of the opposite end of the spectrum.

In a clever dissertation, Hansen (1991) observed that as people think about problems and issues there is a pattern to how they probe situations pursuant to seeking ways to improve. Whether they termed it a problem, a need, an issue, or a concern, they identified common elements in their analysis—what is the current status, what should be, and the discrepancy between the two. These are consonant with needs assessment.

There were other findings, but the above were pronounced. The data were subjected to different cluster analysis techniques with the same results. There is exact alignment with discrepancy thinking. This may be an artifact of research coming from a needs perspective, but on the other hand the study was striking since it was done in five distinct fields and generally identical outcomes were realized. The implication is that it may be impossible to fragment how we approach development by wearing blinders (restricting the field of vision) and limiting thinking to needs or asset/capacity building. The conceptual mechanisms relate, and separation would be artificial. Neither should be ruled out, and could they be linked together?

So how should we operate in the real world? Should asset and resource assessment take place before we determine need, or should the logic be reversed—identify needs and then, as McKillip (1987) proposed, locate resources and figure out what could be adapted or applied for the resolution of needs? Or, should both be done simultaneously via a split personality? Wear different hats and periodically switch them as you go through the process. Sometimes you are the needs assessor, the asset/capacity builder, or both combined into one.

FIRST STEPS TOWARD SYNTHESIS

Synthesis is exactly the reason for this book. If you identify assets and capacity, toward what purpose or goal are they to be directed? This is what needs assessors would ask and why they would criticize the other side. From that point of view, you, either consciously or subliminally, will be considering needs in the equation. Analogously, the challengers of needs assessment are appropriate in that it is negative and may lead to dependency. The critics are right about having a "can do" mind-set and that more will be accomplished by having it. Their stance on the internal drive for improvement is on target.

So is it one, the other, or both with the answer here based on the emerging trend that it is feasible to do needs assessment in a complementary way with a realistic degree of compromise starting with the asset side of things? You are not beginning with negatives, and people will become more involved in processes, procedures, and decision making due to that. As they buy in, introduce needs assessment and, if it already has come up, just let it happen. Hansen's findings indicate that no matter what is done or in what order, needs enter the picture. It is normal and cannot be avoided even as we focus on assets and strengths. The two processes relate to each other.

An illustration of this occurred in a study of community development in Appalachia. Photovoice (Chapter 4) was a technique used with community members. Teenagers and young adults were given inexpensive cameras to photograph what they considered to be the assets of the community and its issues. The community was producing the data, interpreting it, and giving it meaning in its own words and vantage points. The entire endeavor was heavily community led and guided.

Needs and assets were in what was generated. The photographers were asked to write short narratives about what the pictures were illustrating. The photos with narratives were posted for a large community group discussion and an open interchange about the community's current situation, its strengths and assets, its problems, and where it might go. It would be difficult to cast the activity as asset/capacity building or needs assessment without losing a sense of what was taking place. It was a combination of the two beginning from the strengths side of the ledger. It was a merger, and that is exactly where this text will be going in Chapter 2.

A COMMENT ON THE VALUE OF SYNTHESIS

There are examples of the combined usage of needs assessment and asset/capacity building but not an overabundance of them. Given that, is moving toward a synthesis more of an academic exercise with limited practical value? Hopefully not! It is possible to envision many ways of utilizing such a concept via incorporation into the formulation of governmental policies for not only attending to current concerns and issues but planning for a variety of beneficial social programs. This could be done in mental health, public health, and agriculture to name just a few. This is notable and is partly embedded in several of the case studies in Chapters 7 and 8. Moreover, the idea could have applicability to nongovernmental activities, business settings, and joint public and private ventures. Needs assessors and asset/capacity builders will have to understand each specific situation and temper the principles accordingly to make them work.

HIGHLIGHTS OF CHAPTER 1

1. A fictitious conversation was used to start off the discussion for this book.

2. The historical roots of the needs assessment were laid out in regard to criticisms and the expansion of writings about needs assessment from the '70s to the '80s.

3. The journey went into the '90s with intensified criticism of needs assessment along with more writings about its practice. Asset/capacity building was woven into the narrative.

4. The trip was brought to the present with the evolution of needs assessment and by noting that a trend seemed to combine it and asset/capacity building almost seamlessly. A synthesis was taking place naturally.

5. A practical project doing just that was briefly described.

6. The value of a synthesis was briefly noted.

DISCUSSION QUESTIONS

1. Might there be situations where it would be better to not combine needs assessment and asset/community-building efforts? Explain and offer examples.

2. There are drawbacks to starting with needs assessment as noted in the text. What might be some negatives about beginning with asset/capacity building?

3. Internally led projects for improvement were contrasted to projects that are externally directed. Based on your experience, what are the advantages and disadvantages of each?

4. Communities and organizations are always in a constant state of flux and change, so how often should they do one or the other of the activities or do them in combination?

5. Discuss implications of the activities from a fiscal point and from the standpoint of morale and invested energy.

6. Discuss implications of the time required for a needs assessment and/or an asset/capacity-building venture.

7. Do you know of any government programs where a combined approach was implemented? If so, describe them and their success.

2

A Synthesis of Needs Assessment and Asset/ Capacity Building

BASIC DEFINITIONS

Need is a noun, "a problem that should be attended to or resolved" (Altschuld & Kumar, 2010, p. 3). It is a gap or discrepancy between the "what should be" and "what is" conditions, and *needs assessment* is the process of identifying needs (discrepancies), prioritizing them, making needs-based decisions, allocating resources, and implementing actions in organizations to resolve problems underlying the important needs (Altschuld & Kumar, 2010, p. 20).

Asset/capacity building (A/CB) refers to building a culture in an organization or a community so that it can grow and change in accord with its strengths and assets as related to its future. Specifically, A/CB is the identification of the array of assets (organization, community, agency, fiscal, skills of individual people) available or potentially available to a group, and the application of what has been so ascertained to improve the group in a positive way.

A COMPARISON OF NEEDS ASSESSMENT AND ASSET/CAPACITY BUILDING

In Table 2.1 needs assessment and asset/capacity building are compared to demonstrate their relationships and uniqueness on dimensions such as

- vision;

- premise (the thought pattern of those conducting the effort or facilitating it);

- role of external individuals (driving force, participant, etc.), with several entries dependent on where things are in a process;

- context for the work;

- how the work might begin;

- methodology mix;

- who or what groups are involved in obtaining data;

- from whom the data are collected;

- use of results;

- time frame for the endeavor, noting that it is dependent on the context and issues of concern;

- collaboration and/or cooperation required for activities to be successful; and

- other parts of the work.

The simplest way to draw distinctions would be in terms of extremes, and if one is an absolute devotee of one of the camps that would be reasonable, but for the author that is not meaningful. The premise is that there is a trend toward hybrid usage, and explanations within the table reflect that view. The dimensions are in the middle (they are the rows of the table) with asset/capacity building and needs assessment being on the left and right, respectively.

Many of the entries in the table are straightforward and require slight amplification whereas others are not black-and-white contrasts. Philosophical distinctions are made as in rows 1 and 2 (vision and premise of the activity), although in practice there are a lot of similarities between the two endeavors. In rows 3 and 4 (roles of external individuals at the

Table 2.1 Comparing and Contrasting Asset/Capacity Building and Needs Assessment

Asset/Capacity Building	Dimension	Needs Assessment
Some of the individuals involved have a sense of what might be a better future or what should be.	1. Vision	The "what should be" state is like vision although it usually isn't referred to in that way.
This might arise over time, but the idea is present even if vague at the beginning.		When the NA is about the long-term future, there is much overlap with A/CB.
Begins with assets and strengths as the way to go and comes from a can-do, self-reliant attitude.	2. Premise of the activity	Kicks off with a focus that needs (discrepancies, gaps in performance) are prioritized as the basis for action.
Does not start with needs or gaps as they are negative thinking.		Resources (assets) come into play later in the process.
		Starts with identifying the "what should be" and "what is" conditions and gaps between them.
Facilitators are catalysts for the community or organization and help whomever they are working with to find their own direction for capitalizing on assets and strengths.	3. Role of external individuals at the beginning of the endeavor	Probably early on NA is more externally directed and led. It may be that the external person or group narrows the focus and direction of what is to be studied.
Assumes that communities and groups are ready to lead the endeavor, and in some instances externals may have to exercise more leadership.		The above was true 10–15 years ago, but now the organization or agency is more involved at the onset via a needs assessment committee (NAC), which makes more decisions about focus.
		Needs assessors still are more directive than their asset/capacity-building counterparts.

(Continued)

Table 2.1 (Continued)

Asset/Capacity Building	Dimension	Needs Assessment
The involvement would be continuous, but from a "Rogerian" stance the individuals and groups are in control and will find their path toward change and improvement. The catalyst is the same throughout the entire process.	4. Role of external individuals as the endeavor progresses	What the needs assessor does changes as the NA gets into prioritization of needs, selection, and implementation of solution strategies—more local aegis then becomes apparent. The needs assessor during the latter stages of the process becomes more of an advisor with the control being in the organization or agency. Over the course of the assessment ownership becomes the province of those in the organization.
A/CB occurs often in community settings such as health care, public health, and community development. The ideas generalize if one thinks of an agency or a business as a small community.	5. Context for the work	NAs seem to be done in agencies, organizations, institutions, businesses, and companies. The context is usually narrower and somewhat less complex than working in communities.
A/CB and NA may be very similar with regard to initiating factors. Some groups or individuals in a community have a sense that change is required. The focus may be due to the hierarchy although this is usually less so than in NA.	6. How the work might begin	NA and A/CB often commence in the same way, but here it tends to be in response to problems. One difference may be that the impetus initially may come from the administrative level.

Asset/Capacity Building	Dimension	Needs Assessment
Heavy reliance on the use of qualitative methods such as interviews, observations, and focus groups. Some studies are mixed in method, but qualitative methods seem to predominate. Doesn't get much into causal analysis or prioritization strategies.	7. Methodology mix	Surveys and database analyses were noticeable in the past and are still used extensively, but multiple methodology is emphasized more now. More variety of methods than A/CB including causal analysis and prioritization.
The community or group has to be fully committed to the endeavor and may define what data are collected and may even do the data collection. Other data might be used, but the emphasis is as just described.	8. Who is or what groups are involved in data collection?	As the NA gets off the ground, the needs assessor usually does more of this. If an NAC is involved, it has a major effect on what issues are looked at, what sources and people are considered key, and so forth.
Primarily the community and groups, even including the nature of the physical environment. Other sources may be used and are important, but the stress is as above.	9. From what individuals or groups are data obtained?	NA collects data from 3 levels, direct recipients of services, providers of services (teachers, health workers, etc.), and the management of an organization. Data are most often obtained from the first two levels mainly by surveys.
Results inform community discussions about next steps and future directions. The community may be part of the interpretation of the data and is an active decision maker.	10. Use of results	Results lead to identifying the biggest and most important needs (discrepancies), which are prioritized and causally analyzed as to what activities or programs would be undertaken to rectify them.

(Continued)

Table 2.1 (Continued)

Asset/Capacity Building	Dimension	Needs Assessment
Time depends on what has been learned and the size of future efforts to be undertaken. Since cooperation and collaboration across community groups are inherent in this process, it is assumed that they will take more time than NA. Time is predicated on whether the community has engaged in similar efforts previously so the learning curve is not so steep.		The needs assessor with the NAC would usually do the above steps. Less broad group participation is apparent most of the time.
	11. Time frame with understanding that it varies with context and issues of concern	For smaller, less severe needs the estimate to complete the three phases of NA would be perhaps 3 months, not including implementation of solutions. For major and severe needs the time would be longer, and if cooperation or collaboration across groups is required for their resolution, it will escalate. Like A/CB, communities have differential readiness for NA, so time is variable.
In enhancing communities, cooperation and collaboration are essential. Collaboration (shared vision, input, and decision making) is more intense than cooperation and mandates trade-offs for organizations and groups.	12. Role of collaboration and/or cooperation required for activities to be successful	There are cooperative and collaborative NAs, so there is overlap with A/CB. Here, the two camps might be close together.

beginning and as the endeavor progresses), the facilitator in A/CB is a catalyst, a person who guides but is not controlling or directive. For NA in the past the facilitative aspect was less prominent. With a recent emphasis on forming a needs assessment committee (NAC) and having it integral with decision making and implementation of procedures and solutions, the needs assessor would also have to be a facilitator as a group goes through the three phases of the process. Whether it is a community, an organization, or an agency, when activities move into new programs and services or restructuring existing ones (Phase 3), control is less the domain of the needs assessor. Then the community or group must commit to the entire endeavor, and in that regard A/CB and NA are in a similar middle ground. Modern NA fits this pattern.

For row 5 (context), assessments are predominantly observed in organizations and agencies. A/CB is more difficult because it is across a community, not so much in a bounded space. Yet there are instances where assessing needs will be like the supposedly opposite end of the spectrum as in public health or emergency preparedness. The resources and assets of health care organizations, police and fire departments, and groups with heavy equipment will have to be considered (especially if there is an earthquake with many collapsed buildings), and water and utility companies, charitable organizations that provide assistance, the military and national guard, and others will have to be cataloged as assets. For a large emergency (as on September 11, 2001, in the United States), the complexity of working across a set of providers is apparent.

So the problem that confronts NA in regard to disaster planning, and what might be done from the A/CB perspective, is nearly identical. Analogous thinking occurs when looking at collaborative needs spanning organizations, and that is the reason for the category in Table 2.1. More will be said about that later in the discussion.

One other point here: Can NA continue to look inside and not externally? Do organizations exist within cocoons without taking into account an increasingly complex and interdependent society? The author doesn't think so, but he was more restricted until working with Witkin who apprised him of a vista to which he is now committed (see Altschuld, 2004).

How does a needs assessment or an asset/capacity-building effort begin (row 6)? There is limited research to guide an answer. The entries are an educated guess based upon experience and perception. Usually a few individuals or a small group, possibly even from the hierarchy, senses a problem or has a feeling that change would be good for the community or organization. They are the initiators in NA and A/CB. They might be akin to the early adopters/adapters of an innovation. In 2010, Altschuld and

Eastmond speculated about how a needs assessment gets going (small group concerns, external press, accountability demands, problems that arise, a bottom-up, grassroots emerging body). Somehow there is a sense to do something different and move forward. The level (high or grass-roots) may differ, but it is likely that, if investigated, the two processes will be comparable.

As to methodology mix (row 7), a balance is now more common. In 2004, the author made a strong case that needs are not understood from solely quantitative sources such as databases; they are useful but insufficient. Watkins, West Meiers, and Visser (2012) treat both types of data in an equal fashion. Some needs assessors may favor certain methods, but a mixed approach to procedures is being promoted. That could be said, but perhaps to a lesser degree, for A/CB projects. Initial work is more qualitative in feel and includes cataloging of resources and their locations. However, recent articles from the A/CB perspective contain greater usage of quantitative methods including surveys and analyses of existing quantitative data. If the order of what was done was not factored in, it would be difficult to distinguish a needs assessment from capacity building with the proviso that the former are probably more deficient in determining resources. A conclusion is that methods are coalescing and will continue to do so.

Who is involved in data collection (row 8) and who provides data (row 9) would 20 years ago have afforded sharp distinctions. Needs assessors then would have been the prime collectors via surveys, focus group interviews, interviews, and epidemiological or database studies. Other methods were there, but these would have been the main ones for Phases 1 and 2 of assessment. Methods dealing with causality, prioritization, and solution strategies were also employed later in the process. By contrast, in asset/capacity building the community is the major player in regard to methods and data collection, not so much the facilitator.

This picture has changed in the last 15 to 20 years for needs assessment as there has been movement away from the needs assessor directing and controlling the process. If an NAC is active, more of the assessment, the decision making, the questions to pursue, and the collection of data become its province. The external person will be more supportive than was the case previously.

For row 9, the sources are a bit different, but in current practice some asset/capacity-building endeavors are collecting data from groups and sources that are along the lines of a needs assessment (i.e., it is suspected that the three levels of needs assessment are there for A/CB but perhaps not fully explicated). There is a great deal of overlap in the use of results (row 10) for A/CB and NA: The goal is really identical, to improve the organization or community and see positive change occur. Utilizing results and who makes the ultimate decision of where to go next are dependent on how the situation unfolds. In capacity building, the power should reside in the community or organization based on strengths and resources that have been identified. In NA it would be lodged more in the hands of the assessor, the external consultant, but practice is changing, and it is now more open, particularly in Phase 3, where choices are made as to improvements or new programs to be implemented. Thus decisions in the two approaches possess many of the same characteristics.

It is difficult to compare the two entities on time frames (row 11) since each has its own distinct nuances that make estimating somewhat tenuous. Many needs assessments are of short-term duration whereas building a community requires much longer. One conclusion is that needs assessments tend to be quicker than their counterpart. NAs may be narrower in focus, done within a limited community (an agency or a business), not across so many groups and organizations. Altschuld and Kumar (2010) placed needs assessments into two time categories: short term (a year or less) and long term (three years or more). The complexity of issues to be attacked determines how much would be needed. Although there are long- and short-term needs, it is safe to say that asset/capacity building is lengthier, which is reasonable when row 12 (cooperation and collaboration) is taken into account.

For needs assessment, why should anything but limited attention be directed toward cooperation and collaboration since so often it is done within the boundaries of a prescribed organization or institution? Numerous aspects of the situation are already well known and understood. We don't have to attend so much to the concerns of others and institutions outside of ours. The focus is internal, and the problems and needs are ours, not those of somebody else. Cooperation or collaboration can only add to the headaches!

The view is more inward and in some cases applies well. But in an interdependent society will this lead to effective change and growth, especially for some of the concerns confronting us? Certain contexts demand that cooperation or collaboration occur as the norm, not the exception. Establishing lines in the sand doesn't work as in public health preparedness and the requirements for collaboration it places on all involved parties. Consider Exhibit 2.1.

Exhibit 2.1   Cases Where Cooperation and Collaboration Will Be Mandatory

Think of public health preparedness in relation to the assets for dealing with catastrophes—epidemics, earthquakes, tsunamis, and terrorist attacks (9/11, the bombings at the Boston Marathon in 2013). Obvious questions include:

Can any single organization or group handle what might occur?

Does any organization have at its disposal the resources to deal with a problem of this magnitude?

A catastrophe presents different types of issues to be resolved, so will one organization by itself be equipped to treat everything?

What kind of organization and service provider cross-coordination must there be for maximizing success?

Does every provider know its assets and strengths and those of other groups so that help will flow smoothly?

In this vein, look at air pollution, water quality, transportation, delivering cost-effective higher education in times of mounting financial difficulties, and so forth. All of these are not solvable without the sharing of resources, energy, and expertise.

For needs assessment there are social and economic issues that press for going beyond the boundaries of one's safe personal and institutional space. What of the asset/capacity building? Cooperation and collaboration are its heart, its inner core. As stressed by Kretzmann and McKnight (1993), the essence is an in-depth assessment of a wide array of resources. What businesses are in the community, and what do they do? What could they contribute to strengthening the community, and how could they be built into what is to be done? What organizations such as clubs or religious groups are there, and what is their potential involvement? Are there areas in which they could complement what the businesses can do?

Bring in educational resources and government ones (community centers, agencies), and the landscape becomes stronger but more complicated. Tie in the skills and abilities of individuals in the community, along with volunteers, and it is clear that asset/capacity building entails forging this mix into a potent force for improvement. Needs assessment and asset/capacity building are alike on this dimension. Without cooperation and collaboration, they would be less or of diminished impact. What does this mean?

View cooperation and collaboration as being on the ends of a continuum. An assessor or an asset/capacity builder might be conducting a study and would desire your *cooperation* in collecting data and ask for help via questions such as these:

- Could you help in identifying those who have insight and understanding about the community?
- What might be some good ways to get them involved and offering their thoughts?
- Do you have any ideas about questions that might be included?
- What are some of the smaller or unique groups in the community we should have in the study?
- Could you assist us in contacting them and gaining entry into their organizations?
- Your assistance in collecting data would be very much appreciated. Could you help?
- Would you endorse our study and lend the name of your group in support of it?

These are cooperative queries. We value your assistance to do the work, but it is primarily that, cooperation, not collaboration or a low level of it. See Figure 2.1.

Collaboration goes deeper. Cooperation has to be there but ratcheted dramatically up beyond just providing help and assistance. Now the collaborating organization is a full partner as to what the data are about, how the data will be used, what kinds of decisions might be made from the data, what new priorities might be initiated, and so on. Cooperation frequently takes place but full collaboration not so often. Issues come into play. It connotes that a group or an organization give up a measure of control. Compromise is in order with the potential of losing some of a precious commodity, turf. This can be psychologically difficult as a trade-off for ultimately greater, more positive outcomes. It goes counter to the grain of us as persons, and the level of exchange and working together may not be achieved.

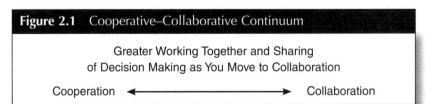

Figure 2.1 Cooperative–Collaborative Continuum

Greater Working Together and Sharing
of Decision Making as You Move to Collaboration

Cooperation ⟵⟶ Collaboration

What are other implications of collaboration? In 2010, Altschuld and Eastmond examined the specifics of collaborative needs assessments across institutions and organizations based on needs that are mutual and of high enough interest to each participating entity. Table 2.2 from their work is about the pros and cons of collaboration in needs assessment, and it could be extended to asset/capacity building by simply changing terms. The entries come from students with generally many years of experience in school systems, educational institutions, or social or government agencies who were asked to identify reasons for and against working together. This exercise was repeatedly used with about the same results each time. Interestingly, the positives and negatives were always close to equal.

Table 2.2 A Sampling of Reasons For and Against Collaborative Needs Assessments

Reasons For	Reasons Against
Shared resources lead to economies of scale for the needs assessment and for actions taken to resolve needs.	Fear of loss of turf or control of same.
Money saved could go to new and/or additional services (more resources).	Unless the setup is perceived to be fair, there could be acrimony.
Better use of staff skills across organizations. Not having to duplicate work.	Limited exposure to working together across entities.
Not operating in a competitive environment.	Sometimes plans developed across entities by committees will not be very good. Negative connotations of a committee product.
Improvement of available services that are poorly done at the present time.	Activities and actions will be difficult to sustain when many parties are involved.
Cross-fertilization of ideas across organizations and groups.	Some groups due to size and other factors will dominate the collective (lack of parity).

Reasons For	Reasons Against
Creating opportunities and even new job possibilities.	Eliminations of jobs and reductions in force (job insecurity).
Collective actions could lead to promising responses to problems.	If perceived as above, there could be an unwillingness of individuals and groups to give honest and frank input.
Establishing or enhancing channels of communications across organizations and groups (very positive outcome).	Normal competitive spirit will emerge.
New experiences, meeting people, fresh ideas, stimulating growth and change.	Way too much hassle and not worth the effort.

Source: Adapted from Altschuld & Eastmond (2010). Used with permission.

The conceptual base for collaboration (and cooperation for that matter) is that we do better joining forces and using assets and resources in a united fashion. That is obvious, but there are powerful forces against doing so. Going from cooperation to collaboration requires ways to ease or reduce negatives. Altschuld and Eastmond (2010) suggested guidelines for achieving collaboration in needs assessment, which are valid for the hybrid framework:

- Given that opposing forces will be encountered, collaboration will take more time. (Frustration will occur, so patience is in order.)
- Protection of turf is a major concern, so take it into consideration when going for collaboration.
- Find ways that different parties and groups can share so that they have an enhanced sense of ownership and commitment.
- Make sure that whatever the groups and individuals are collaborating on is of high importance for all of them.
- It might not be at the top of everyone's list, but it has to be of sufficient value for buy-in, commitment, and action of some sort to improve the situation.
- Collaboration requires coordination to be successful. It doesn't occur spontaneously and might not be sustainable without it.

- What is helpful is for the individual or group leading the effort to have worked previously across organizations in collaborative ventures. What problems did they encounter, how were they resolved, which strategies for resolution worked best and which did not, what did overall success look like, how was it determined, and so on? This type of background will help in smoothing rough spots and building a spirit across involved parties.
- The *criticality* of leadership cannot be overstated for it is at the center of asset/capacity building or of any collaborative needs assessment.
- Keep in mind that when looking at the resources held by not just one organization but many, the door is open for creative problem solving.

This whole topic is vital to needs assessments and asset/capacity building, and the same will be true for the hybrid framework.

In this vein, it should be noted that in other contexts the concept of collaboration has a slightly different look, and the term that might be used is *partnership*. Lepicki, Glandon, and Mullins (2013) perceived it that way when working with Adult Basic and Literacy Education (ABLE) programs in Ohio. They created the Partnership Evaluation Model with five levels of development to describe partnerships (collaborations in the context of this book). They are in Figure 2.2. What these authors have done is formalized the idea of working together to enhance the delivery of ABLE programs across diverse regions of the state. Similarly, partnering in community involvement in youth development and school success was promoted by the Harvard Family Research Project (2013). For them, there are seven key elements (shared vision of learning, shared leadership and governance, etc.) with many similarities to the ABLE schematic.

The idea of partnering or collaborating underlies a funding program currently in the state of Ohio for innovative ways that local governments could work together to enhance citizen services (Siegel, 2012). The premise is that costs of provision can be significantly reduced across jurisdictions while maintaining quality and service levels. The savings could be as large as 70%. Logistical problems in doing this are to be expected, and the state will assist those who are funded for a smooth transition across groups.

Interestingly, Friedman (2013) has commented about the need for collaborative efforts in government, citing successes in the extremely competitive environment of Silicon Valley. He begins by noting the positive

Figure 2.2 Partnership Evaluation Model

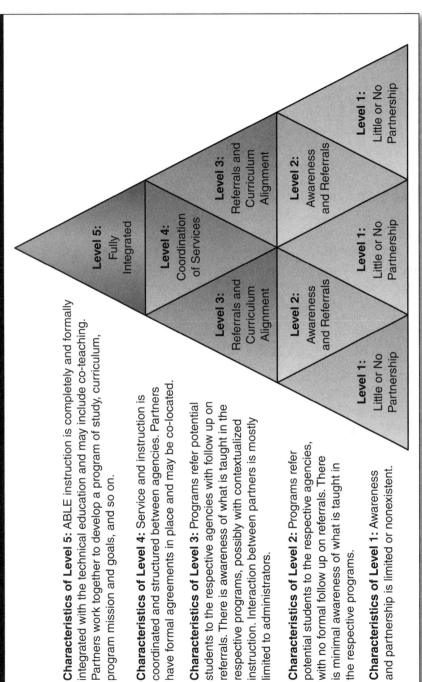

Characteristics of Level 5: ABLE instruction is completely and formally integrated with the technical education and may include co-teaching. Partners work together to develop a program of study, curriculum, program mission and goals, and so on.

Characteristics of Level 4: Service and instruction is coordinated and structured between agencies. Partners have formal agreements in place and may be co-located.

Characteristics of Level 3: Programs refer potential students to the respective agencies with follow up on referrals. There is awareness of what is taught in the respective programs, possibly with contextualized instruction. Interaction between partners is mostly limited to administrators.

Characteristics of Level 2: Programs refer potential students to the respective agencies, with no formal follow up on referrals. There is minimal awareness of what is taught in the respective programs.

Characteristics of Level 1: Awareness and partnership is limited or nonexistent.

Source: Lepicki, Glandon, & Mullins (2013). Used with permission.

connotation of the concept and a shrill negative one, being a collaborator as in Nazi-occupied countries in World War II. The positive side occurs where there is a climate for it and where the ultimate good of the client, the consumer, or the culture is foremost for all parties. The observation is insightful, and when we push for working together, groups might be reminded of this important fundamental.

As another example, the mayor of Columbus, Ohio, assembled a coalition of a wide cross section of the community to establish directions for the public schools (Coleman, 2013). This was partly in response to a major crisis but in addition seemed to be motivated by a sincere desire to improve. In a short span of time the group collected much information about the operations of the district, engaged 1,000 citizens in various activities to solicit input, worked to identify new and dynamic leadership to replace the retiring superintendent, and took other first steps to propel positive and meaningful change. The collaborative aspects are noticeable, and the activities of the coalition parallel portions of the hybrid framework that will now be described.

DEVELOPING THE HYBRID FRAMEWORK

In reviewing literature a number of asset/capacity-building and needs assessment projects were located. The drive behind them was not needs assessment, but needs were not neglected, and resources were at least partly going to be attenuated by them. The two activities were used in tandem to help organizations.

Common patterns popped up frequently across what were thought to be different procedures, processes, models, and frameworks. A consistent theme was there—listening to the voice of the community or organization. It went much further. That voice was prime in terms of what information was collected and seen as important, what were sources of pride and what were concerns, what were the strengths of the community, what were its important components, what might be future possibilities, what would be good things to do, and so forth. Subjects weren't targets but main players in the enterprise. The persons collecting data also were voices in the drama, and the facilitator was catalytic, not controlling. This stance was inherent in empowerment and participatory evaluation and evaluation capacity building. Whether it was from evaluation, asset/capacity building, or collaborative needs assessment is not of concern, but it is the emphasis that matters. The focus is on community and how it is fundamental to improvement and change.

One other strand of thought impacting a hybrid framework is strategic planning (Figure 2.3). Obviously, needs are part of it with the left and right anchors being its two prime elements—"what is" and "what should be." Between them are internal and external screens (strengths, weaknesses, opportunities, and threats—SWOTs) through which the current status is examined in relation to the future situation. Strengths and opportunities are like concepts in asset/capacity building, and weaknesses and threats are closer to needs assessment. The final piece for the hybrid framework comes from the three-phase model of needs assessment expanded by Altschuld and Kumar (2010).

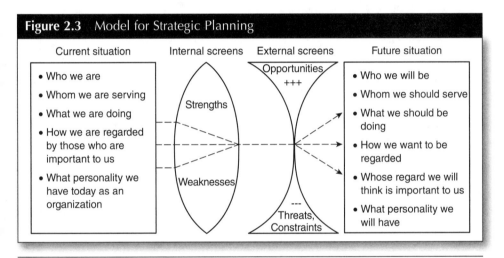

Figure 2.3 Model for Strategic Planning

Source: From Witkin & Altschuld (1995), originally from Nutt & Backoff (1992) and used with permission.

THE HYBRID FRAMEWORK

The hybrid is a prototype, not an absolute. It is to be used, tested, refined, and refined again. It is a framework, not a rigid model, for the intent here, and that is why the softer word fits better—think of it in that light. Table 2.3 contains an overview of it.

The first step doesn't start from a needs or assets/resources stance. The idea is that as communities or organizations raise questions about improvement or where they might be going, they often don't really know or aren't certain as to what might be required and what to do. Watkins and Guerra (2002) observed in needs assessment that when groups originally asked for assistance, they were more into evaluation than assessment.

Table 2.3 The Hybrid Framework

Step	Purpose	Comments
1. Scoping the context	Probe into the situation by a variety of means to determine what might be the best course to pursue. What emerges—needs assessment, asset/capacity building, or a hybrid?	Whether in needs assessment or asset/capacity building, scoping is essential. Form a working committee to find basic information about the context.
2. Decide on what actions should be taken	Determine what to do: • nothing, • a needs assessment, • an asset/capacity-building endeavor, or • a hybrid approach.	Depending on what has been learned, there are numerous possibilities for action. The working committee, not the external person or group, is the key to making the decision.
3. Divide the working group into two subcommittees	Identify resources, strengths, and assets as well as needs at the same time. Subcommittees work independently on needs or assets.	It is important that the charge to each subcommittee is clear. If the overall committee is not large enough for division, start with the asset (positive) side of the equation.
4. Subcommittee(s) *independently* place key findings in tables or figures	Portray findings and what is being learned into formats that facilitate discussion about how the information can be used.	Tables or simple figures should enable better decision making. Too much information can overwhelm, so strive for simplicity.
5. Subcommittee(s) exchange what has been found and then meet to discuss how to use results	Align the two parts—assets and resources with needs. Come to agreement as to where the assets and capacity aspects could be applied to resolve needs, if there is congruence.	There should be a fairly good understanding of needs and assets, generated separately and arrayed to promote discourse and an honest exchange of ideas. Each subcommittee should review the work of the other before group discussion begins.

Step	Purpose	Comments
6. Develop a strategy for improvement based on assets and needs	Build off the prior step translating what is now understood into mechanisms for development and positive change.	The information available establishes a foundation for action plans. Sufficient group chemistry should be there for this activity to proceed smoothly.
7. Implement plans, monitor, and evaluate as to how well they are moving forward	Put into effect the activities that have been planned, see how they are functioning, and see what the outcomes are.	Determine that plans are translated into real programs and events. Formative and summative evaluation should be done.
8. Recycle back to earlier asset and needs findings to add more pieces to the improvement package	Pick up other facets of improvement that could not be done as first or initial activities.	Usually there will be too many pieces to proceed, so revisit previous results and move ahead with selected ones.

They devised a simple rating instrument with alternatively ordered items, half about needs and half about evaluation. If the ratings were higher for one half than the other, that tipped off where the group was in its thinking and what it might do.

The same idea applies to "scoping the context." Shuck blinders and constraints and be open-minded as to what might be the best way to go. It is hard to do, but it is the course to follow. An example of keeping an open stance occurred when the author was contacted by a state agency (natural resources) to help with a needs assessment. They knew the needs, and there was nothing of use that he could offer. They didn't require an assessment, but weren't sure about the causes of the needs and were puzzled by how constituents perceived some watershed problems. It was easy to suggest that they do a straightforward survey, focus groups, or causal analysis with subsamples in specified regions. The author did not get a consulting contract but made recommendations that were attuned to the situation, not what he *a priori* could do.

In a hybrid approach, as early as feasible, community members or organizational staff should be included in the process. As explained in Chapter 3, they might interview others, seek reports and prior studies, or observe in the setting. Whatever those activities are, they most likely will have two components—assets and strengths, and needs that arise in the course of preliminary investigation—and what comes from them are grist for the second step (deciding on action that might be taken) in the process. A facilitator or facilitating group pulls together what has been learned about needs and assets so that a discussion ensues about what is understood about the community, organization, or agency. The information, summarized, probably in factoid sheets, is distributed to everyone in the group. To get the discussion going, ask questions such as the following:

Assets and Resources (Strengths)

- What are the strengths and resources that this community or organization has?
- What has been done before that improved this community or organization?
- What activities, events, and so on are liked and appreciated?
- Has anything come up about what was done quite a long time ago that perhaps should be tried again?

Needs

- What are problems and issues confronting the community or organization?
- Which among these is most pressing or urgent to resolve?
- If we were to resolve some of them, which ones do you think would be of most interest to the community or organization?

From there the group considers whether it would be best to more fully assess needs, to explore resources and strengths and how they could be utilized, or to do both. Depending on the discussion, the decisions are:

Do Nothing Enthusiasm is lacking to proceed further, and nothing much will be accomplished, so end here. There are resources and needs, but they are not important enough to warrant further action or the investment of time and energy.

Focus on

Assets. We are positive about our assets, resources, and strengths and sense that there is much to gain by putting time into learning more about them. Our effort should go into this.

Focus On

Needs. There are needs that we are aware of in this community or organization that should be looked into in greater depth. Definitely needs assessment is what should be done.

Do a Hybrid

Approach. We don't know enough about the assets and needs. We should do both activities and work to improve our situation from the knowledge gained.

If the group is undecided, start with assets and later investigate needs. Look at what is there rather than concentrating on needs. Beginning with assets puts a positive spin in motion. But eventually needs will arise.

Steps 3–5 (collecting information, arraying it for decision making, using the results) are the natural course to be followed after decisions are made to do a hybrid investigation. Community members, organizational staff, or agency personnel would be formed into working committees to collect and analyze preliminary information (data sources, reports) that is located. As much as possible, seek existing sources of information, and that is a reasonable expectation. There are census data, regional planning documents, educational status reports, and chamber of commerce studies that should be used to the fullest extent. If some data are missing, think of shortcut (cheap and quick) ways of obtaining them, or at least give indications of what full data might reveal. Placing the information into a utilitarian format for guiding deliberations is not an easy task. It is described in detail in later chapters (see Chapter 3 and particularly Table 3.3).

This is not to be externally led since it is the province of those most concerned and affected by how the results are used, but someone or the group has to take responsibility for guiding the process. It has to keep it moving apace and getting what is being garnered into reasonable tables and summaries for later use. This doesn't take place by magic, and a subtle dimension of facilitation (being a catalyst) is necessary for a successful effort. Notice it is best to have subgroups working simultaneously/independently on assets and needs; otherwise, the two components could contaminate each other prematurely.

When there is enough information to initiate thinking about next steps, schedule a meeting of the two independent groups. (It may take some time to come to this point, depending on what is found and how it informs understanding and potential change.) It is important that the data and main findings are set up so that it is easy for everyone to see what is known about assets and needs. This might be by short tables or figures in which the findings stand out to the reader. Present results not in so much detail that their digestion is difficult and can lead to an upset stomach. Place the needs and assets/resources into categories to help participants in their review. Provide each of the groups with summaries of the others' findings for review as a small group and then go to a large group session. For the small group reviewing the needs or asset findings use thought generators like the following:

Needs Review Group (the individuals who looked at assets)

- How realistic do the needs seem to you?
- Were there any that surprised you?
- Are there others that seem to be missing?
- Which one or ones stand out as highest priority, and why?
- Which ones could be resolved or improved in the short run, and which are going to take a long time?

(Add in the next questions only after they have completed the prior ones.)

- When you think about what has been found about resources, are there places where you think they could be put to good use?
- Are there ways to combine resources for resolving needs or for interesting ways to move ahead?

Assets Review Group (the individuals who looked at needs)

- Were there any of them that surprised you?
- Are there others that seem to be missing?
- Which one or ones stand out as having the highest likelihood of access and being used?
- Which ones could be used in the short run, and which are going to take a long time?

(Add in the next questions, but only after they have completed the prior ones.)

- When you think about what you found about needs, are there places where the assets could be put to good use?
- Are there innovative opportunities to use resources that would enhance the community, organization, or agency?

Now the seeds have been planted, fertilized, and watered, and growth can take place. The last three steps (defining the action strategy, implementing and evaluating it, recycling back to areas not previously attended to) in the hybrid are where the payoff occurs. The process has moved to formulating plans for applying assets to a need or set of needs, or it can use strengths creatively—an exciting part of the journey.

One suggestion is to begin small before going large. Doing so takes less time for implementation and demonstrating outcomes. Groups require reinforcement, and shorter endeavors can produce results that satisfy the requirement. Evaluation should be built into any new activities for monitoring and demonstrating outcomes. In terms of the evaluation, pose questions to the group along the following lines:

- What should the activity look like in practice, and how will we know that it is taking place as planned?
- If an outsider were seeing it in operation, what would this person be observing?
- What is the nature of the change?
- If we were to say that the new project or effort was successful, what would that mean?
- What are indicators/outcomes that should be expected?
- How many people might be affected, in what ways would they be changed or different, how could we demonstrate success to ourselves and others, and so on?

Success might be that two or three community or organizational assets are working together where previously they haven't. Other indicators include greater participation in services, continuing work or planning for the use of resources, or the longer-term resolution of needs.

The emphasis is on smaller, more immediate initiatives, not ones that require more time and input of resources. This incremental approach is not a dodge from major concerns. Certainly a number of them have come up previously in the hybrid framework and undoubtedly are in some of the work products of the subcommittees. They are not being dismissed or forgotten but are being revisited as the group grows with success on what are admittedly easier-to-achieve objectives and starting points. If too much is attempted and not enough progress occurs, enthusiasm may weaken, and momentum will be lost and hard to regain. Avoid this at all costs.

Indeed the final step has been included for just this reason. There will be a demand to move to higher and more expansive efforts as time passes.

A lot of energy has been expended to date, so instead of beginning anew return to prior findings. What short-term and long-term projects might we now undertake? Given what we have done, could we enhance or build from it? What seems to be missing, and what might have the biggest bang for the time and resources we might devote to it? How much would it take to enhance what we currently do? Let's move to new and higher outcomes or other parts of our communities and organizations.

In most cases there will be areas like these that have been identified but not focused upon. Take a second look and see where good can be done. As the group begins that second review, more data and information on a specific area may be desirable, and it might relate to assets, resources, and/or needs. If that is the case, don't reinitiate the entire hybrid approach again. Think about what data are required and what might be shortcuts for attaining them. Heavy and long involvement in data collection may slow down things too much, dampen fervor, and be detrimental. The group should be the judge on how to keep moving and maintain momentum. The hybrid framework and its steps have been covered briefly. The latter in depth will be the substance of Chapters 3, 4, and 5.

HIGHLIGHTS OF CHAPTER 2

1. Key terms of needs assessment and asset/capacity building were defined. It is important that they be distinguished from ECB (evaluation capacity building).

2. Needs assessment and asset/capacity building were compared showing overlaps as well as differences.

3. Attention was directed to a cooperation-collaboration continuum, and needs assessment and asset/capacity building are similar on this dimension. This concept might be termed *partnering*.

4. A hybrid framework (not a rigid model) to span the gap between needs assessment and asset/capacity building was proposed.

5. The steps in the framework were overviewed, and decisions that a group might encounter were noted.

DISCUSSION QUESTIONS

1. Even though only eight steps were described, are they a sensible characterization of how the process (working within the hybrid framework) might occur?

2. Are some of the steps incorrect or out of place? If so, which ones, where, and why should changes be made?

3. Are there steps that should be added? If so, what are they, why are they necessary, and where should they be placed?

4. The process outlined in the hybrid framework must be managed in order to be successful. Who should do it, and how should it be done to keep the flavor and the spirit of involvement?

5. When you review the framework, where might it not work well, and what are your thoughts about what might be done at those points to ameliorate the situation?

6. If you have been involved in a collaborative venture before, what were its ups and downs?

7. Can needs and assets and strengths be separated in a meaningful way? What are your thoughts?

8. Community- or organization-enhancing approaches often can get bogged down if they go on for extended periods. Where might the process be shortened, and what would you suggest to shorten it?

3

Looking Closely at the First Three Critical Steps in the Framework

As people age and enter into different facets of life, they consider ways to pass property to spouses, children, and grandchildren in a legal, tax-propitious manner. This could be in a trust that allows estates to be distributed with fewer tax consequences than if that legal protection was not in place. Establishing such a trust is a two-phase process. The first phase details who benefits, what categories of things are in the trust, when it will take effect, who the trustees are, at what point their responsibilities begin, and assorted clauses and features. The trust provides a basic structure through which its provisions are implemented. This is similar to what must be done for the hybrid framework that bridges the gap between needs assessment and asset/capacity building. More explanation must be there for its steps.

In the second phase of a trust situation the classes of assets or the fields within it must be populated. What you own is placed in the trust. What are tangible assets such as a home? Are there checking and savings accounts? What about paintings, artwork, china, cars, or other items? Are there investments, and are any of them complicated? What about businesses in which you may be involved? What debts will the trust and trustees have to resolve? How does the trust relate to other legal documents (will, living will, power of attorney, health care specifications such as "do not resuscitate")? For the trust you have to fill its various sections and areas.

The analogy to the hybrid framework holds but not entirely. Table 2.3 in Chapter 2 has many cells that require populating but with differences from a trust. They consist of methods for the steps and where a group or community would be in the overall process of change and improvement. This is akin to the legal document but with a significant distinction. Generally, property and possessions fall nicely into categories. In needs assessments and asset/capacity-building endeavors, methods may align with one category or match separate parts of the framework depending on how it is implemented and the depth of information to be collected. One method may not solely reside in the realm of one step.

Many texts in needs assessment (Altschuld & Witkin, 2000; Watkins, West Meiers, & Visser, 2012; Witkin & Altschuld, 1995) speak to the placement of methods in the process. This is helpful, but there is slippage in practice, and methods are creatively employed across activities, so placement in the hybrid is suggestive, not prescriptive. The methods are borrowed liberally from what needs assessors and asset/capacity builders do in their specialized domains. When procedures may seem identical, questions will focus more on assets, strengths, and resources or more on needs. Be flexible when thinking about ways of collecting information.

METHODS FOR THE FIRST THREE STEPS IN NEEDS ASSESSMENT AND ASSET/CAPACITY BUILDING

Table 3.1 has the first three steps with suggested methods but not an exhaustive set of them. This provides a good overview of the framework and its implementation, but neither all procedures nor all the details of how they are done, for whole books could be devoted to such descriptions. Only a glimpse is here. Certainly other procedures could be used. Be open in methodological choice and consider ways to cheaply use or adopt techniques.

STEP 1. SCOPING THE CONTEXT—GENERAL CONSIDERATIONS

When scoping a situation, whether one is internal or external, questions have to be raised about the interest and motivation for improvement: Who are the key actors? What is causing the concern? What are the issues? How long has the situation been like this? What has been done or not done so far? What is the history? What are the skills and strengths we can build on

Table 3.1	First Three Steps in the Hybrid Framework With Possible Methods/Strategies	
Step	*Purpose*	*Methods/Strategies*
1. Scoping the context	Probe the situation to determine what course of action to pursue. Do preliminary needs assessment or asset/capacity building.	Informal reconnaissance Casual interviews Observations Informal discussions Micro-ethnology Cultural audits Review of existing information Other related strategies Usually done by a working committee
2. Deciding what actions should be taken	Determine next actions such as doing nothing, or conducting a needs assessment, an asset/capacity-building endeavor, or a hybrid approach.	Collation of what has been found Array of information to facilitate group decision making Individual and group review of the information Group discussion and resolution of what to do next: • nothing • needs assessment • asset/capacity building • hybrid approach
3. Dividing the working committee into two subcommittees	Subcommittee 1 conducts a needs assessment. Subcommittee 2 identifies resources, assets, and strengths.	Assignments and responsibilities for each subcommittee are specified. (If the overall group is too small for subdivision, start on assets—accentuate the positive.)

to move forward? What are the good things that could be taken advantage of to accomplish outcomes? Are there untapped assets in our community that could be used?

Usually some small group in a community or in an organization begins to think that something has to change. These thoughts might come from the administration, a grassroots group, or some combination. *The company is no longer competitive and could go out of business. We are losing jobs to other locations here or abroad. Our community is having problems in relation to crime, maintenance of property, deteriorating infrastructure, services not being as plentiful or as good as we would like, and other issues. We have to act; we simply can't stand still. The quality of work or community life isn't what it should be. What can we do?* The group perceives a future that it doesn't like, becomes agitated about it, and meets to talk about what might happen. Exhibit 3.1 is an illustration of how this might occur.

Exhibit 3.1   The Historical Case of German Village in Columbus, Ohio

When the author was studying organic chemistry in graduate school at Ohio State, he was invited to an undergraduate assistant's home for a Christmas dinner. What a wonderful offer, and for a starving graduate student one that was readily accepted. The family's home was comfortable and in an area of Columbus that was originally settled by Germans (not exclusively) and had brick streets and houses of an older-1880s up to early-1900s European style. It was quaint but showing age and in the next few years would be in decline. It was 1962, and a good time was had by all.

Anyone who has visited Columbus over the last 30-plus years knows that this is German Village. It is a trendy part of the city filled with the same homes that were there in 1962, but many have been refurbished and restored while preserving their old-style demeanor. The houses now go for high prices.

There are shops and restaurants and an alive feel to the place. The narrow brick streets are still there and reflect the time when the village was coming into being. The author always takes friends from out of town to dinner in the village, and they fall in love with it.

How did this renewal (if that word is appropriate) get started? Was it a needs assessment or an asset/capacity-building effort, a mixing of the two, or something else? A small group of individuals who lived in the area had a cherished affection for it. They saw what might be the situation in the future if nothing was done (in needs assessment the discrepancy between what is and what might be).

This small, motivated group was the impetus for the revival and resurgence. It was a grassroots, bottom-up endeavor and has become immensely successful. Now when you go to Schmidt's Sausage Haus, a popular and large eating place dating back to the 1880s, at the peak dining hours, be prepared for a serious wait.

But was it needs assessment or asset/capacity building? It would have been easy to just focus on needs and go into the negative dependency mind-set noted by Kretzmann and McKnight (1993). That was far from the reality of the group. In terms of *assets*, they saw wealth. The houses were unique in style, the narrow streets were distinct for the city, and the village was located close to downtown Columbus, so location, location, location was very good.

And what about those not-very-wide brick streets and what eventually would be seen as a lack of parking? From a needs perspective wouldn't it be better to change them into modern thoroughfares? That would be in conflict with the farsighted, *asset* vision of the group. And, to this day, the streets remain crowded, narrow, bricked, and hard to maintain. Without them, something would be missing. Being seen as an asset was a positive factor, and if the needs basis for action had predominated, it could be quite a different scene today.

The question persists: Needs or assets—what is it?

In some fashion as the enterprise begins you have to conduct what is called friendly reconnaissance, not scouting out an enemy but learning what is going on and is there. Even though the initial premise is different, needs assessors and asset/capacity builders do comparable things— observe; informally interview; go to the web to look for reports, newspaper articles, blogs, and other reports; attend community meetings; and others. The idea is to get a sense of what community members or organizational personnel view as strengths and needs.

This overarching rubric is what Altschuld and Eastmond (2010) called micro-ethnology. A small cadre of people has to learn about the situation of interest. What is on the minds of those who live in the community or work in the organization? What do they like and dislike, and why do they have these perceptions? What do they see as the strengths and needs? How much do they care about their work or residential area? Are the streets clean, does the work space seem inviting, are houses maintained, and are there warm feelings as well as concerns? What are our thoughts about where we live and work; are we upbeat and do we see potential, or are we dispirited?

In the same vein, what has been said about our community—what are its ups and downs? What kinds of things are being noted by others? What data exist about the context, and what do they say about it? Where is the information to be found? How can we organize to get improvement going, and who will be doing this work? What has been done or proposed previously for change? Who played important roles before, and are they still active?

Another area to be probed is what cooperation or collaboration work has gone on or is currently taking place. In an asset/capacity-building study of four small neighboring communities in the United Kingdom, Balogh, Whitelaw, and Thompson (2008) perceived that only two were likely to move ahead, those with people or groups already working together. This affords a stronger base for improvement as compared to situations where such is not there. (This is a salient factor, and Donnermeyer, Plested, Edwards, Oetting, and Littlethunder [1997] and Edwards, Thurman, Plested, Oetting, and Swanson [2000] have suggested surveying a community or group in terms of its readiness to progress.)

Who directs the investigative effort? This might seem pushy, going against the inclusive stance inherent in the hybrid framework. It is important and has to be answered. In asset/capacity building and needs assessment the consultants and others like them are guiders with the focus on organizing for progress, not controlling the process. For needs assessment this view is evolving, but it is not new for asset/capacity building.

The small group that is eager for change and looking into the setting constitutes the fact finders and pulse takers, and involved external folks are facilitators lending expertise about data collection and collation, good or potential sources of existing information, and so forth. They might lead initial discussions about what we already know, what we should be learning, what questions we should ask, what should be observed, whom we should talk to, how the information and facts should be put together, and other related content. But a delicate balance must be there for community buy-in and ownership. As much as possible, the community or organizational staff should be the force behind the endeavor. Concerns from this group drive the process and how information is obtained. Group members should be a big part of data gathering for they know the context better than external persons, are like those whom they are engaging in casual conversations, have a feel for what to observe and where to probe, and have rapport. Guidance for them is useful, but it is always against the above backdrop and an understanding that the project is the community's.

The external individuals understand methods and process skills but do not have the intimacy and sensitivity. They may also collect data and do some of the work. Are they seeing what the community members do? If not, what are they missing? What unique insights and angles might be added? Their efforts would be a somewhat independent verification of what community members find. Or they might with small group members assist in exploring reports, records, and epidemiologic sources that aid in scoping the situation. Here they could be very helpful.

Under the aegis of the group members they could organize and portray data. Putting what is being found into a meaningful format for decision making is critical and does not happen by itself. Without a coherent picture the group could lose interest and the endeavor dissipate without any visible results. In assembling what has been garnered from numerous and useful pieces of data, think about the following:

What are the assets and strengths in the community or organization?

What are the weaknesses, what individuals and groups are associated with the assets, and what individuals or groups are most affected by needs?

What has been done earlier, and how successful or unsuccessful was it?

Were there instances of groups working together to promote change?

Have outside factors come into play that impacted the community or organization, and how have they been handled?

What historical events can we build into our thinking about change and improvement?

What is the context, and is it ready for change, or are there major obstacles to be faced?

Are there other communities and organizations whose experience could help us?

What should come from all this effort is a rich collage of what scoping has revealed about the situation! It is not a road map for change, but it does lay out the landscape and its human dimensions.

STEP 1. SCOPING THE CONTEXT—WAYS IT COULD BE DONE

Numerous techniques could be used to determine the social contours of the community or organization.

1.1 Micro-ethnology and Preliminary Interviews

The micro-ethnology perspective is the eyes and ears of the individual or group (Altschuld & Eastmond, 2010). As you walk through the organization or community, note what is going on and is there. In a school, for example, what is the condition of the building, what instructional technology do teachers have access to, do students and teachers seem friendly, are you able to go around in an unescorted fashion, what is on the bulletin boards, and the like? Think of micro-ethnology as doing informal detective work (see Figure 3.1).

Figure 3.1 Sherlock Holmes Doing Micro-ethnology

Source: iStockphoto.com/Tomacco

The same strategy would apply to an organization or a business. What does the eating area look like, is it clean, are the restrooms clean and maintained, are the staff members free to decorate their work spaces, is the place welcoming, is there an appropriate amount of human interaction, and what is the overall texture and feel? Are there noticeable disparities in different locations within the organization, and what might they be?

Extending this to a community is reasonable, but a community is considerably larger than a school or most businesses. What catches your attention when you drive or walk through the streets? What kinds of business establishments are there, and depending on the day of the week how busy are they? Are there some that should be there that perhaps are not? What is the condition of apartment buildings, homes, and other residences?

Do homeowners take care of their properties? Do you see signs of deterioration or what the neighborhood might be like in 5 or 10 years?

Coupled with your observations are the people in the community willing to share with you. Identify who you are and your purpose in being there. Being a member of the community is helpful for street credibility, and a sense of trust could lead to honest insights and useful opinions. Indicate that you are working with a team that is looking at ways to improve the community—to learn what its strengths are, ideas for change, what has been tried before, what has or hasn't worked, what might be issues, and similar questions.

State that the data will be put together by others from the area, that all comments will be kept confidential, and that individuals will not be named in any report, and encourage frank and open comments. Ideally each member in this scoping activity would talk with 5 to 10 people, and with 5 to 10 in the group there could be up to 100 casual conversations. This could be done by teams with one member asking questions and the other summarizing what is being said by interviewees. (Later on, scoping would tend to be more formal such as in structured interviews, but for now the process is informal to get a quick view of what the community is like and what residents are saying.)

For the interviews, there should be a range of respondents from younger to older residents with the older ones, if they have lived there a long time, having a better understanding of history and change over the years. The time perspective of the younger ones is much shorter. Make sure in summaries that age and length of time in the community of interviewees are recorded, since responses might be variable. (Exhibit 3.2 is an example of what can be learned from a few simple interviews.)

Exhibit 3.2 What Can Be Learned From a Few Casual Interviews

A few years after the author began teaching needs assessment, he thought that a good way for students to get into the topic was to interview people in their workplaces or university departments via a few questions, and what they found would be discussed in class the next week. The inquiries were:

Did the interviewee know of or recall any such assessments that had been done?

(Continued)

(Continued)

If so, what actually happened (methods, procedures, review of data, etc.)?

What was found, or what were the main findings?

What was done with the results? Did anything change?

The author asked the same questions of a colleague in an adjoining office. He had been at the university a long time and had seen a reorganization of the college and the relocation of their small academic unit. He had a good idea of what had gone on in the past.

What did this activity produce? It revealed the lay of the land but with disappointing results. For the small class, most students reported no needs assessments or limited efforts. A few surveys had been conducted, and that was about it. The colleague remembered one survey some time back with no changes or new directions emerging from it—not what the author wanted to hear.

But on the positive side with just a few interviews it was possible to learn about the nonexistent baseline for needs assessments. Interviews like this are easy to do and have high information value.

The interviewers should have a list of questions to guide them and a recorder for capturing the comments of those being interviewed. A form for jotting down comments or observations would be helpful. This is a casual 10-minute conversation, so many detailed questions would not be in order. The team members should have five to six key areas to probe after finding how long a person has lived in the community and related demographic information. After completion, thank the individual for offering his or her thoughts. If any interviewees would like a report across interviews, send them one. When the interview is over, the team (if two people were involved) should debrief/discuss what has taken place. What stood out, what was interesting, what kinds of things were stated, and so on? Once four or five interviews are done, were there any trends or patterns repeated? Highlight them as well as other aspects of the community or organization that have arisen.

To find interviewees, look for locations where persons gather such as shopping areas, parks, community festivals, churches, community meetings, or other gathering places. There could be sampling bias, but this is an exploratory scoping activity to get an initial feel for the community. When the findings are examined, it may be that more has to be done.

Review the interviews in a grounded theory type of way. Are there common categories of responses in regard to strengths and issues in the community and/or organization? What are historical events that have come up, and to what extent might they still be influencing current perceptions? What has been tried before, and what new ideas have been mentioned? What have the interviewers observed? They should be given some instruction in thinking about what the interviews contain and how to analyze them as they are active participants in the process.

1.2 Cultural Audits

It might also be advantageous to consider what has been called the Cultural Audit (Altschuld & Eastmond, 2010). For needs assessment you would go into a company or an organization to get an overview of how it operates, what it currently does, how receptive it is to change, and so on. The procedure consists of casual yet focused conversations with main categories such as the following:

1. Organizational Assumptions

2. Practices—Formal and Informal

3. Communication Channels

4. Anomalies, Problems, and Exceptions

Table 3.2 is a summary of typical questions, and Exhibit 3.3 is an example of an application of the technique by Eastmond and his students for their university department. The content in the table has been modified to make it more suitable for the hybrid framework. The table and exhibit could be adapted for a community with suitable questions as appropriate. The audit format is also a way to organize and present findings, and the categories are utilitarian.

Table 3.2 Categories of a Cultural Audit With Areas for Probing

1. **Organizational Assumptions**

   Motivation of those involved

   Commitment across levels to change

   Expectations for change

   Degree of respect across segments of the organization/community

   Understanding of what segments do

   Opportunities for action across the collective whole

2. **Practices—Formal and Informal**

   How services and products are delivered

   How people are contacted

   Nature of interactions

   How funds are distributed and financial matters handled

   Shortfalls in finances

   Other related questions

3. **Communication Channels**

   Whether people know and understand one another

   Existence of a spirit of working together

   Hierarchical dimensions to communications

   Clogged communication channels or reasonableness

   Comfort levels in sharing

   Healthy climate

   Other related questions

4. **Anomalies, Problems, and Exceptions**

   Unrealistic expectations

   Cliques and groups that would make working together difficult

   Enough time to accomplish things

   Ideas are open and challengeable (not feeling intimidated)

   Factors working against achieving group goals

   Other issues

Source: Adapted from Altschuld & Eastmond (2010). Used by permission.

Exhibit 3.3   The Cultural Audit Applied to a University Department

1. Organizational Assumptions

   All parties are motivated to improve.

   There are bright graduate students and faculty.

   Working together is valued, and excessive competition is not.

   There are high performance expectations.

   Respect for others is important.

   There is a low failure rate for students.

   Faculty members are able to teach well and publish.

   Products are the primary criteria for performance.

2. Practices—Formal and Informal

   Portfolio assessment is prominent.

   Few tests are given.

   Lots of hands-on connections to the real world are made.

   It's fine for students to be paid for work.

   Interaction between faculty and students is encouraged but occurs more for students on campus and in cohort groups.

   Funding from outside sources affects a lot of the educational experience.

   Socialization into professional associations is promoted.

   Responsibility for finding a job after graduation is more on the students.

3. Communication Channels

   Students know each other particularly in the cohort as well as faculty.

   Generally there is less separation between faculty and students in this department than in others.

   Hierarchy is not too prominent.

   Communication occurs through organizations and electronic mailing lists.

   E-mail communication is generally the mode.

4. Anomalies, Problems, and Exceptions

(Continued)

Exhibit 3.3 (Continued)

Sometimes there are unrealistic expectations for students especially if they work for more than one professor.

Group projects with international students are somewhat more complicated.

Not having many right answers in the field leads to unease.

Socialization expectations are difficult for some students.

The cohort system makes some feel uncomfortable.

There is a feeling that some people "work" or game the system.

Religious differences between faculty and students make sensitivity imperative.

Many international students raise security issues (the audit was done a number of years after 9/11).

Marriage patterns in the state mean that more local students are married at a much younger age than others in the program.

Changes in program requirements cause problems.

Depending on undergraduate training, the level of student technical skills is quite variable.

Given job market conditions, there is some degree of angst.

A kind of inbreeding occurs with few interdisciplinary students.

Source: Adapted from Altschuld & Eastmond (2010). Used by permission.

The details in the table and exhibit could be modified to fit varied situations. In a completed audit the environment is readily noticeable from a short document. This is summary power and would be useful for a discussion of the entire group involved in needs assessment or asset/capacity building. Consider the technique for gathering data as well as for portraying key findings.

1.3 Existing Data and Other Related Sources

Extensive data sets and existing information can be easily located and accessed, so take advantage of them. Remember from the first chapter that Kamis (1979) noted that a criticism of needs assessment was reliance on what was available with its hard-number social indicators. Some of the concern is still valid, but there is no reason to avoid looking into what is there especially when tied to interviews, observations, cultural audits, and so forth. Also keep in mind that resources and strengths are now entering into the picture.

If we are looking at a community, there are regional planning offices with data on employment, demographic trends, housing, educational attainment, and the like. There would be similar information about businesses—starts and failures. The department of transportation has many details on public transport and traffic patterns in an area. The reports and records of the police and court systems would help in understanding the community. Social agencies often have databases that contain much value. If there are enough members in the group, some should interact with departments and agencies for what may be there and accessible. It is not only about what they have but about whether they would be willing to help in the improvement effort. Do they have staff who could assist in data or report access for special information needs? If such support can be enlisted, it is beneficial.

What trends are in the region and the larger society? Counties or states routinely collect educational, financial, and social statistics in state departments of education, rehabilitation services, veterans' affairs, and others. A treasure trove is there, and sometimes by asking the right questions it is amazing what can be uncovered.

Before turning to the business side of the ledger, don't forget newspaper articles by knowledgeable reporters. They offer insights that may differ from what was just described—what communities are doing, who the movers and shakers are, what has been done in the past, what were concerns some time ago, and what is the present situation. Reporters for newspapers or on television might even be part of the interview process. Lastly, as communities, organizations, and agencies strive to improve, they might perceive that they are the first to do so. While each instance is unique, many features are not. There is writing on what others have done in their localities. What did they find, what information did they collect, where was it, what did they do, what problems were found, and how successful was the implementation of new directions?

This is benchmarking, and it is particularly pertinent when deliberations move closer to making decisions about improvement strategies. (This may seem premature as the emphasis is on scoping the situation, not on resolving it. Why is it here? Things will be observed that are for later steps in the hybrid framework and could throw off the perspective. If brought up now, they could be disruptive and derail the train, but that doesn't mean they should be discarded, ignoring their utility. Keep track of them for later referral.)

How does this all apply to organizations not in the public sector? The processes are easily adapted to businesses and private enterprises, but sources might differ. For newspapers there might be local business dailies or, on a larger stage, *The Wall Street Journal*. Look at specialized agencies and groups that have data relevant to what companies do. Employment statistics are routinely issued by government entities. The Department of Labor has all kinds of data and reports and can provide employment trends and what is happening in the workforce. The Department of Housing looks at new-home construction and the sales of existing homes. The Better Business Bureau is another source.

Health organizations (local, state, and private) monitor factors related to the well-being of local and national populations. These include heart health, diabetes, obesity, and so on. The National Health and Nutrition Examination Survey (NHANES) is an extensive and accessible database especially focused on children (Centers for Disease Control and Prevention/ National Center for Health Statistics, 2013). It contains information on key variables for youths ages 5–19 as collected by means of valid sampling and measurement procedures.

Another area that could be considered is the population of senior citizens. Departments of aging at state levels and offices in cities can provide tons of data. A trip to the library for a quick search can be of great value. In 2007, for a needs assessment workshop for the California Department of Aging, the author did just that, and what came from it was incorporated into a well-received session. He is in the relevant age group but did not know much about the issue, and without the search (a day to find and review materials) he would have been lost.

How much can be done in the preliminary scoping activity? Don't spend inordinate amounts of resources (people, time, money, motivation) but explore enough to get a sense of what is there. The group may go back later for more depth as it deliberates and discusses what might be desirable to do. But it is wise to do this after the initial scoping is probed for insights.

1.4 Other Techniques to Consider for Use With Step 1

The techniques and methods in Table 3.1 are just illustrative of what could be done. A few comments about other methods are useful. Lauffer's

(1982) *environment mapping* exercise for community development uses a one-page figure where the organization, agency, or collective is placed in the middle, and then there are sides representing clients and consumers for goods or services of the organization, who collaborators might be, where resources came from, and so on. Lines are extended from the middle to identify existing or future communication channels, the amenability to change, and other features. This is very similar to some of the concepts in asset/capacity building.

A second technique is the *photovoice* procedure, which was mentioned in Chapter 1 and will be covered in Chapter 4. Developing *detailed lists of assets* à la Kretzmann and McKnight (1993) would work, but its placement is not seen as being in the first step. A third technique that might be included is a quickly administered survey, and if you are in an organization, the use of SurveyMonkey or a related technique will be applicable. Generating instruments could consume considerable resources here, so these should be rough in nature and short. A couple of pages could easily be administered in a shopping center or a place where people congregate. The questions could be about areas of needs and assets and strengths. It might even be wise to have different versions for each. Sampling would not be random, and results might not generalize. More surveying might be desirable down the road.

The cruder survey is to get ideas about what the community and its members might be thinking. It should have an open-ended question or two to let respondents state their own ideas. There are also specialized forms that determine the readiness of a community to engage in development. This might be important where there is no prior history of such activity as compared to settings where there were long-standing traditions of working together.

In the realm of possibilities a type of focus group interview (FGI) could be employed. The concept is to have the questions firmly in mind and when the opportunity arises begin to ask them in a casual manner. The interviewees might not be aware that a focus group is being conducted, which is exactly what the author did with a group of teachers at a work session. He was at a table as they were working and saw that he could ask questions without ever formally establishing the group and the rules.

When the time was right, he said, "What are some of the things you think about when planning the science, technology, engineering, and mathematics curriculum for middle school students?" The the moment was perfect, the teachers jumped in, and he asked if they would mind if he took notes. From there he proceeded to ask other questions and had a lively discussion (FGI) without ever directly indicating he was doing so. The comments were more open and frank than what would have been obtained from a formal procedure. It just depends as to when this could be done. The upshot is to be flexible in regard to how data and information are obtained. Sometimes that will take you to methods and procedures that haven't been thought about, but that is perfectly acceptable.

Lastly, there are neat tools arising from our ever-increasing technology. For example, in *The Week in Healthcare* under the heading "Technology," Jaimy Lee (2013) observed that there is a major effort under way to enroll 1 million people with smartphones. The phones would monitor vital signs and report the same back to researchers and investigators. This would create a massive real-time database. What an exciting way to collect information with the nation as the community.

Along the lines of applications, the author's son offered another example. He and his family are planning a special vacation and located an app of the area that contains virtually all of the major recreational opportunities it offers. They are planning to rent a car, and the program even provides GPS capabilities for getting to whichever recreational site they select. If one were cataloging resources in an asset assessment, the purchase of this app would be a very inexpensive and time-efficient way of obtaining the information. Similarly, there are many computer-based utilities for looking at real estate and even ones that afford good maps of the location of a home and the wider area in which it is situated. (See Chapter 4 for more details about this.)

Maps are also useful for studying crime and its prevention. The author recently reviewed a manuscript for a major journal where perceptions of various types of incidents were obtained from student surveys at a large metropolitan university. The prevalence was compared to computer maps of the vicinity as to what might be done for the expanding campus. Where would it be beneficial to put in more lighting? What about pedestrian flows? How might student safety be protected at night? These are some of the needs that could be addressed by the combination of surveys and technology. Usages like those just described will definitely increase over time.

Now assume that Step 1 has been completed and the group has tapped into the critical "building blocks" of information that will be revisited when going through the eight-step process. It, with Step 2, forms the bedrock of the hybrid approach and should yield dividends.

STEP 2. DECIDING WHAT ACTIONS SHOULD BE TAKEN

This is possibly the most important step in the framework. Everything that has been collected has to be put into a picture for the decisions to be made:

- Given what has been gleaned to date, we simply don't feel comfortable about planning any new efforts or programs and should not do anything more.
- We need to explore more and need additional information about certain topics.
- We know a lot about the situation, the needs, and the assets and strengths, and we would like to examine potential strategies for improvement. What have other communities, agencies, or organizations done that we could adopt and/or use?
- We have learned enough to plan a new program that will help the community.

The first decision could happen but isn't likely; the second seems probable. The third and fourth ones may occur, but the second is what is expected. So how do we get to that decision, and what is the key to facilitating the group in a rich discussion of what has been generated?

Getting What Has Been Collected Into a Utilitarian Decision-Facilitating Display

So far the group has interviewed a variety of people to learn about the community. Group members have talked to many individuals and learned about strengths and assets. They have been asking about needs: What should the community be attending to, and what are the main problems? The members of the group have made observations and notes about what they have seen and learned. Existing information in records and databases has been examined, local media have been looked at, and history and facts pertinent to the situation have been reviewed. Surveys may have been conducted. All of this must be analyzed and arrayed, in a fashion that enables discussion and decision making. It has to be placed into a logical structure; if not, much good work will go for naught. Who takes the lead in this, and who is involved?

Ideally, if some initiating members have relevant skills and experience, that would be a big plus. They can be a sounding board for how the data are being treated and depicted. They can be internal detectors of subtle biases and be a form of checks and balances on those compiling the data. When this is not the case, an outside facilitator will guide the process. Handling this appropriately retains the locus of control in the community or organization and does not shift control to whomever is analyzing and portraying data. The hybrid framework demands that members of the group have to be active players as much as possible. Outsiders should be selected based on their ability to work this way so that the collaboration process is fair and inclusive of community members.

Getting a coherent sense of what is there can be daunting given the multiple sources of distinct data, an issue often seen in needs assessments. Multiple sources, multiple groups, quantitative results, and qualitative results make pulling results together a tricky proposition. Whether in needs assessment or in asset/capacity building, the concern is the same, making meaning from the many types of information that has been garnered. Altschuld and White (2010) suggested the following general rules for doing this. First, keep all summaries short and focused. Second, treat each source independently and analyze it from that point of view. Interviews would be separate from observations as would a review of existing data. In each summary, include main findings that are supported by data as well as others that may be less well held or supported. Once all summaries are done, look for patterns or similarities across them. This strengthens findings—multiple ways of collecting data are corroborating one another. Then move to more tenuous results and conclusions. Altschuld and White proposed a format per source for reporting, Exhibit 3.4. Exhibit 3.5 is an example of one created for German Village long after the fact.

Exhibit 3.4 A Format for Reporting Findings

Summary of the Method Used

What did you do (interviews, surveys, reviews, observations)?

In general, what were the questions for which you were collecting information?

From whom did you get information?

How were the data analyzed?

What were the main findings?

Use bulleted sentences or phrases for the things found.

If ideas about assets, needs, or even solutions came from the data, place them in appropriately labeled categories.

Identify if there were contradictory findings, where there was not agreement or where there were differences of opinion or views.

Draw conclusions as to what the findings might mean for improvement efforts.

Other Comments

These might pertain to the fact the articles reviewed were somewhat dated, not enough people were surveyed, more detail and information would be desirable, and so on.

Source: Adapted from Altschuld & White (2010). Used by permission.

Exhibit 3.5   Sample of What Might Be Included in a Summary Generated for German Village After the Fact

Methods Used

A small number of random interviews were conducted in several locations in the village.

About 25 people were casually interviewed (roughly equal numbers of men and women).

Casual chats were initiated about what they thought about the area, its good points, and what needed improvement.

Other questions focused on what they thought could actually be done to improve.

Main Findings

Most people thought that the village had interesting architecture.

Some of the restaurants were a key feature of the area and were known all over.

(Continued)

Exhibit 3.5 (Continued)

Many observed that the area was deteriorating and neglected in the city's thinking.

Without action being taken most perceived things would go downhill.

Several remembered renewal efforts, but they seemed to produce not much.

Contradictory Findings

The people interviewed were divided about the brick streets.

While most interviewees appreciated the community, some seemed to be overcome with ennui as to whether anything could be done to improve the area (a give-up attitude).

Other Comments

A number of interviewers expressed the idea that a broader and more probing set of interviews needed to be conducted.

Keep the summaries to several pages or less. In Exhibit 3.5, a conjectured summary is given of what might have been highlights of informal interviews. A full, more detailed account would be longer. The main findings dealt with assets, needs, and some aspects of prior efforts in the community, all important for understanding context.

If voluminous numerical information was obtained, include only key tables in the summary—don't inundate the group with data. If four or five total sources were part of the data set, there should be between 10 and 15 pages of summary to digest and discuss. If the analysis went further to common patterns across sources, then it might be closer to 20 pages, which is a lot for a group to consider for decisions about what to do in Step 3.

Since group members participating in the hybrid framework may have been involved with one source, they might review summaries of others. Develop a compilation for all sources regarding issues and assets that pop up again and again. Each member of the group should receive the summaries with instructions to think about what might occur next a week or so before a full meeting of the total group. If a summary across summaries was done, distribute it for group review. An example is shown in Table 3.3

to illustrate how to inform deliberations. Remember the goal is to promote utilization of what has been learned.

Please note that Table 3.3 will be referred to in later chapters. It is a touchstone, an anchor, for recording progress in hybrid endeavors and for making decisions related to moving ahead. Its importance cannot be underestimated. (For other interesting summary tables, see McDavid, Huse, and Hawthorn, 2012.)

The first row in the table is where the history of an area or organization would be given. It is the backdrop in which innovation and change will occur and is necessary for focusing the look at needs, assets, and new endeavors. While the past has bearing on the future, keep it in perspective. Change is an ever-evolving part of the environment. History is important, but there have been significant events over the last 50 years.

One is that the population is not the same as it was and is evolving. More professionals who work in the downtown now live there due to proximity to government institutions in the heart of the city. A major education center has moved in as have some new large employers. These developments have been gradual over time. History sets the tone but is a moving target.

In the table, assets, strengths, and resources are in one row separated from past cooperative/collaborative efforts, but aren't these assets? Why the separation? Many improvements in communities and organizations have been dependent on such relationships as part of their fabric. Separating them ensures that they don't get lost in the shuffle of a lot of information. It underscores them as potential ingredients in subsequent projects and endeavors.

There is a subtle aspect to the table that could be overlooked. It captures elements in a way that invites comparison and contemplation of assets and resources, needs, and reflections on improvement. Groups should review them. The table is offered not as a prescription but to generate thought. Other columns could be added such as what other data would be useful, where they exist, how they would be obtained, in what order they should be sought, to what extent they are critical, who should be charged with learning about them, and so on. Structure the table in the best way to foster a rich discussion of the group. It is anticipated that the table will have gaps and sketchy entries. These are fruitful for what to do next as they point toward where more understanding is needed.

Table 3.3 One Potential Format for the Cross-Source Summary

Topic of Study	Main Findings	Information Sources	Other Info Needed?	Comments
Relevant history	Originally a German population with some retention but now more diverse Parochial schools in accordance with background of early Germans Restaurants retain a German cuisine Other facts	Interviews Newspaper accounts Library readings Internet Micro-ethnology	Some additional history might be useful.	History gives a feel for the richness of the area and its influences on the current situation.
Assets, strengths, and resources	Unique eateries Some interesting shops Many professionals in village due to closeness to downtown Unusual home architecture Active churches and religious groups Brick streets	Observations Interviews Newspaper features Cultural audits Micro-ethnology Some census data	More thorough and complete catalog of resources is desirable. Only a surface sense of the assets and strengths.	There is a base of assets and strengths that could be tapped into if the right mind-set is developed. This is critical for any new efforts or programs in the community.
Needs and/or issues	Brick streets have problems. Homes are in need of maintenance and upgrades.	Observations Interviews Census data	As with assets more information about needs is warranted.	Trends over time should be determined to see what projections might be.

Topic of Study	Main Findings	Information Sources	Other Info Needed?	Comments
	Some of the businesses are on shaky ground. Portion of population is aging. School population is decreasing. Other needs	School populations published in newspaper Cultural audits Newspaper articles	Aging population and declining school population must be examined in detail.	
Past or suggested collaborative and cooperative efforts	Over the years community groups have formed for renewal but with limited success achieved. Most recent ones were four years before, but initiative dried up. Concerns about area have also been discussed at city council.	Interviews Discussions with city council members Newspaper articles Micro-ethnology and cultural audits	Some of the involved parties are still around and should be contacted and interviewed. Need a more intense look at what was attempted before.	Most initiatives have positives and negatives with much to learn from what was done before. Some of the same ideas might come up again.
Improvement ideas	One involved beautifying the area by planting flowers and trees. Another was getting volunteers to clean up and enhance Schiller Park on the south end of the village. Enlisting the involvement of the business community was also promoted.	Discussions with long time community members and activists Newspaper articles	More information is absolutely needed. Would be good to see what other cities have done and what has and hasn't worked.	The literature can be a valuable source about projects and strategies. Over time it would be useful to do some benchmarking of successful endeavors.

75

GROUP MEETING, DISCUSSION, AND DECISION MAKING: COMPLETING STEP 2 AND ENTERING STEP 3

When tables and displays have been created, distribute copies of materials to group members. Approximately a week later have a meeting (it might be fairly long, so allocate sufficient time and have a comfortable space with refreshments). There should be appropriate board or wall space to show what the group is talking about or to hang worksheets for everyone to see.

The distributed materials should be accompanied by instructions that give guidance as to what might be looked for and what might be done. These might be:

1. Please review the brief summary for each source of data and be prepared to ask questions or make comments.

   Do the results make sense to you?

   Were there any findings that surprised you, and if so, what were they?

   Are there other questions that should have been asked, or is there other information we should be seeking?

   Do you think anything is missing?

   How useful and valuable is the information that we have obtained?

2. Based on your review be prepared to ask questions or make comments.

   Does the summary table (3.3) make sense?

   Are there other things that should have been in the table?

   Does it seem to have captured what was in the summary of each method?

   Do we have enough information and understanding of the situation to proceed to an action plan, or do we require more?

   If the answer is no, what should we be doing to learn more about our assets, strengths, and needs?

   Do the less-filled-in parts of the table provide suitable direction for what we might do next?

What are options we should be considering?

Do you have any ideas as to how we can make our assets work better or more efficiently?

Are there needs that seem more pressing than others?

Do you know or recall anything about improvement efforts in the past?

When you look at assets, needs, and improvement and enhancement strategies, does anything stand out to you as to how they might be aligned?

When group members receive the materials, stress examining them prior to getting together. Remind them that decisions reside with the group as representatives of the community or organization. The meeting will be a lively exchange of comments and views and will lead to next steps in exploring community development and enhancement.

Start the meeting with welcomes and go over each source in turn using questions as above. Take note of additions and concerns to update tables and summaries after the meeting. To the extent possible there should be relative consensus on changes, corrections, and so forth. Make sure, as they are made after the meeting, that a date is affixed to the more final document. This is an easy way for recording the work of the group. All dated documents provide an accountability/audit trail and will be helpful to groups in the future.

When the separate sources of information have been completed, move to the summary across sources (which will be longer and in more detail than what is shown in Table 3.3). This should engender a lively discussion. If the exchange moves into the juxtaposition of assets, needs, and solutions, record what is being said especially for later steps in the hybrid framework.

STEP 3. DIVIDING THE WORKING COMMITTEE INTO TWO SUBCOMMITTEES

Once the interactions slow down, project Table 3.3 on the wall with a new sixth column on the right. Title it "Next Steps" (this is Step 3). Provide the participants with a handout that shows the table with the new column. Have them jot notes on what those actions should be and go around the group in round-robin fashion getting everyone's ideas and note with tally remarks how many had the same thought.

Now the group is in a position to think about how it might organize for Step 4 of the framework. Ordinarily what happens is that more information about needs, assets, or improvement strategies will be required. We are not ready to go further into the hybrid process without knowing more. We don't want to jump the gun! Seek agreement for what seems to be most pressing and how more knowledge might be obtained. Assignments are made, and everything is in place for moving forward.

One other question: What about the size of the group, and is it up to its new tasks? So far a small, highly motivated one has been behind data collection, analysis, interpretation, and making decisions. Chemistry and cohesiveness are there, but more human resources may be required to get things done. A middle ground has to be reached between the ambience of the group and its ability to tackle next steps. It may be necessary to expand by several individuals who are independently minded yet would share the enthusiasm and work ethic of initiating members. The latter would nominate those who fit and bring energy and vitality to the effort. Can new members cooperate and collaborate? Do they have specialized expertise? Have they worked with data? Have they used databases and other methods? What organizations in the setting do they connect to? Do they have time to devote? Would they be helpful? Since only a few more are needed, a group discussion should suffice for soliciting involvement, and when on board separate them across tasks with old hands providing orientation and assistance.

HIGHLIGHTS OF CHAPTER 3

1. To bring the hybrid framework to life, methods or procedures were suggested for the first three steps. They were not exhaustive but rather showed ways to accomplish steps.

2. From there, the rest of the chapter contained mostly a detailed discussion of the steps.

3. Stress was placed on Steps 1, 2, and 3 as the foundation of the hybrid framework.

4. Step 1 focuses on scoping the context, Step 2 is pulling the information gained into a logical summary and making decisions about

what the group should do next, and Step 3 is then organizing to implement decisions based on progress to date.

5. How the overall framework might get started was explored followed by a general description of what informal scoping is about and issues that might be probed.

6. From there a sampling of methods for scoping was given— micro-ethnology, cultural auditing, interviewing, use of existing data sources, and how emerging technology might be employed.

7. Step 2 examines what is collected in terms of analysis, interpretation, and further use.

8. Emphasis in Step 2 was put on how to portray the findings in a manner that facilitates decision making. Table 3.3 was provided just for that purpose. Questions to guide the deliberations of the group were suggested.

9. The chapter ends with the group organizing (Step 3) for Step 4. Here it may be desirable to expand group membership to carry out new work and assignments.

DISCUSSION QUESTIONS

1. Only a sampling of methods was provided. Do you know of others that might be applied? If so, what are they?

2. It might be informative to look at how needs assessments, asset/ capacity-building efforts, or hybrid approaches start. Is there a difference between successful and unsuccessful ventures? Discuss this and, if you were to conduct research, how you would do it and what kinds of questions you would ask.

3. What is the best size group for initiating efforts like these? At the chapter's end, enlarging the group was covered especially in relation to Step 4.

4. Emphasis is on an informal scoping of the situation as the first step. Would it be better to do this more formally at the beginning? If so, why? What are the advantages and disadvantages to starting informally or formally?

5. Data presentation is critical for decision making as the group works on Steps 2 and 3. Since the data will be qualitative and quantitative from many sources, this is difficult. Look at ways to summarize information in the chapter. Do you see alternatives for doing so without overwhelming a group? Make suggestions.

6. Are there additional issues and concerns that might be raised about the content of the chapter and the hybrid process? Can or should needs and asset work be combined?

4

Step 4 in the Hybrid Framework

A method as noted may relate to several steps depending on its implementation and the depth of information to be collected. It does not solely live in one house. There is flexibility with procedures being innovatively employed in a hybrid assessment. Placement is only suggestive. Table 4.1 includes methods for assessing needs and identifying assets. (For some other interesting methods, the reader is referred to Stevens and Ortega, 2011.)

Table 4.1 Step 4 in the Hybrid Framework

Step	Purpose	Methods/Strategies
4. Conducting the hybrid assessment in greater depth	Committees develop sharper pictures of needs and assets and resources as related to thinking about improvement.	For needs assessment, use many of the activities for Step 1 but in greater depth: • emphasis on collecting/using existing information as feasible • photovoice • combined needs/solutions surveys • many other techniques For asset/capacity building, use some Step 1 procedures but in greater depth: • location/categorization of assets • photovoice • combined needs/solutions surveys Subcommittees prepare summarized reports about needs and resources.

OVERVIEW

The group has decided to dig deeper into needs and assets/strengths simultaneously and has divided into two small groups (with five or six people in each) for the tasks at hand. The best place to begin is with the last activity at the end of Chapter 3. Look at Table 3.3 and the columns added for the purpose of Step 4.

What do we know, what is missing, and what would we like to know? What new information would be useful to collect? What questions might it answer? In what sources might it be located, and how would we access them? What might be the expense (time, funds, people) of getting more data? Are there inexpensive ways to do so? These are just a few questions to consider. They are posed with the understanding that a lot is already known about needs and assets from earlier activities. That is why Table 3.3 is so important. It shows what we have and don't have. It may take several meetings to formulate what the group feels is the best direction for in-depth understanding of needs and assets.

STEP 4. THE NEEDS ASSESSMENT PART— LITERATURE/LOCAL DOCUMENTATION

One thing that might be done is to return to the literature and local documentation that has been reviewed. See what is there and find more in archives, at the library, or on the web. Does what we now have tell us enough? Does it provide ideas about the causes of the needs and ways in which to resolve them? If new sources are found and voluminous, scanning is appropriate. Read a few completely to see if they offer anything unique (information is often similar). Note the procedures used in them to obtain data. If surveys were done, what were the results? What were the items, and who was surveyed? Are they available for use or adaptation to the current context? What were the main topics, and how utilitarian were the findings? Were there any recommendations for what to do the next time needs were to be ascertained? Were any special techniques employed such as DACUM (Norton, 2011) in a business or industry setting or a Delphi survey (Hung, Altschuld, & Lee, 2008) of a community or an organization? Overall, what was helpful, and were the results insightful?

The web is a great resource. It was a large part of the author's research for this book. He queried it and reread his own materials in terms of asset/

capacity building and needs assessment. As time passed, his search expanded. Without such access (and the assistance of students and colleagues) the effort would have been more difficult. He additionally talked to others about the topic, which is like scoping the context. This led to many other reports. It helped to demonstrate the shift toward a hybrid framework being advocated.

STEP 4. THE NEEDS ASSESSMENT PART—PHOTOVOICE

This is a technique that provides much useful information for understanding needs. It is a form of observation and is described in the asset/capacity-building part of this chapter.

STEP 4. THE NEEDS ASSESSMENT PART—SURVEYS

For Step 4 the surveys are more sophisticated than those for Step 1 of the framework. Ordinarily for needs they consist of two scales—the first asks respondents to rate usually on a 5-point scale (from 1 on the low side to 5 on the high) the importance of "what should be" for a community or an organization. Second, the same rating is done for present status. This produces average values per item and discrepancies via a subtraction of the two. There are many examples of such scales from various settings. But there is an issue, for when both scales are on one instrument, the return rate and the number of completed items drop for groups (Altschuld & Hamann, 2012; Hamann, 1997).

Another suggestion is to include sections on the instrument about possible solutions or improvements that could be made and barriers that work against new initiatives. This is contrary to the commonsense idea of keeping questions and content focused on needs, not other things (Altschuld, 2010b), and thus not confusing the situation for respondents. Clarity of intent and content should help in getting surveys completed.

Why, then, break with orthodoxy? Remember that the survey is not the initial step in needs assessment for the hybrid framework. Effort has already occurred, and much is there about needs, so doing a survey is not starting from scratch. Now we want to probe more deeply into needs. Surveys are often done only once because of costs related to development, design, implementation, and analysis, and if a community or an organization's staff members are required to take a second survey, they may balk and not be enthusiastic. Maximizing the one-time endeavor ensures a high information yield, and if the survey is not too long, it might be wise to look into solutions and barriers.

Another reason for doing this was given by Hunt et al. (2001). In that public school setting the audience became more involved in the process. Particularly, as issues and suggestions that it raised appeared on the survey, ownership increased. Since the research team had prolonged exposure to the site, what it did may generalize only to a confined context like a business or an agency rather than a community. Nonetheless, it was an interesting use of a needs assessment survey. Adaptation is dependent on the nuances of each local situation.

There is one other caution about questions dealing with barriers in that they may appear negative. In organizations and agencies, management could see them as a referendum on what it is doing or has done and thus feel threatened. They necessitate openness and receptivity on the part of respondents and the organization as to what may come from them. From the author's 40-plus years in evaluation, bristling at such questions is more the norm than the exception. Therefore, be careful in their wording. What factors tend to make success less probable? A softened alternative may be the course to follow. The purpose is not to dissuade from this content but to make sure there is awareness of and sensitivity to a delicate issue.

It might be desirable, especially for communities, to have two surveys, one for "what should be" and the other for "what is." Design a version with "what should be" items to be rated and with possible solution or improvement strategies. For the latter consider scaled items or open-ended prompts for ideas. A second form would be the "what is" items with questions dealing with barriers to improvement. Examples of questions and formats are provided in Figures 4.1, 4.2, 4.3, and 4.4.

Figure 4.1 Example Items for a "What Should Be" Survey

Some Items and a Scaling Approach for the "What Should Be" Condition for a Community Needs Assessment Survey

Item	Scale
Community agencies work together.	NA 1 2 3 4 5
Communication of issues/concerns occurs across community agencies and organizations.	NA 1 2 3 4 5

City services (police, fire, etc.) communicate with   NA 1 2 3 4 5
groups in the community.

City council members are fully aware of   NA 1 2 3 4 5
issues/concerns.

Indicate the degree to which you disagree or agree that the item *is important* for this community to progress and move forward. Use the following scale:

NA = not applicable or don't know, 1 = strongly disagree, 2 = disagree, 3 = neither disagree nor agree, 4 = agree, and 5 = strongly agree.

Figure 4.2   Example Ways to Ask About Solutions

Some Items and Formatting for Solution Strategy Questions for a "What Should Be" Survey

OPEN-ENDED VERSION

When you think about what might be important for this community to progress and move forward, what ideas can you suggest for the items that you agreed with most strongly in Figure 4.1? Provide a few phrases or short sentences.

Idea 1

Idea 2

Idea 3

CLOSED-ENDED VERSION

Below are a number of ideas that have been suggested by community members for improving our community. For each suggestion please indicate the degree to which you feel it is a good idea.

Idea 1   NA 1 2 3 4 5

Idea 2   NA 1 2 3 4 5

Idea 3   NA 1 2 3 4 5

(See the scale described in Figure 4.1.)

Figure 4.3 Example Items for a "What Is" Survey

Some Items and a Scaling Approach for the "What Is" Condition for a Community Needs Assessment Survey

Item	Scale
Community agencies work together.	NA 1 2 3 4 5
Communication of issues/concerns occurs across community agencies and organizations.	NA 1 2 3 4 5
City services (police, fire, etc.) communicate with groups in the community.	NA 1 2 3 4 5
City council members are fully aware of issues/concerns.	NA 1 2 3 4 5

Indicate the degree to which you disagree or agree that the item *is currently being achieved in this community* in relation to progress and moving forward. Use the following scale:

NA = not applicable or don't know, 1 = strongly disagree, 2 = disagree, 3 = neither disagree nor agree, 4 = agree, and 5 = strongly agree.

Figure 4.4 Example Ways to Ask About Barriers

Some Items and Formatting for Questions About Barriers to Resolving Needs

OPEN-ENDED VERSION

When you think about what might prevent this community from progressing and moving forward, can you provide a few examples? Use short phrases or sentences in your examples.

Idea 1

Idea 2

Idea 3

CLOSED-ENDED VERSION

Think about barriers that might prevent this community from resolving/ improving problems or issues as suggested by citizens. For each suggestion please indicate the degree to which you agree with it.

Barrier 1	NA 1 2 3 4 5
Barrier 2	NA 1 2 3 4 5
Barrier 3	NA 1 2 3 4 5

The figures give the general tone of questions. Next, which individuals and groups should be responding? The author has emphasized that there are three levels in nearly all contexts. *Level 1* consists of those who directly receive services or the intended beneficiaries of any improvement efforts. In a community they would be community members. *Level 2* is the individuals or groups (teachers, nurses, schools, service representatives) who provide services (teaching, health care) that alleviate or reduce needs. *Level 3* is management or the structure that supports Level 2 and, in turn, Level 1—those individuals and groups who make decisions or provide the administration, funding, and other resources that enable Level 2 to do its duties so Level 1 is enhanced or improved.

The three level designations are a handy way to think about sampling for the survey. It works for community surveys and those in a business or an organization. Surveys are distributed most often to Levels 1 and 2 and less often, or later in the process, to Level 3. One consideration is that you may need different versions of questions for levels. Why might this be important? Level 1 directly receives services or products and has a firsthand seat for responding. What do these look like, how well are they implemented, and so forth? The perspective is unique, and no one else has it. Level 2 delivers service but does not directly experience it in a visceral manner. The questions may be similar but have to be tailored to where this group resides in the hierarchy of levels. This was the case in a study of college students and faculty (Altschuld, 2010a; Lee, Altschuld, & White, 2007). If different question wording makes better sense, consult these sources for guidance.

Moreover, groups may not agree on needs. In the Lee et al. (2007) citation they did not. That is neither good nor bad, merely reality, and it shows where groups have not reached a consensus. This should be made clear and entered into the discourse about needs. Should one group's responses be valued more than another's? Perhaps! It could be argued that Level 2 responses are the most important since these individuals/groups are direct providers, and if they have different views that will affect how they go about their work. But can we neglect the values of Level 1 in a democratic society? If views vary, report them and let the small group decide their meaning in regard to needs.

Let's pretend that the data have been collected and analyzed in terms of discrepancies as well as barriers and solutions. What do you do with the results? Go back to the summary table (3.3) in the prior chapter. It is a work in progress with holes to be filled in with new findings as they are uncovered. Take what has been learned and add it into the appropriate places so that the picture is richer and more complete. To ensure that the text is distinguishable from previous entries, use alternating colors. When the table is reviewed, everyone will have an immediate sense of new information and how it enhances the results. It is also wise to put a new date on the table to aid in the review process and to monitor progress.

This underscores the criticality of a table such as 3.3. Without such tables the process could easily disintegrate into chaos. With them utilization-focused decisions based on findings are facilitated. In this context there is one other technique that is frequently used.

STEP 4. THE NEEDS ASSESSMENT PART— EPIDEMIOLOGICAL ANALYSES

Elements of epidemiology are the prevalence of a condition at the present time and what it might look like (incidence) in the future. In disease, for example, we have the current rate of obesity in children and what might be trends in five or ten years if there are no interventions regarding the condition. Chiasera (2005; Chiasera, Taylor, Wolf, & Altschuld, 2008) studied just this and predicted correctly that major problems would occur. This was from data in the National Health and Nutrition Examination Survey (Centers for Disease Control and Prevention, 2013a, 2013b; Centers for Disease Control and Prevention/National Center for Health Statistics, 2013). The concept here is that extensive data exist in accessible forms, and as we computerize input from health care systems, employment, insurance, education, communities, and others, such data will be even more available. This technique opens windows to identifying needs and should be used.

But there is a caveat. Data are always accurate and truthful and do not lie! Or do they? In 2012 and 2013, it was observed that a big-city school district had possibly been misreporting its attendance figures for a seven- to eight-year period. The significance of this could have been serious and underscores that blind acceptance must be preceded by hard questions as to how data come into being. Some students were dropped and later reenrolled, and if done at certain times during the year, their test scores were not counted in the school's performance on the state tests. The effect was to remove low performers and produce misleading (higher) results. Schools looked better, and judgments about them were incorrect (Bush, 2012; Bush & Ferenchik, 2012; Bush & Smith-Richards, 2012; Smith-Richards, 2013).

On the other hand, there may be problems and issues with data entry due to delegating responsibility, lack of explicit directions for placing data into the system, or staff who are overworked and pressed for time. There may not be nefarious intent, and therefore only corrections are required to improve how things are done. Without further investigation the nature of the problem, if it is one, is not evident. Thus, the other side of epidemiology is to learn what is causing a discrepancy by further probing, which may involve the use of qualitative techniques.

So raise questions about data. How were data put into the system, what personnel were involved, and so on? Below are a few others that might be asked:

- How were data collected?
- Who entered the data (in the school case this was an extremely important question)?
- Have any basic definitions of data terms changed over time (especially important if trends are examined)?
- What issues are there with the system (what concerns have been raised)?
- Are there errors or problems with the data that warrant attention when interpreting results? What are they?

Recall the German Village example in the previous chapter. Expanding the preliminary epidemiological data that were located in Step 1 would now be appropriate. What existing data would be highly useful? It would be desirable to know a lot about the people in the area. What is their age, how long have they lived there, how many are retired, what types of work are they doing, what is the nature of in- and out-migration, how many own homes, and so on? Almost all data like these would be found in existing sources.

This is a big mouthful for the small needs assessment and asset/capacity-building group to swallow. It may not have the capability to access and work with databases and interpret results. The task might seem insurmountable if the group will be undertaking it. That is not being suggested; rather, approach the assignment from the mind-set that assistance can be obtained. There are organizations and groups that regularly deal with such information and will probably help if the request is not too detailed. They may even do so without remuneration.

For German Village, it might be as simple as contacting some local Realtors for advice, guidance, and expertise. The author and his wife recently moved to a condo, and what can be found on the web is amazing. They built in parameters that were important to them and, through Zillow and other sources, were able to limit going to homes that did not fit their requirements (see brief mention of this in Chapter 3). The electronic resources offer a dramatic contrast to when they last (37 years ago) bought a home. They used Google Maps to get views of neighborhoods, what they looked like from overhead and on the ground. They could find comparable home prices. Their Realtor was computer savvy and aided them. Going further, there were mailings from other Realtors regarding available properties, asking prices, and features of the condos. The latter was crucial since the author's spouse had an ankle problem that made a one-floor plan an absolute requirement.

Analogously, the office of the county treasurer maintains many records via its property tax assessments and collection duties. Many cities, counties, and regions have planning offices that monitor changes and developments. They know the demographics of communities. The Census Bureau collects information that is used by municipalities and government agencies. Community United Way organizations are attuned to these data, and the suspicion is that so are insurance companies and public utilities.

Given what is there, the group should be trying not to get new data but to capitalize on what is extant. Ask individuals that routinely deal with such sources for assistance. To do this the group should have its goals and ideas identified as it gets the input of those in the know and who have access. The following steps should be helpful.

1. Identify your needs for information as best you can.

   How many own their homes, what is the market like in this area, who is buying homes, why are they buying in the area (may not come from records), and so on?

It often may be that different groups and individuals have to be contacted.

2. Brainstorm where the information may be located. For housing it probably is with Realtors, for demographics it may be government planning groups, and so forth.

3. The small group might split into teams, each charged with finding and making appropriate contacts.

4. Meet with these contacts and explain the overall purpose (grass-roots efforts to improve the community) and then get to the more specific questions.

   Sophisticated epidemiology can be complicated, requiring time and expertise. That is not what will be needed in most cases, with a basic level of information being fine. See if there are already pre-pared reports that fit closely enough to do the job.

   Ask for other help should it be required and if they will provide it.

   Thank them for what they can do for you.

5. Review what is there to see what insights it offers for the needs assessment effort.

How should the group use the information? Build easy-to-read, straightforward tables that capture it at a glance and make the decision-making process flow smoothly with pertinent facts and data. Table 4.2 is one example of this; others are possible. Its content could be briefly summarized for entry into the continually-in-progress big summary table (3.3), even with reference to Table 4.2. It depends on how much is there and what is important for the decisions to be made. If there is too much, put the excess into appendixes instead of swamping the channels.

The table is a snapshot rather than a massive set of numbers. That is deliberate. If more quantitative details are desirable, have them available as needed. A lot of information is not a problem but can be when it bogs things down.

Notice how the discussion keeps returning to that overall summary table. Progress is notable in such a table and by the incremental filling of its cells. As before, dated entries are a record of the assessment, about needs, and, as will become apparent later, about assets and resources.

They could also serve for presentations to the broader community or organization. They are a focal point for input and actions that might be

Table 4.2 Information From the Expanded Epidemiologic Data Gathering Effort

Information Area	10 Years Ago	5 Years Ago	Present Time
Age of Population	Population somewhat older than metropolitan area	Population noticeably older than metropolitan area	Age disparity is getting greater
Home Prices	Somewhat lower than other comparable areas in city	About the same as 5 years previously	Disparity in home prices has accelerated
Demographics	Primarily due to older population, more single-person households than other areas	Trend is becoming more pronounced with the passage of time	Trend is still there, but some younger people seem to be moving in—important to monitor if that becomes prominent
Rationale for Home Purchases	Relatively low costs due to conditions of homes	Same as 5 years ago	Low cost remains the motivating factor, but now some reasons due to location near work
Other Variables as Deemed Important			

based on the findings. They would be helpful in situations where funds are to be raised. Before turning to assets and resources, there is one other facet of needs that must be discussed.

STEP 4. THE NEEDS ASSESSMENT PART—A COMMENT ABOUT TYPES OF NEEDS

When attempting an assessment, a basic question is what type(s) of need(s) is (are) the center of attention. In 1972, Bradshaw asserted that there were four classes—normative, expressed, comparative, and felt. Kaufman (1992) referred to mega, macro, and micro needs. Perhaps the most extensive listing is in Altschuld and Kumar (2010) where seven distinct ones are postulated. Among them are short- and long-term considerations, severe and slight needs, and collaborative circumstances across organizations and groups, with asset/capacity building being yet another category. Other writers would characterize gaps or discrepancies in yet other ways.

How in this context would it be best to think about them? What constitutes their nature? It is hard to speculate, for each hybrid is unique and will go in its own direction. Certainly, time will be a factor, and pressing immediate needs will be identified, but more major ones necessitating large projects and the commitment of serious resources will be the norm. This is just what will be observed in the six cases in Chapters 7 and 8. The discrepancies in them are diverse related to crime, community health, community development, and services to be delivered by a state agricultural agency. Consistently, they are about important issues—severe, unlikely to be resolved in the immediate future, and likely to entail considerable resources for resolution—and demand collaboration across entities in the local situation.

The sample is small, but a conclusion is that this pattern will tend to pertain to other cases as they begin to appear in the literature. It is only a partial answer to the question about types but does seem to be a logical one.

STEP 4. THE ASSET/CAPACITY-BUILDING PART—INVENTORYING, LISTING OF ASSETS AND RESOURCES

Surveys for needs have been discussed in some depth. It is fairly easy to adapt the principles to assets, so they will not be repeated here. Now the focus is to inventory or list assets and resources and/or learn about them through photovoice. Resources can be thought of in terms of educational institutions, government agencies, religious organizations, businesses and industries, and individuals in the community. In the movie *The Shawshank Redemption,* Andy the protagonist is in prison and always mentions needing a person who is good at finding things, who has the pulse beat of what is going on, and who knows how to get stuff done. That person is Red. They become close friends, and eventually the story takes off from there. How is this relevant to the idea of assets? Consider Exhibit 4.1.

Exhibit 4.1 The Case of Melvin and the Remodeling and Repair Experience

About six years ago, we needed some work done on our former residence. I was introduced to Melvin, a jack-of-all-trades—rebuilding, plumbing, basic electrical work—you get the idea. We contracted with him for what we needed, and about three years later he remodeled the condo that became our new home. He has become our go-to person, our Red, for most things.

Recently, a ceiling fan in the kitchen was having a problem with a small support rod. Melvin took it apart and saw that the rod could not be repaired, and there began the asset/resource odyssey. Melvin and I went to several big-box hardware stores and found that they did not carry the part since fans had changed in the past 10–15 years. We were advised to contact the manufacturer or buy a new unit to replace it. What a pain!

Melvin was of a different mind. Like Red he is good at finding things. We embarked on a journey to many parts of our city that I had never been to and didn't even know existed. All the stores and establishments were gracious, and because Melvin asked, they allowed us to rummage through their odds-and-ends parts boxes.

We went to the Habitat for Humanity outlet where they sell all kinds of goods and building supplies that have been donated to the organization. Up to that point it was quite an adventure but an unsuccessful one. Everywhere we went we asked for recommendations as to where to look next.

The last one had us at a lighting and fixture store that was located in an out-of-the-way place. The young lady behind the counter examined the defective part and said that it was from an older fan. She could not match it, but she had an idea. She went to her odds-and-ends basket, pulled out a piece that was close to what was required, dabbed some antique-type paint on it, and solved the problem. She would not accept any money for her assistance or the part.

Problem solved—all because Melvin is a person good at finding things.

This was a lot of to-do about getting one small part for an older fan, and it would have been easier to skip all of that and buy a new one. But the old one fit the décor of the room, and a new one might not have been right. Recognize, like the author's experience with Melvin, that the trip to identify and catalog resources and assets may be arduous and take some time.

In a community we can learn much about how to seek out resources and assets from Melvin. One thing for sure is that key informants in the area are invaluable as a starting point. He is really a small contractor and has contacts throughout the community. People like him, who have been in business for years, certainly know their areas well and where resources (materials, expertise) are. Notice how we went from one business to another until the part was located. This means that the first thing to do is ask around in organizations and businesses for people who are the "Melvins"—the informal conduits into communities. Find them and seek their help. Rest assured that strengths are all around you, but you may not be aware of them.

Realtors are another extremely important source. As we were looking for our new home, we had to have some work done on our old one (eventually Melvin made the house presentable for sale). The Realtor proved to be a godsend. She had a comprehensive website (she had been in information technology previously). It was a wealth of information regarding services that would be of value, and she had tremendous personal knowledge that aided us immensely. Because Realtors are intimately aware of the communities they sell in, they are another key source for identifying assets, strengths, and resources.

Ask them about transportation in the area. What do they see as the activities there for children, and who provides them? Ask similar questions about senior citizens. What are the religious and civic organizations in the vicinity, and what do they offer? What government offices are around, what do they do, and what contributions do they make? What are the educational institutions, and how do or could they enhance the community? While Realtors are part of the buying and selling process across communities, they usually are better acquainted with some locations than others.

Personnel in agencies and organized groups in communities (especially those who are there on a daily basis) have good insights into assets. Tap into them with questions like those above. Most police departments in big cities and even medium-sized ones have officers devoted to community relations. See them as a resource; if approached thoughtfully, they may be willing to assist. Enhancing and further developing the community should make what they do more effective in a positive way. Similarly, fire personnel and emergency medical teams in firehouses can add to the picture. One question particularly applicable to them is in regard to the cooperation and collaboration they have seen among groups and organizations. If organizations are working together, that is valuable input for thinking through improvement.

Here it also seems apropos to adapt and use the ideas proposed by Kretzmann and McKnight (1993), a map of community assets divided into main parts, such as

local institutions (schools, libraries, businesses, etc.);

citizens' associations, such as churches, cultural groups, and others; and

the *gifts, talents, and special skills of individuals.*

Each of these categories contains many subgroups. For example, in the latter one, there are youth, senior citizens (who could be broken into many age ranges), skilled workers, artists, and others with talents and skills. Kretzmann and McKnight provide detailed forms and questions that can be used to find out details about assets. In their voluminous reference they show countless diagrams about resources and how they might connect or interrelate. Included is also a community assets map.

Looking at assets goes beyond cataloging what is tangible to working relationships across groups, a spirit of cooperation, and even collaboration. It includes a volunteering ethos in a community. These can be the make-or-break factors in the success of a joint asset/capacity-building and needs assessment venture. In Chapter 7 a history of working together is cited as a reason why some small municipalities are better suited to doing both activities as compared to others that do not have such experience. In Chapter 8 volunteering is so crucial that it is studied in its own right. How to determine and measure such variables is no easy matter and complicates the identification of assets, especially for large jurisdictions.

For states or major metropolitan areas, the task of cataloging and assembling lists of assets is not a simple one. Consider State Independent Living Councils, which are found in every state in the United States. If assessing statewide needs for those who require assistance to live independently is extended to assets, producing what those resources are is more difficult to comprehend. Determining resources and strengths is not so straightforward and will take considerable time. The size of the undertaking must be taken into account when doing a hybrid study. If the working group is small, perhaps only look into a portion of the assets or seek help in ascertaining them. Many times, this will be more complex than assessing needs.

On the other hand, if we are inside an organization, an agency, or a business, the task is notably easier. To learn about assets and strengths ask current staff members. The knowledgeable ones have over time found many useful resources and may not have been queried about them in a systematic way. They are a hidden or tacit but invaluable bank of knowledge.

Tell them you are trying to identify the assets and resources available to them or ones they might have used. "When you think about our organization and the strengths it has, what comes to mind? Take a few minutes to jot down your thoughts, and then we'll discuss them." With small groups the same kind of question (or questions) could be used to start a focus group interview. Inquire about work with other organizations, institutions, or specialized groups. This will help in pinpointing meaningful existing interactions. Whom do they seek out for help with problems, what resources do they often utilize, and so forth? This is reminiscent of Lauffer's (1982) community mapping technique for developmental settings.

The author used a version of this in a strategic planning effort he conducted in a university-based national center where he was its evaluator. In advance of a retreat, he and other colleagues gave staff forms to fill out about the current status of projects and how they aligned in percentages with the center's research and service foci. Then the staff were given four open-ended forms about strengths, weaknesses, opportunities, and threats in the situation.

They had not done this before, nor was it anywhere to be found in the initial thinking and proposal that led to the center being funded. They jumped into the task, and the 10 people produced an enormous amount of information in a short period of time. The data were reviewed and collated to depict the current status of the center and what was arising from looking at the four dimensions.

The worksheets for staff were open-ended. There were general directions such as "We are seeking ways to learn from each other to enhance the future of our center. Ideas are neither right nor wrong. Responses will be grouped together and kept anonymous. Provide your ideas about the strengths, opportunities, and so on that you feel we have and can build upon" (Figure 4.5).

The results were remarkable. All ideas were shown in total group session along with a collated summary. How many were in common, and which were unique? A specified amount of time for discussion and interchange of each was allotted, followed by a zero-sum game voting procedure for prioritizing. The staff then engaged in conversation about what might be done next to make the center better and more sustainable.

Figure 4.5 Example Assets-Related Questions Used in Strategic Planning for a Center

Strengths (briefly describe the strengths of this center in terms of our connections, location in this university, resources we do or can tap into, nature of our projects, and so forth)

_____

_____

_____

_____

Opportunities (describe what aspects of what we are now doing or what we could do in the future can be capitalized on or used as positive springboards to enhance the center)

_____

_____

_____

_____

STEP 4. THE ASSET/CAPACITY-BUILDING PART—PHOTOVOICE

Photovoice is a technique uniquely suited to getting a feel for the assets of a community (Downey & Anyaegbunam, 2010). It works especially well when used in conjunction with other data sources, brings the contextual milieu into perspective, and helps community members better understand their environment (Man & Mandel, 2012). It can detect needs, but the emphasis here is mostly on assets. There are major advantages and disadvantages to it as shown in Exhibit 4.2.

Exhibit 4.2 Some Advantages and Disadvantages of Photovoice

Advantages

- Data collection is solely in the hands of the community or group members, with outside or external involvement minimal.

- It's a novel way of obtaining data and may turn on those participating in it.

- It can be relatively inexpensive since community members are getting the basic data (in comparison to doing surveys that may be more costly).

- In many instances, it is a quick way to obtain very useful data.

- It can provide an intimate picture of the assets and issues inherent in the organization.

- Data analysis and interpretation rely heavily, if not exclusively, on community members who write interpretations in their own words, not those of a third party.

- It may be a terrific jump start for the entire community or organization to get involved in thinking about improvement.

- Pictures are said to say a thousand words, and this fits the adage.

Disadvantages

- As with any technique, the hope is that it reveals a valid portrayal of what the community or organization is like, but it could be biased.

- It will require some orientation of the individuals taking the pictures to ensure that everyone has the same general parameters in mind.

- The technique may work better in some contexts (say, rural communities) than others.

- Collecting the data may be easier than interpreting it and writing up what it means.

- Usually it is good to buttress what it produces with other information such as surveys or demographics (rely on what is produced, but don't overrely).

- It will require skillful leadership to move the larger community or organization into meaningful discussion about what is being depicted.

There are three distinct parts to photovoice. First, people are provided with disposable cameras and asked to take pictures of what they see as the good things in their community or organization and, since it could be utilized in needs assessment, what are the issues and concerns (see Figure 4.6).

Clear instructions are absolutely essential to get the activity going and to challenge participants. The working group wants to obtain a balanced view of the subtle features of the setting. (This technique could also be used with the CPTED concept presented in Chapter 1.)

Figure 4.6 Community Involvement in Photovoice

Source: Can Stock Photo Inc. / Antikainen

Then the individuals are encouraged to go around the community to take it in and get what they, not somebody else, consider as representative of the positives and the features that are not so positive. A variation of this might be to have teams do the assignment, with perhaps one person doing the photography and the other taking notes, or to separate the photography group into halves—one for positives and one for negatives. Or, instead of disposable cameras, capitalize on the fact that many now have camera-equipped cell phones. They are quite accustomed to taking pictures and might readily accept and rise to the challenge.

Second, and this is where the fun comes in, have a session where the photographers are given what they generated, they engage in an open discussion, and then are asked to write a short paragraph depicting the nature of the photograph and interpreting what it is showing or denotes. To do these activities, copies of the pictures could be mounted on boards or on the wall, with tentative captions, and clustered into negatives and positives as suggested by the individuals who produced the images. Have the photographers look over what they and others have done. From there, move them into general discussion of what they are seeing, and only after that have them begin the writing exercise.

Guessing that there are perhaps 12 people involved, provide some guidelines for writing (It may be helpful to provide a sample or two of a description,).

- What is this a picture of?
- Where was it taken?
- Why did you choose to take it?
- What stood out to you?
- Would others share your perceptions?

- Does it represent an asset/strength of our community or a need?
- What other comments, if any, would you like to make?

The third and last activity in photovoice is the most exciting. The photographs with their explanations serve as the foundation for a larger community or organizational discussion and exchange. This is analogous to what is often done in organizations, sometimes with captions but often without. Pictures of major events—parties, receptions, prominent visits, and so forth—are neatly displayed for staff and visitors. The displays are quite popular, people always stop and look at what they contain, and they are part of the culture. They are a public record or demonstration of what has happened. Pictures allow people to project themselves into the scenery. They almost come alive.

Keep the photos separated into strengths and positives and things that should be improved. The community will really get into the discussion, which will take on a life of its own. The moderator will have to sense when to let it run and when to bring it into focus. It can be insightful and illuminating and the basis for getting everybody in the community involved in what it means to them. Stress that this is what fellow community members, not outsiders, are feeling. Raise some good discussion questions about assets, resources, and strengths:

- Does this accurately convey the strengths and values of our community or organization?
- Do you have any comments about the way in which a photograph was interpreted?
- Do you know of other examples of strengths or assets that weren't observed?
- Do these photos provide a good description of our community or organization?
- Do you feel that the sample represents us?

The process is repeated for issues, concerns, and needs. Don't dwell on negatives. Have the community or organization initially look at what it has, what it might need, and what might be some directions in which to go. That is the concluding section of the photovoice meeting. What suggestions does the community or organization have, where might it go from here, and how could the resources and what it brings to the table be put to good use for its improvement? It might even be desirable to have small, facilitated break-out groups discuss separate aspects such as issues and strengths.

The meeting should be recorded and notes taken. After it is over, the small group should analyze how it went, ideas about the process, and what suggestions should be looked at in regard to how it could expand what is known on the grand summary table (enter these suggestions into Table 3.3). The now-expanded understanding of assets and needs is becoming evermore complete. We are building by increments.

That is where the hybrid framework is now taking us. We want to use the information that has been collected to date that is pertinent to needs and assets. Most of it is in the table. As there may be an excess of information, it may be necessary to have a few key tables appended to the overall summary. It depends on what has been learned and deemed important. Strive for balance. Too much detail could overwhelm a group's ability to gain a comprehensive understanding of needs and available assets, and too little is not enough to consider meaningful ways to proceed.

Seek a few individuals who are concerned about the community or organization to take a look at the synthesis. If there is a spectrum of constituencies, pick a few individuals to do the review. Ask about such aspects of the summarized materials as the following:

- Are the summaries clear and understandable/?
- If not, what isn't?
- Would a larger group as we proceed into the future be able to grasp the meaning of what has been found?
- Is there too much to fully get a feel for the needs and assets?
- Is there anything missing that should be added?
- What might be the reaction to the status of the community or organization?
- Are there aspects of what has been observed that are surprising?
- Have we covered all the bases?
- What recommendations might the reviewers have?
- What else would they like to offer or suggest?

Once this input has been collected and utilized, the process is moving toward Step 5 of the hybrid framework, the action plan for improvement that will emanate from a group decision session. This will be covered in the next chapter.

HIGHLIGHTS OF CHAPTER 4

1. The group is organized well enough to divide into subcommittees assigned to needs assessment or the identification of assets.

2. Both activities are predicated on earlier scoping activities.

3. For the needs assessment, short explanations were given of surveys and Level 1 (service recipients), Level 2 (providers of services or goods for the community or organization), and Level 3 (those who enable Level 2 to serve Level 1).

4. A number of other strategies for conducting the needs assessment were highlighted. They were ones that are frequently seen in the literature.

5. A brief comment was offered about types of needs in hybrid work.

6. Then the text shifted to assets and started with a description of what parties might be able to spark thinking about assets and resources. They were gatekeepers or knowledgeable individuals with insights on such matters.

7. The Kretzmann and McKnight idea of a community map of assets was briefly mentioned, as were the categories of assets to be ascertained.

8. If the situation was more internal to an organization or institution, an example of determining strengths via open-ended key staff forms was presented.

9. The last technique for assets (and also for needs) was photovoice. Its advantages and disadvantages, as well as how to use the data, were provided.

DISCUSSION QUESTIONS

1. Not much attention was paid to the size of the originating group involved in needs assessment and asset/capacity building. How large or small should each subcommittee be, what might be optimum, what might be most efficient, and so on?

2. There is a lot to do for Step 4, especially for a volunteer effort, should outside help be sought. What should be its involvement, where might seed funds be obtained for this purpose, what might be the drawbacks to doing so, and so on? Discuss the issues.

3. The identification of assets can be quite complicated, particularly if on a sizable basis. Considering that, describe what you might do to locate such assets. And, if you have done anything like this, what did you do?

4. Photovoice has strengths and weaknesses. How might it be done in a big city, what would you have the photographers do, how would you instruct them, and should they be divided into teams with one seeking problems and issues and the other strengths?

5. The amount of information collected in the hybrid framework can be too much. A grand summary table (3.3) has been proposed to deal with this. Can you recommend other ways to put the information into a meaningful format?

6. One important lurking issue is leadership. We want full, open, and democratic participation, but given what is to be done, leadership is required; otherwise energy and motivation can dissipate. (We've all been in groups where this has happened, and the work went for naught with the effect of decreasing participation in future such endeavors.) So questions are:

Who should lead?

What should be the nature of that leadership?

Should it change as we go from the initial steps in the hybrid framework to the later ones?

5

Steps 5–8, Completing the Hybrid Process

T able 5.1 contains the last activities for needs assessment and asset/ capacity building. The community or organization decides to take action, and the digesting of assets and needs is by and large over. Let's get going to improve.

Step	Purpose	Methods/Strategies
Table 5.1 Hybrid Framework for Needs Assessment and Asset/ Capacity Building With Possible Methods/Strategies		
5. Using what has been learned to make decisions for possible new programs	Align the two parts of the improvement picture. Agree if alignment is the best way to proceed. Determine if more data and information should be collected.	Each subcommittee does an independent review of the other's results. Develop a matrix to see where needs and assets overlap and where they don't. Consider use of group procedures: • check in/tune in • what/so what/now what • concept mapping/ mind mapping • others

(Continued)

Table 5.1 (Continued)		
Step	*Purpose*	*Methods/Strategies*
6. Developing a strategy for improvement	Translate findings into action plans for development and positive change.	Use a variety of techniques: • success mapping • fist to five • multi-attribute utility theory • others
7. Implementing and evaluating the action plan	Conduct planned activities. See how well they are functioning and what their outcomes are.	Use to-do lists and responsibility sheets. Conduct formative and summative evaluations of activities.
8. Recycling back to first steps for expanding the improvement package	Pick up other facets of improvement that could not be done as first or early activities.	The group revisits previous findings and moves ahead with those it selects.

AN INTERESTING EXAMPLE OF MOVING FORWARD

In the suburb where the author lived, an expanse of open land was ceded by the school district to ensure borders with the neighboring urban district. In trade, a big revenue-producing area was given to the latter, and harmony was forever after—or was it? The space that had long been fallow underwent rapid growth with the construction of homes, condos, apartments, restaurants, companies, and office buildings. Many more children had to be educated, and since major tax dollars were given away, the burden was on less rich sources to support schools.

The pressure on the elementary and middle schools and the one high school intensified. When the author's youngest son was a senior, crowding was so bad that teachers had to direct traffic during the change of classes (to prevent class clowns, the author's son included, from acting out). The number of school-age children rose to more than 11,000, close to double what it was before.

Needs were apparent, but so were opportunities. Was a needs assessment called for, or would it be better to think about asset/capacity building? How to proceed? Exhibit 5.1 is a synopsis of what happened with the name of the district changed, and Figure 5.1 is an adaptation of one of the drawings that the schools used when approaching the public with their work.

Exhibit 5.1   The Illustrative Case of the Westington Schools

Administrators, teachers, the board, and community members began to meet, and the consensus was that thinking about the future must start. Data gathering and planning efforts would be required. This led to a committee consisting of teachers and community members. From the start, the stress was on needs being created by a population press and that it was a unique opportunity to build on positives for the future. It was a nexus of needs and assets.

The suburb was close to a state university with many members of the faculty calling it home, including one experienced in planning processes and who was an active parent with the schools. She consented to lead the endeavor and was very good at creating involvement, which was instrumental in the success that was realized. This was a key factor. (Leadership and facilitation were absolutely mandatory for establishing the right ambience. Whether it is needs assessment, asset/capacity building, or a combination, this is the deal maker. A committee or an individual can do it so long as there is good sense of how groups work.)

What was done? The initiating group sought information about needs and assets. Questions were raised to focus the undertaking.

- What are the strengths in the schools and in the community (assets/resources)?

- Is it possible to expand the current facility and take advantage of a readily available resource?

- What might happen as the student population gets larger (needs)?

- What have other districts done when facing similar situations (benchmarking for needs and assets)?

- What does the formal and informal literature say that would be helpful?

- What does our community (within and outside of education) think? The voice of the community is important.

(Continued)

(Continued)

The guiding group with its exceptional leadership did the following:

- Subgroups looked at literature regarding the future of education and trends in the field.

- An architectural study of the high school was commissioned to see if it could be expanded to accommodate burgeoning numbers of students. The finding was negative, with huge costs to be incurred if the school were enlarged or reconfigured. It might be best to tear it down and build anew.

- Local newspapers were examined for what was happening or likely to happen in the community and the overall urban area.

- Committees began working with the community in small group discussions using what was found and summarized from the literature and other sources.

- Brief scenarios (one or two pages in length) dealing with trends in education and the society were handed out to participants. The idea was to get people considering what the future might mean for the schools.

- Larger community meetings were held to consider issues.

- Results from these efforts were collated into four options for the district to pursue.

- The district identified individuals (the author was one) to take the options to the community. Pairs were formed, usually a respected teacher and a community member, and trained to conduct community meetings for about 50 people per session.

- Using handouts, the teams led community meetings, which were highly publicized. The purpose was to explain what had been done and learned, and potential new directions. (This is similar to community forums in needs assessment for soliciting views and perceptions about what has been learned and next steps.)

- As each meeting was ending, a survey was administered to attendees. The four options were shown in pictures, two of which in adapted form are in Figure 5.1, and participants were asked to rate them.

- Nearly 1,000 forms were completed, representing about 3% of the entire population in the district. It was not random, but most respondents were the parents of school-age children.

The work paid off in a big way. In the following years the district passed a new bond issue, built a modernistic second high school, and made changes to the existing one and to the curriculum.

It is doubtful that this would have gone as smoothly as it did without the procedures described above. The initiating core/working group created a milieu highly receptive for action, and all of this came about from an involved citizen base that was well led.

Figure 5.1 Depicting High School Possibilities by Simple Descriptive Drawings

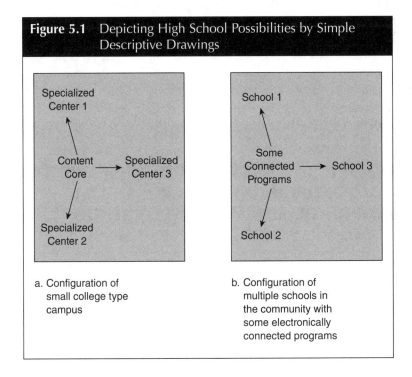

a. Configuration of small college type campus

b. Configuration of multiple schools in the community with some electronically connected programs

How does "Westington" stack up against the hybrid framework? Was it needs assessment, asset/capacity building, or both? Needs assessment was there in terms of the current status being measured against the population changes and what they would do to the system over the next decade.

Assets were examined, not in the detail of Kretzmann and McKnight (1993), but they were reviewed. Many methods were used to obtain data and perceptions.

The most striking aspect was immersing the community in the decision-making process. Some of this was after the fact since the four choices were proposed by the district, but they were openly brought to the community for discussion and debate. The meetings about them were lively, with many thoughts expressed. They were in the spirit of building communities from inside, and the purveyors were not those heavily vested in what might happen.

Even with extensive volunteer participation, the overall effort was not inexpensive—meetings, training, architectural study, reviewing the literature, and benchmarking required resources. Investment from the school board and in-kind contributions of many individuals were essential. The district was an upper-middle-class one, the expenditures were deemed worthy, and the outcomes supported that position. Without such a financial base, this would have been more difficult, so what is realistic for a different environment should be carefully examined. Implementing the hybrid framework at some point requires funding. This should not be a deterrent, and probably Westington did not know what it would cost when it embarked on the venture.

STEP 5. USING WHAT HAS BEEN LEARNED TO MAKE DECISIONS FOR POSSIBLE NEW PROGRAMS—BEGINNING TO DO SO AND PREPARING ACTION PLANS

Go back to Table 3.3 in Chapter 3. Look at the identified needs and assets. Is there a match between them? Go to the literature for past actions that have been proposed or tried. If benchmarking was done, how did comparable communities or organizations handle needs, assets, and issues?

What did they experience?

What actions did they take in terms of people, finances, and other related factors?

How did they organize for action?

Who were the prime movers, and how did they manage to gain support?

What structures (committees, working groups) did they establish?

What activities and programs did they implement?

What snags did they run into, and how did they handle them?

What seemed to work, and what did not?

Is the effort still in operation?

Did they do any evaluations of their efforts?

> What did they find?
>
> Did they do any cost-benefit analyses?
>
> What changes did they make based on the data collected?

Were new programs and projects sustained after their initiators were no longer involved with enthusiasm and energy? Are the new endeavors still there?

What are things to avoid doing?

Were there any unique uses or combinations of resources and assets that might be applicable to what we have been studying?

Did they leverage resources on the margin for a larger impact?

What would they do differently if given a chance to do it over?

If you describe your situation, do those being benchmarked have any insights into how to proceed knowing the constraints and opportunities available to you?

A lot of information has been gathered and is in focused summaries. Individual committee members prior to a meeting of the group should review what is there. *How should we move forward? What are the most pressing needs? What are the assets and resources? Do they align, or would it be better to go outside the box and form unique combinations of ideas?* Be open rather than constrained.

Encourage the group members to jot down their thoughts in abbreviated form for the meeting. It might include features such as those specified below.

- Needs or problem areas in consideration
- Assets/resources that could fit here or be applied in innovative ways

- The gist of the action strategy
- Where it is coming from (community suggestions, benchmarking, the literature, etc.)
- What the action strategy might look like—what actually would occur
- In the short term
- In the long term
- The pros and cons of the idea

Participants would bring their efforts to the meeting, or ideally they would send them out three to five days before everyone gets together. Action-oriented strategies would be generated by each person for what might be accomplished in the short term and down the road. They are input for a discussion, and if new directions arise during it, they are fine.

It is important to have ground rules for the meeting. View the session as guided brainstorming that will propel the group closer to solutions or improvements.

1. First, all ideas are welcome. There is not a bad one. There may be ways to think about using ideas in a manner not previously considered. Everything proposed is valuable.

2. Second, individuals will be asked to briefly describe what they are suggesting and its merits. Stress brevity, not a polemic about what they have come up with. It is not to be defensive, and when questions are raised, it is not to be perceived as a personal issue. We are just trying to get to possibilities for moving forward.

3. Third, as part of Point 2, all strategies have pros and cons, so they are to be mentioned in a straightforward manner.

Allot about 90 minutes for presentations and subsequent interactions. Excitement should be noticeable as the group is getting closer to action items. The prior work is moving the organization or community to a higher level of functioning. Notes or highlights of what has transpired should be kept. The moderator(s) of the session should give a short recap of what is to be pursued and eventually offered to the community for consideration. Coming to this point is an important step.

Since the group is not large and has been operating as a collective, one way to do this is to ask for a simple vote (show of hands) on what seems most propitious. Tally the results, and select the top options. Another version is to give out colored pens or Post-it notes to each individual. Then ask participants to assign points to each option with no more than 3 out of a total of 10 points being given to any one choice. This zero-sum game forces examining all options rather than focusing on one. Or suggest that people not vote on what they have developed. This could bring to the surface choices freer of bias and vested interest. Ratings are to be done independently. As the group gets ready to choose, state that ideas can be modified/combined later for what will be brought to the community at large.

The author did a procedure like the one just described with a state-wide organization when its board was doing strategic planning. Possible new directions (one per sheet) were listed on poster paper with subheads, and then the papers were hung on the walls of a conference room. Each person reviewed them and placed independent votes on the sheets. In addition to the votes there was a draft of what options required. Here is what happened as the election proceeded.

People quietly started scanning. They were familiar with the content, but now they had to put their money (votes) on the table. It was "put up or shut up" time. The mood was somber.

No one rushed. The charge was important and was done in a serious manner. The process took about 20 minutes and produced much agreement about where the organization should be going over the next few years.

Some board members felt so strongly about an issue that they assigned most of the points to it. That is neither good nor bad, but it is why only a certain number should be allocated to a choice. It makes for a fuller inspection of all the ideas that have been generated. The group reviews the votes, and the top three choices are identified.

STEP 5. USING WHAT HAS BEEN LEARNED TO MAKE DECISIONS FOR POSSIBLE NEW PROGRAMS—OTHER PROCEDURES FOR COMING TO A DECISION

A few other ways give the flavor of what can be done. If more are desired, see Stevahn and King (2010) in which there is a compendium of 24 ("double dozen") techniques tied into needs assessment. Adaptations of several (check in/tune in; what/so what/now what; concept mapping/mind mapping) that apply to the hybrid framework will be overviewed.

Check In/Tune In

Group members are asked reflective questions and given time to consider answers prior to discussion. They bring to the surface group perceptions. Questions could be along the lines of these:

What is your biggest "aha" moment, or what revelations are coming to mind about what we have come up with?

How well do you think that we are making connections across ideas?

Have we linked important ideas together?

What insights do you carry away from this work?

What do you think is the most innovative vision we have?

Are there any questions that we perhaps should answer before moving ahead?

This pause is useful for thoughts about the solutions that are now in front of the group.

What? So What? Now What?

Divide the group into triads and then give the "so what" and "now what" part of the exercise. *"So what" do the solutions or new programs mean for our community or organization, and "now what" are the next steps? What concrete measures and activities will we have to undertake to make it a reality?* This may seem to be jumping the gun since we are in Step 5, not Step 6, of the hybrid framework. True, but thoughts like this are probably on the minds of individuals. Why not capture them as we move to implementation plans and conducting activities? After sufficient time for small group responses, pull the total group together for an exchange of thoughts and record them for subsequent input to options.

Concept Mapping/Mind Mapping

The goal is to develop a map of a new program or structure for change. Divide the group into triads. For each solution option, ask group members to create a description of key elements or aspects of it. Who are the key stakeholders or groups involved, and who would be impacted by new services? The group might also suggest resources to be incorporated into a solution. The essence of the task would be placed in the middle of a diagram, and then the participants would individually or as a group complete the diagram (see Figure 5.2). This is followed by a large group exchange of ideas.

Figure 5.2 Sample Maps

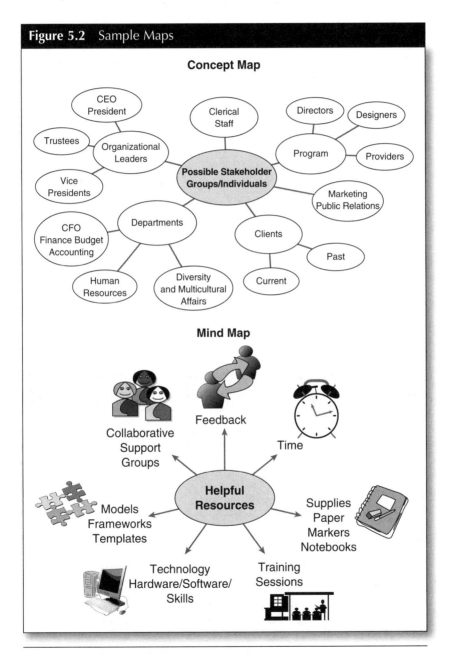

Concept Map

Mind Map

Source: Stevahn and King, 2010. Used with permission.

STEP 5. USING WHAT HAS BEEN LEARNED TO MAKE DECISIONS FOR POSSIBLE NEW PROGRAMS—FINISHING THE OPTIONS

Small groups subsidiary to the larger one expand/examine the options in more detail, looking into advantages and disadvantages (pros, cons) and what a program might look like in the short and long run, how it might be started, what resources are necessary, where assets and monetary support could come from, and so on. The final product is not a full plan but a five-page explanation of it. The pros and cons are vital for how it will be portrayed to the larger community, as will be resource decisions. If someone in the small group has drawing or sketching ability, provide a depiction of the main theme of an option. This was done effectively in the Westington example to convey ideas to the entire community.

Keeping pace is critical because the committee should be energized. Motivation is high and maintaining it important. The suggestion is that the small groups do their work over a week. What they produce leads to an overall discussion about how to get the community/organization involved and what its reactions might be. This session is a biggie, and much is riding on it! It is best if all participants have reviewed the more finalized options prior to meeting. Get recommendations for modifications, and after that the meeting will move to two main activities. Exhibit 5.2 is one of them.

Exhibit 5.2   Role-Playing as to What Might Happen With a Change or New Direction

The author was part of a committee of staff, administrators, and faculty members looking at the personnel evaluation practices for 450 employees and graduate students in a major college of education. The undertaking was large, and evaluation of this type is always tricky.

The committee reviewed the literature, looked at past and current practices, benchmarked with other colleges, surveyed different groups, and did other research. These efforts led to a new system to be proposed. The committee wanted additional input across the college as it vetted the new strategy. It was far from a done deal.

What the committee had been doing, its findings, how it had arrived at the system, and what it would mean were to be explained in open forums. In a sense this is parallel to what the initiating group for the hybrid framework would do.

Fortunately, the committee was facilitated by two internal university consultants who participated in its activities and meetings. They knew group processes and what it might take to sell a radical change to members of university staff, some of whom had been there for many years and were protected by the civil service system.

The committee proposed a fun way to anticipate what could happen. Participants were put into role-playing situations. Pairs were formed (other variations could be used), and each person was given a role card. For example, the author was a 30-year staff member who had never been evaluated and was negative. The other individual was a new employee who did not have much in the way of formulated opinions. The new employee interviewed the senior one.

Roles are not difficult to create. Needless to say, this was not an ordinary activity, and everyone quickly got into it. In some cases, the role-playing was conducted in front of the committee. The interviews sensitized everyone as to what might be encountered when taking its work to groups in the college. It also made the committee think more about the new procedures.

All in all the experience was a hoot! (See Altschuld & Lepicki, 2010a.)

The technique in Exhibit 5.2 could easily be used with the hybrid framework. Remember that the initiating group consists of individuals who have been chosen to represent the heartbeat of the community or organization. They are aware of concerns and issues, and it would be a simple matter for them to come up with types who would be in attendance at community forums and meetings, such as

naysayers—those who seem to always be negative about everything and will undoubtedly be in attendance;

resource questioners—who think, "We'll never have the resources to do this, so why even think this way?";

those who tacitly agree—the nodding ones who appear to be in agreement and supportive, but you don't know what what is on their minds;

talkers—when talkative people get the floor, they can run on and in effect destroy a meeting;

nontalkers—those for whom you have no indication of what they are thinking and whom you may have to draw out into the discussion;

uninvolved individuals—who for some reason came to the meeting but have no interest in and are doing things (texting, reading materials that are not pertinent) that have no relation to the intent of the assembly (they can be disruptive); and

others—recall meetings in which you have participated, and the people in them, that have led to less-than-successful outcomes (a long list could be generated).

The role-playing should be helpful for going public and dealing with what might happen. Have strategies for tabling comments from those who are long-winded, from those who will have to be drawn into the discourse, and so on.

STEP 5. USING WHAT HAS BEEN LEARNED TO MAKE DECISIONS FOR POSSIBLE NEW PROGRAMS—TAKING ACTION PLANS PUBLIC

What is needed for bringing plans to concerned audiences is in place. If you are in a large organization, set up meetings with areas or departments—make sure that they are not so large that people will feel inhibited. If in a community, get publicity about the meetings and activities to the local media and schedule sessions at times that will draw well from residents.

When a meeting begins, welcome everyone and explain the purpose of looking at new directions that have been explored and obtaining feedback from the community/organization. Set ground rules (everyone is encouraged to speak; you may have to briefly summarize what a person is saying so that others can state views; the moderator must keep everything flowing; the agenda will give a sense of what will occur). Table 5.2 contains a possible agenda (time, materials) with meeting length approximately two hours.

Having someone take notes to capture the highlights is worthwhile. When the meeting ends, use surveys for rating options and expressing perceptions. Simplified drawings are useful for understanding choices. Since the tone is positive, don't offer the negatives of an option, but if questions come up, be ready to respond. (This fits with the asset emphasis on the positive.) Note that each course of action has provisions for short-term and fuller implementation.

After all meetings are concluded, pull together the collected data and inputs that were offered. It is hoped that one or two options are preferred

Table 5.2 Agenda, Time Allotment, Materials, and Comments

Agenda	Time Allotment	Materials	Comments
Introduction	5–10 minutes	Handout, packet, name tags, refreshments	Preparation and planning are critical for success. Establish ground rules and stress that input will be sought and welcomed.
Description of what has been done previously	10 minutes for presentation 10 minutes for questions and comments	Packet containing short, clearly labeled summaries	Make it obvious as to where the initiating group is coming from. Don't overdo but ensure a feeling of what has been done. Be open if someone disagrees or has alternative views.
Discussion of the options for action	40–60 minutes for questions and discussion	Option descriptions in the packet	Make sure that distinctions among options are clear. Ask for what the attendees are thinking as they review the descriptions.
Closure	10–15 minutes	See above	Summarize what transpired. Make sure that all complete the survey with ratings for the options.

via ratings and what participants said. This provides an impetus for moving forward. The results should be communicated to the media and the organization that eventually will be involved with the change.

STEP 6. DEVELOPING A STRATEGY FOR IMPROVEMENT

Nearly everything is in place for final plans for improvement. It is possible that there is enough without having to do much more. Step 6 is just for fine-tuning options and generating detailed plans for proceeding. Here are other things that might be done.

First, the initiating group should review what has come from the community or organization meetings. What suggestions were made that could be in the final plans for the highly rated choices? What possibly could be deleted from them? If we did the "what/so what/now what" and "concept mapping/mind mapping" activities, what do they mean in terms of implementation? Who are the stakeholders and involved parties, and are they currently on board? Are they organized for new efforts, and if not, what would it take? As for resources, how could they be accessed for improvement? What about the immediate and long-term features? What would be best to get us going? When should we begin—what are the time frames? What should we be doing right away to start? Should we enlarge our capacity (people, organizations, financial resources) to do all of this? What are concrete next steps and activities? Earlier work has led to many answers to these questions. These are just examples of group deliberations. For the sake of argument, the text is going to move to three techniques that deal more with the nature of final plans.

Success Mapping is a one-page pictorial display of the project or new endeavor that shows how its components relate to each other.

Fist to Five is a rating technique for a solution or parts of a solution along continuums such as from least to most important; needed, doable, feasible; and so on.

Multi-Attribute Utility Theory (MAUT) is a procedure for selecting the best solution strategy based on its likelihood of satisfying rank-ordered criteria.

Success Mapping

Success mapping, a one-page map, sets the stage for what is to be undertaken. It does not show all the minutiae but lays out basic elements uncluttered by tons of details. It is simpler than a logic map or an activity responsibility table that might be seen in planning efforts. It is an overview device for people to comprehend the whole picture before getting into the nitty-gritty. Sometimes there can be too many specifics. They are needed, but the success map would be the constant reference for group members when they think about the new direction or effort. What does it look like?

Figure 5.3 is for the performance improvement and evaluation system for the major college of education. Figure 5.4 is for a nationwide moving company fitness program intended mainly for males working on the trucks.

Figure 5.3 Success Map for First Tryout of Performance Management System

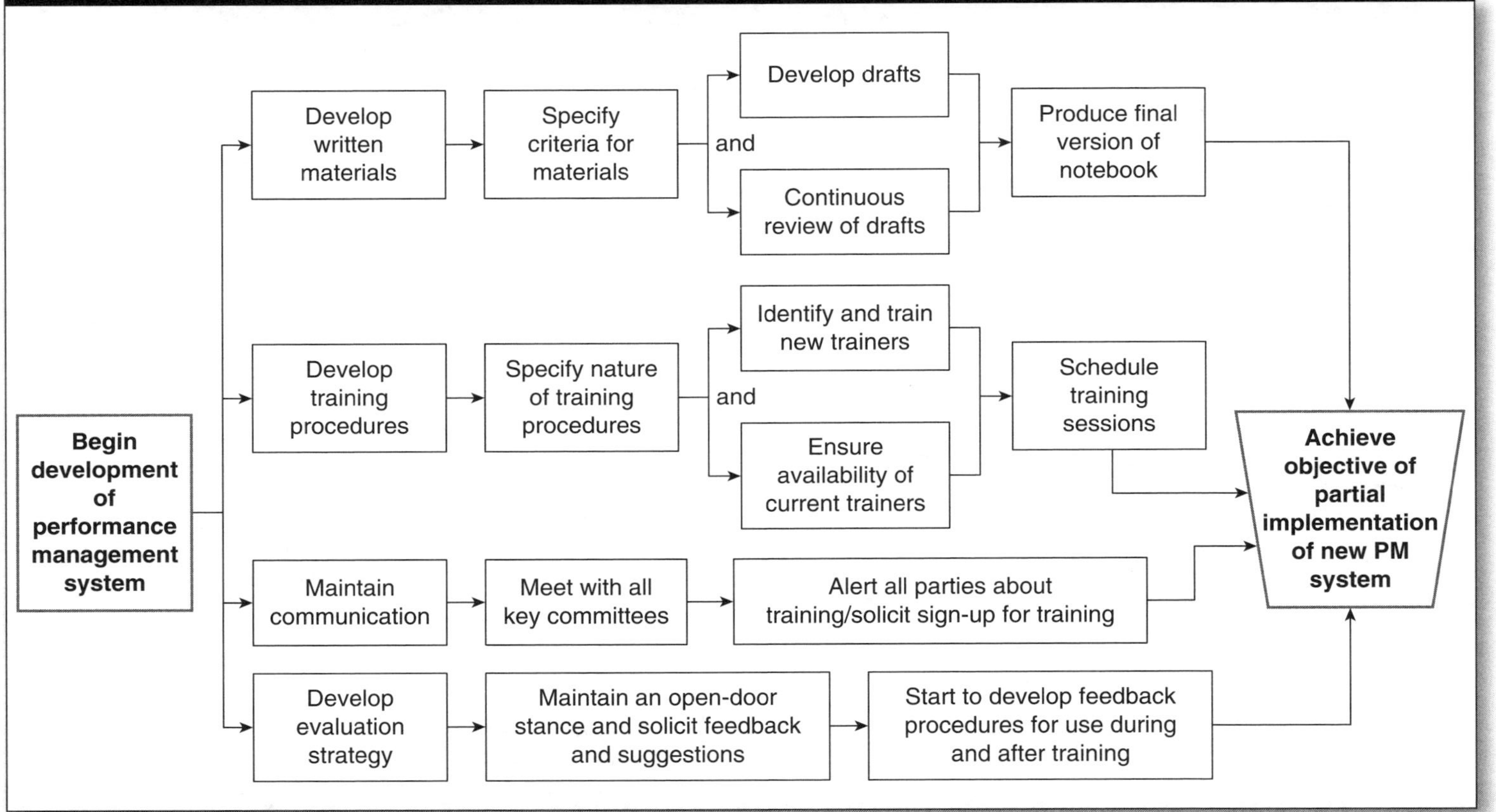

Source: Altschuld and Kumar, 2010. Used with permission.

Figure 5.4 Rudimentary Success Map for a Program Designed to Reduce the Back Problems of Employees of a Nationwide Moving Company

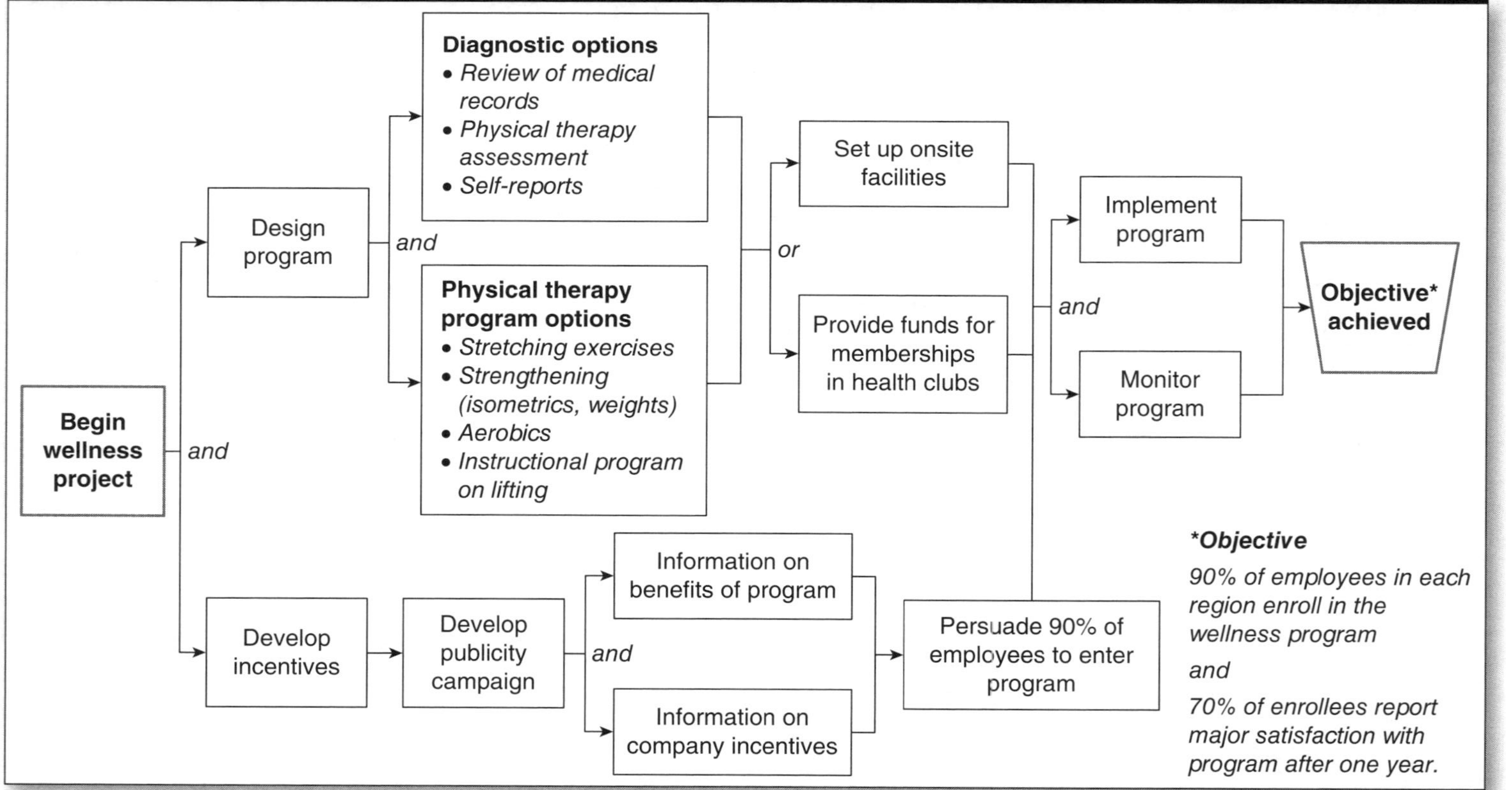

Begin wellness project

Design program

and

Diagnostic options
- Review of medical records
- Physical therapy assessment
- Self-reports

Physical therapy program options
- Stretching exercises
- Strengthening (isometrics; weights)
- Aerobics
- Instructional program on lifting

and

Set up onsite facilities

or

Provide funds for memberships in health clubs

Develop incentives

Develop publicity campaign

Information on benefits of program

and

Information on company incentives

Persuade 90% of employees to enter program

Implement program

and

Monitor program

Objective* achieved

*Objective
90% of employees in each region enroll in the wellness program
and
70% of enrollees report major satisfaction with program after one year.

Source: Altschuld and Kumar, 2010. Used with permission.

(These examples come from needs assessment but fit the hybrid context.) In the figures, key parts of what is being proposed are apparent. In Figure 5.3 the second column contains four facets that must be done to get the new system developed and running. In 5.4, there are two such entities that propel the wellness initiative. Some things are important to note. The end objectives with standards may be displayed, thus pinpointing what is to be accomplished. Another is that the page gives a feel for formative and summative evaluation. Mapping like this is invaluable and highly recommended, and coupled with "fist to five" its impact is magnified.

Fist to Five

Paraphrasing "the best laid plans of mice and men" can go astray. Success maps are only plans, and they can be off the mark and fail. There are several ways to probe for failure such as cause-consequence and fishbone analyses with the former being least sophisticated. Fault tree analysis (FTA) is an in-depth but more complex technique. All these approaches for determining failure are valid, and each has plusses and minuses. (See Witkin and Altschuld, 1995.)

"Fist to five" is a quick way of getting to sources of failure. Remember that the small working group has been investigating needs and resources for some time. Why not have it do the exercise? Review the overall success map (Figures 5.3 and 5.4) and ask group members to rate feasibility, the importance of what is being suggested, ease of implementation, and so forth. They would use a 5-point scale going from low to high, and the ratings, done independently, would be collated.

An even better way to do this would be to look at subparts of the system and subject them to the same kind of analysis. The four parts of Figure 5.3 could be rated on variables such as those above to identify the weakest links in the proposed new direction. It would not take much time and could lead to a productive conversation that had not occurred before. Interestingly, for Figure 5.4, the author and B. R. Witkin in 1995 did an FTA and perceived that the system would fail on the incentive side. If "fist to five" came to the same conclusion more easily and in much less time, that would be a good result.

One thought about looking at solutions in this way is that it might have the negative cast of needs assessment that was vehemently criticized (Chapter 1). That is partially correct, but if the goal is to have a stronger design for moving ahead, the benefits outweigh the tint of negativity. Another consideration is that there is a side benefit to doing this type of activity. At some time as resources are applied to problems and issues via new developments, the ugly head of evaluation will be reared. What bang are we getting for the work we have done? Is it making a difference, in what ways, and what evidence can be collected about impact and effectiveness? Who or what is changing in accord with what has been implemented? If more resources for the new effort are warranted, how can they be justified to investors in the public and private sectors?

These are legitimate inquiries, and the techniques in this section are useful for evaluation. They help in spotting what might go wrong and suggest where to target evaluations—critical points in systems. We might even go so far as to consider whether there are differences in short- and long-term solutions, and if the long term is more problematic, perhaps the effort should be concentrated on the near or immediate time frame.

Multi-Attribute Utility Technique

The multi-attribute utility technique, or MAUT, is applied where multiple solution options have been proposed. Which of them would work best against criteria that the group established for a solution? Here are a few:

- Number of people in the organization or community impacted in a positive way
- Dealing with a concern that is of great importance to a large number of individuals
- Length of time for implementation in the short and long term
- Complexity of the option with the less complex being more desirable
- Whether the option, if implemented, would impact more than one issue (a new library program for a school-age population might spill over to senior citizens—an instrumental effect)
- Cost factors in the near and longer future
- Demonstrating a positive outcome, galvanizing support, motivation, and involvement
- A situation that requires immediate attention and for which delaying would not be reasonable

- An option that could lead to unique ways of combining existing resources and strengths
- Community or organizational willingness and enthusiasm to change
- Feasibility of implementation
- Others

More criteria could be added, so the list could get quite long, and deciding on options against all of them would be difficult. That is where MAUT comes into play. It uses the Pareto principle or, as implemented in MAUT, the preserving of ratios. Examples of Pareto would be if you have a large group involved in a meeting, a small number of people do most of the talking, or if you have identified many causes of a problem, only a few are the real ones. As applied to choosing the best option, it would be that just a small number of criteria are what we should be concerned about. There is a formal set of rules in MAUT for reducing the number to four or five (Altschuld & Kumar, 2010; Altschuld & Witkin, 2000). Here, a simplified version is being offered.

Convene the committee and explain how criteria would help in choosing the best strategy. Show a few criteria as a seed to start a brainstorming session on important ones. As they are generated, list them and then have the group consolidate the list into a more manageable entity for rank ordering. Assuming that there are 15 criteria, have group members pick what they see as the top 5 and put them in rank order. Stress that they be very careful in deeming their top 5 inasmuch as MAUT works best when criteria are limited. If a consensus is not there, quickly discuss issues for reconciliation so that everyone agrees and can live with the result.

Look at the rankings and starting at the bottom or lowest one give it an arbitrary value or weight of, say, 10. Then move up to next lowest ranked one and give it a value of 20, and proceed through the list in this fashion. This is preserving ratios in a formal MAUT. Enter these values into a table as shown in Table 5.3. Preserving ratios means that if a 10 is given to the lowest ranked criterion, then by assigning 20 to the one immediately above it, Criterion 4 is twice as important as Criterion 5. Criterion 1 is 5 times as valuable as Criterion 5. The weights for the criteria are all ratios of the lowest one. The starting weight of 10 was arbitrary, and one could start with a different weight and the ratios would be different as well, such as 25 for Criterion 4 (2.5 times the lowest weight), 35 for Criterion 3, and so on. A quick discussion can resolve the weights.

Table 5.3 A MAUT-Type Structure for Deciding on Best Options

Criteria with weight (x)	Option 1	Option 2	Option 3	Option 4
Criterion 1 (50)				
Criterion 2 (40)				
Criterion 3 (30)				
Criterion 4 (20)				
Criterion 5 (10)				
Total				

With weights and the criteria in rank order, the table is now to be completed. Each person looks at each option in terms of the criteria and says that Option 1 has a .60 probability for meeting it, Option 2 a .45, and so on down to Option 5 where the probability is .08. The probabilities are averaged for the group per option in a cell, the average is multiplied by the appropriate weight for the row, and products are summed down the column. The higher the total, the better the option is, and the more likely it is the choice for the group to pursue.

There is a very beneficial feature of doing this. Some options may fit well with some criteria and not others. Different patterns of satisfying criteria may be observed. An option may work for one but not another. This presents an opportunity for the committee that another procedure might not. Look closely at how the options function and what might be behind a lesser preferred option highly satisfying a certain criterion. What does it have in it that another one does not, and could it with modest tweaking be built into the option that received a higher total? Could this be done without much cost while maintaining the integrity of the higher option?

This aspect of MAUT is intriguing and is related to something brought up previously. Could an option have an effect on more than one issue or subgroup within the population, as with a new library program for the school-age population spilling over to senior citizens? This aligns with a premise of asset/capacity building and needs assessment and is called an instrumental effect (Sork, 1998). This in the hybrid framework represents an ideal outcome.

STEP 7. IMPLEMENTING AND EVALUATING THE ACTION PLAN

The group developed a success map from techniques such as MAUT, fist to five, and other activities. Everything has been discussed with constituencies, and it is now ready for action. One caution before beginning! The worst thing that can happen is to try to do it all at once on a massive scale and get bogged down. When this occurs, the energy of a group can quickly flit away. People get discouraged, motivation drops, and things grind to a standstill. It may be better to start smaller, more incrementally, and build up over time. Demonstrate success on a limited scale to maintain morale. Then it becomes easier to ratchet up and expand. In some cases the wisdom to go slower may not be valid. Assess the local conditions before deciding to go big or small.

At this time it might be prudent to solicit some participants with experience in translating plans into real-life events. The group could be enlarged with individuals with management experience who blend into the existing group structure and dynamic. If the effort is a volunteer one, consider assistance from retirees in the community or individuals from the organization who would be willing and able to contribute to the endeavor.

From there, carefully review the success map, asking questions such as the following:

- What are essential things that must be done right away to get going?
- What are the human and financial resources and assets that can be applied to the new venture?
- Concretely, who should be doing what, and when should they be doing it?
- What would be indicators that the process was going as planned, and what would be indicators of success?
- What kind of data or evidence would be useful for demonstrating what we are doing, what we have done, and achievement of outcomes?
- If we are starting small, what would the next phase look like, and what resources would it entail?
- What would the schedule look like?

- Where might we encounter snags?
- How should we manage the program or project?
- As we move off the starting block, how often should we be meeting to see how things are progressing?
- Are we organized in a manner to proceed?

The answers imply the use of Gantt charts, schedules with due dates, planning techniques, and establishing responsibilities and roles for various actors.

One basic suggestion that has merit is from the work of Stevahn and King (2010; see Figure 5.5). It is straightforward for making assignments and scheduling and can easily be adapted. It is appropriate at this point since in general the program would be limited in scope as the community or organization begins to take action. Some of the above questions are particularly important for action and will be further explained.

Starting with the last question in the above list, activities don't just suddenly appear by chance. They are the fruits of thinking them through and having the building blocks necessary to change from a plan into an actuality. Who is going to be responsible for managing what should occur? What would they be doing? It could be a small subset of the original group with the necessary skills. This may seem top down, but it cannot be avoided, and it is critical for movement forward. Or it could be by the addition of new members who have the experience, blend with the chemistry of the group, and are catalysts, not disruptive forces.

Leadership is embedded in the questions. One of its functions is a gentle or at times a more sharply focused pushing of those doing the work to keep going. Another is to make sure that everything is on target with what is described on the success map and, when it isn't, what corrective actions must be undertaken. In the "Westington" example there was excellent leadership; without it, failure was to be expected. Also in that case, leadership was long-term. This is important even if the initiative is not very large. A consistent and steady hand at the tiller eases the journey even in the face of problems. This is a major consideration and must be given careful attention.

One of the other questions deals with resources. As we move from a humble beginning to an expanded set of activities, the concern shifts to where support will come from. This is being posed not from a

Figure 5.5 "To Do" List

			Meeting Date: *Year/Month/Day*

Committee Name
"To Do" List
Date _____

Task (description)	Who (person responsible)	Target Date (for completion)	Current Status (progress/completed)
1.			
2.			
3.			
4.			
5.			
6.			
7.			
8.			
9.			

Source: Stevahn and King, 2010. Used with permission.

dependency mind-set but from a practical one. At the base of almost all things we do is money. The initiating group must talk and deliberate about the longer term and what will be required to get there. What agencies, groups, or individuals could be providers? Are there pots of resources that could be tapped? What persuasive arguments might be employed to get access to them? What information could influence decisions this way?

This links to concerns about *evaluation*. The choice of indicators and ways to portray them will play an important role in the unfolding advancement drama. Many of the steps in the hybrid framework dovetail nicely with evaluation. From the start, queries were made about what was done before and how well it worked. What evidence is there of effectiveness, what indicators have been measured, what different programs or approaches have been done, and what led to results? Go back to benchmarking against other situations, and note in some of the probes there is a heavy amount of evaluation.

Look at the success maps and the idea about outcomes and how they might be measured. The discussion of causal analysis has overlap with formative and summative evaluation. These aspects of hybrid work add much to assessing the enterprise. When the committee gets to evaluation, things have already come up or are in place, and it is not a new albatross around the neck.

A couple of other things done before are also helpful. One is the recommendation that important tables and products be dated and kept as feasible in electronic form for easy access and retrieval. Dating is a running process record of what the committee has been doing. It enables the group to reflect on what it has produced and allows those in the future to see how issues were studied, what was learned, what was pursued and what was tabled for later review, what key variables were studied, what kinds of data and information were found, and so forth. This documentation is a simple way to collect valuable data from day-to-day operations.

The second thing is to think outside the box. There is a neat example of this that came up several times in previous chapters. It is the technique of photovoice. In the newspapers of most major cities in the United States, there are often photographs of sections of the city in "then" and "now" format. German Village photos over time would confirm an effect. Current pictures would show that on the edge of the village new large office buildings have been constructed. This could be adapted to other situations, and with the advent of easy computer storage this is an excellent way to evaluate.

This does not negate the need to do other evaluation activities. Continuing with German Village, one could monitor population trends in the area over time. The same would hold for property values. Have they increased, and what does the path forward look like? New surveys could be conducted about a variety of issues and developments and to ascertain the perspectives of individuals who have lived there a long time or more recent residents. For the former, some questions could be about how the area has changed.

The seeds for many variables that could be assessed are planted at the beginning of the hybrid process and embedded into almost all of its activities. Bringing onto the team someone with evaluation background will be helpful, as will hiring an evaluation consultant. But doing that is not intended to abrogate the responsibility of the group for evaluation or underestimate its potential for doing so.

STEP 8. RECYCLING BACK TO FIRST STEPS FOR EXPANDING THE IMPROVEMENT PACKAGE

The last step in the framework is recycling back through it. Return to how the process began. The goal was to identify and sort through issues related to the community or organization. What are its strengths? What are the needs and gaps? Do they mesh together for change? How do we move the organization and community to a higher level? We gained a lot of information and understanding as the work was being completed. But not everything could be done at once. Many areas of importance were found, and fortunately they have been kept track of, in formal documentation. Go back to see if there are other areas to be pursued. Examine earlier results and ask new questions about what we knew previously.

- What stands out as valuable to now set our sights on?
- Given what we have done for a new program, are there ways we can leverage or tie it to another area of need by using assets at the margin?
- Since the original work was done a year or so before, does the portrait that we painted still seem pertinent? Does it hold up?
- If it has changed, in what ways has it done so, and what do those differences look like?

Review what Steps 1 and 2 produced. Do we need to update the knowledge? This may entail much new work that no one is willing to get into; however, records have been kept, and they contain the instruments and procedures used to collect data. Can we take advantage of this without tremendous expenditures of time and human resources? The group should have a frank discussion about exploring additional avenues.

If it decides to, avoid starting anew. Find ways to use what is there instead of going through the entire process from the top. Be proactive about what has been done and creative about reviewing the information from a unique angle. The one concern is that an issue may have been lightly explored and upon revisitation may seem to warrant an extensive investigation. Do so after careful deliberation since it might require a lot of effort. The compensating factor is that the group is no longer novice but expert.

HIGHLIGHTS OF CHAPTER 5

1. Building from the first four steps in the hybrid framework, there is excitement since the process is now going into an action implementation phase.

2. The "Westington" schools were a case in which a community engaged in an elongated period of study based on needs and assets.

3. Notable in that example was the immersion of the community in the process.

4. In Step 5 of the framework the group reviewed everything done before via questions about needs, assets and resources, and what had been tried earlier in the community or organization. This was for focusing on actions to be taken.

5. Ways to assist the group in coming to a decision about actions were presented: check in/tune in, what/so what/now what, and concept mapping/mind mapping. Also sound out stakeholders about strategies for improvement.

6. Step 6 deals with details for making options operational. Success mapping, multi-attribute utility theory, and fist to five were provided to do this, as was a short overview of causal analysis.

7. Step 7 stresses translating plans into action and evaluating implementation and outcomes. Building blocks for this were embedded in previous hybrid framework efforts. Responsibility for evaluation resides with the group.

8. Step 8 relates to recycling back through the framework with the admonition to not start anew but to take advantage as feasible of what was done before.

DISCUSSION QUESTIONS

1. There is a lot to do in the four last steps with much time and effort required. Do you see places where the process could be shortened without sacrificing quality?

2. What do you think of starting small and incrementally expanding as a strategy? What are the up- and downsides of doing so?

3. At some point the initiating group shifts from visionaries and information gatherers to managers and implementers of new directions. How should this occur while preserving the enthusiasm of the overall effort?

4. Leadership is success. What should the nature of leadership be?

5. What are the major areas in which the hybrid framework could fail?

6. Approaches to help the group in deciding about options for improvement and fine-tuning them were offered. Do you know of others that would be useful?

6

A Checklist for the Hybrid Framework

A lthough philosophically different, needs assessment and asset/ capacity building have been seen as coalescing into an emergent combined approach. This was noted in the top of the pyramid (Figure 1.2) and became the basis for the hybrid framework. A theme running throughout its eight steps is to find out as much as possible about a community or an organization. Numerous strategies to do this have been described. Especially important are write-ups and documentation of what has been done when identifying and resolving needs, finding and cataloging resources, arraying findings, and converting the amalgam of information into plans for action that result in betterment. This is a lot to do, and it is difficult to imagine a pure version that is fully functional and being commonly used.

What is valuable here is a checklist (scorecard) to help a group evaluate other studies. It consists of what should be in a hybrid framework with a system for rating what is located. That is the purpose of this chapter with an application being to exemplars in the literature (Chapters 7 and 8). Another use of the checklist is as a quick reference when a local committee or group goes about its work.

CONCEPTUAL BASIS OF THE CHECKLIST

A way to develop the checklist is to look at the hybrid framework and list variables important for its implementation. To that end, Table 6.1 is a recasting from a checklist standpoint. Variables for each step will be specified,

(Continued on page 141)

Table 6.1 Checklist Variables and Highlights for the Hybrid Framework for Needs Assessment and Asset/Capacity Building

Step	Purpose	Methods/Strategies	Checklist	Highlights/Variables
1. Scoping the context	Probe the situation to determine what course of action to pursue. Do preliminary needs assessment or asset/capacity building.	Informal reconnaissance Casual interviews Observations Informal discussions Micro-ethnology Cultural audits Review of existing information Other related strategies Usually done by a working committee	Concerned, involved group Recognition of two approaches Adequate probing Use of multiple methods Use of existing sources	There is evidence of a concerned group being operational. There is an understanding of different philosophies apparent in the effort. The group is digging in and collecting information. Valuable information is obtained, and its utility is clear.
2. Deciding what actions should be taken	Determine next actions such as doing nothing, or conducting a needs assessment, an asset/capacity-building endeavor, or a hybrid approach.	Collation of what has been found Array of information to facilitate group decision making Individual and group review of the information	Tables, summaries evident Information in usable form Evidence that reviews of the committee have taken place Documentation of decisions from group deliberations Concrete next actions established as well as assignments for same	Summaries of data and information are critical to the process. Via meeting notes, it should be possible to examine group deliberations. Next things to do emerge from the discussion. The hybrid framework comes to the fore.

Step	Purpose	Methods/Strategies	Checklist	Highlights/Variables
		Group discussion and resolution of what to do next: - nothing - needs assessment - asset/capacity building - hybrid approach		Has enough information been found to guide making good decisions?
3. Dividing the working committee into two subcommittees	Subcommittee 1 conducts a needs assessment. Subcommittee 2 identifies resources, assets, and strengths.	Assignments and responsibilities for each subcommittee are specified. (If the overall group is too small, start with assets—accentuate the positive.)	Two working committees are formed, if possible. Each committee is given independent guidelines for doing needs assessment or asset/capacity building. Each group reviews what was done before so as to not reinvent the wheel.	As feasible, the groups work independently on the two facets of the study of the community or organization.
4. Conducting the assessment in greater depth	Develop sharper pictures of needs and assets as related to thinking about improvement.	For needs assessment, use many of the activities for Step 1 but in greater depth:	Documentation of this should show up in summaries or summary tables.	Continued and expanded use of existing sources as well as new ones is essential.

137

(Continued)

Table 6.1 (Continued)

Step	Purpose	Methods/Strategies	Checklist	Highlights/Variables
		- emphasis on collecting/using existing information as feasible - photovoice - combined needs/ solutions surveys - many other techniques For asset/capacity building, use some Step 1 procedures but in greater depth: - location/categorization of assets - photovoice - combined needs/ solutions surveys Subcommittees prepare summarized reports about needs and resources.	Dated entries in tables should demonstrate steady progress of all endeavors.	Without summarized reports and tables, the process could grind to a standstill. The summary tables should now contain much information and data. Lists of assets and resources are being produced. Lists may also indicate linkages between community groups.

Step	Purpose	Methods/Strategies	Checklist	Highlights/Variables
5. Using what has been learned to make decisions for possible new programs	Align the two parts of the improvement picture. Agree if alignment is the best way to proceed. Determine if more data and information should be collected.	Each subcommittee does an independent review of the other's results. Develop a matrix to see where needs and assets overlap and where they don't. Consider use of group procedures: - check in/tune in - what/so what/now what - concept mapping/ mind mapping - others	Documentation of the deliberations of the group as necessary for coming up with action plans Evidence that needs and assets and resources have been compared and juxtaposed Recording procedures that have been used to help group arrive at decisions Decisions listed	Prior work should be coming together so that the groups get more focus about decisions. Solutions or tentative solutions should be emerging. Documentation is critical as related to decisions and the process used to arrive at them.
6. Developing a strategy for improvement	Translate findings into action plans for development and positive change.	Use a variety of techniques: - success mapping - fist to five - multi-attribute utility theory - others	Concrete plan containing such things as schedules and responsibilities Success map(s) that should be clear Additions to initiating group as needed	Plan should be traceable back to what was learned in previous steps. Plan has ideas, if not strategies, for what the evaluation might be and how it should be implemented.

(Continued)

139

Table 6.1 (Continued)

Step	Purpose	Methods/Strategies	Checklist	Highlights/Variables
				Have the community members been informed, their opinion sought, and are they on board with the effort?
7. Implementing and evaluating the action plan	Conduct the planned activities. See how well they are functioning and what their outcomes are.	Use to-do lists and responsibility sheets. Conduct formative and summative evaluations of activities.	Evidence that activities are taking place as planned or changed as necessary Photo evidence if appropriate Collection of appropriate evaluative results Achievement of desired outcomes	Documenting outcomes and process are important for obtaining new funding and expanded efforts. This step establishes the basis for greater involvement and support for more initiatives. A possible new enlarged group is now engaged in effort.
8. Recycling back to first steps for expanding the improvement package	Pick up other facets of improvement that could not be first or early activities.	The group revisits previous findings and moves ahead with those it selects. Usually there will be too many pieces to attend to, so keep some in abeyance, but do not lose sight of them.	Documentation that the group went back to earlier work Rationale as to why group selected one area over another Confirmation that needs and assets/resources were being looked at jointly	A structure is in place for moving beyond previous work. Information gathering from the very beginning is essential to the hybrid framework.

and ones that are particularly notable will be highlighted. This is arbitrary based on the judgment of the author, and it may differ depending on the specific characteristics of a situation and the dynamics within it.

CONTENT OF THE CHECKLIST

Table 6.1 is converted into the checklist in Table 6.2. It's an approximation, not a one-to-one conversion, and the items for a step are suggestive, not absolute. Other ideas could easily be injected depending on local circumstances and what the needs assessors and asset/capacity builders deem appropriate. Modifications are acceptable and expected. For each item, the rating scale goes from 0 (*a very low level of the item*) to 5 (*high representation*). The ratings will be estimates on the part of reviewers and are for guidance purposes.

HOW TO USE THE CHECKLIST

In 2000, Altschuld and Witkin proposed a checklist for evaluating the three-phase model of needs assessment and guiding its process. The premise was that not all phases would be implemented in their entirety. That would be time-consuming and taxing of fiscal and human resources. The model was a structure for guiding the needs assessment process. The authors did not expect that its various features and procedures would be part of all assessments. The checklist contained sections and elements per phase that might be used to consider what should or could be done. What parts of each phase could be implemented given the finances, time, skill base, local politics, and organizational situation? Could we start at a later point in the three phases and not do all of them? Without flexibility, it would be a straitjacket. That view was deliberate and was expressed by the coauthors. There were so many things to observe that if the checklist had been an unbending standard, a lot of items would not have made sense. They would not be in projects and would be rated at the bottom of whatever scale was used.

When that occurred, an incorrect conclusion would have been that a phase or even all three phases weren't there, but the goal was not that every detail of them would be applied or adapted in a lockstep manner for all circumstances. It was an ideal that had to be tweaked in accord

(Continued on page 147)

Table 6.2 Tentative Checklist for Assessing the Degree of Fit With the Hybrid Framework

Framework Step	Items to Observe		Special Considerations
1. Scoping the context	Critical initiating group	0 1 2 3 4 5	This is most important to see if there is a driving force type of group.
	Internally controlled more	0 1 2 3 4 5	Usually there is some sense or vision of the future.
	External involvement but not control	0 1 2 3 4 5	
	Commitment to endeavor	0 1 2 3 4 5	Internal control should be there, or the internal voice should be strong.
	Sense of vision	0 1 2 3 4 5	
	Prior experience in such ventures	0 1 2 3 4 5	External involvement should be there but not control.
	Readiness for self-study	0 1 2 3 4 5	
	Awareness of two approaches	0 1 2 3 4 5	Has the group been using multiple methods?
	Collection of starting information	0 1 2 3 4 5	Are group members learning things about the organization or community that expand thinking and perspectives?
	Clear indications of need	0 1 2 3 4 5	
	Clear indications of assets/resources	0 1 2 3 4 5	
	Mixed methods utilized	0 1 2 3 4 5	
	Quantitative methods used	0 1 2 3 4 5	
	Qualitative methods used	0 1 2 3 4 5	
	Value of information collected	0 1 2 3 4 5	
	Scoping Total _____		

Framework Step	Items to Observe		Special Considerations
2. Deciding what actions should be taken	Preliminary array of info	0 1 2 3 4 5	Look for how the information gathered so far has been put together.
	Evidence of group review of array	0 1 2 3 4 5	
	Documentation of group discussion	0 1 2 3 4 5	Note that the group made its decision based on info.
	Documented decision	0 1 2 3 4 5	A hybrid approach has been favored.
	Hybrid approach chosen	0 1 2 3 4 5	
	Decision Total _____		
3. Dividing the working committee into two subcommittees	Clear charges to each subcommittee	0 1 2 3 4 5	It is important that the subcommittees work independently so bias doesn't enter the process.
	Independence of each	0 1 2 3 4 5	
	Organizing Total _____		
4. Conducting the assessment in greater depth	Evidence of more in-depth data collection	0 1 2 3 4 5	Information should be in greater depth.
	More techniques being used	0 1 2 3 4 5	Usually multiple methods will have been used.
	Mixed methods are in play	0 1 2 3 4 5	With dated tables, monitoring the hybrid process should be possible.
	Summary tables are becoming more complete/detailed	0 1 2 3 4 5	
	If tables are dated, progress is evident	0 1 2 3 4 5	

(Continued)

143

Table 6.2 (Continued)

Framework Step	Items to Observe		Special Considerations
	Expansion of Info Total _____		
5. Using what has been learned to make decisions for possible new programs	Independent review of each group's findings	0 1 2 3 4 5	This is a critical decision-making step in the hybrid framework.
	Comparison of assets/resources and needs	0 1 2 3 4 5	It is very desirable if resources and assets have been compared to identified needs and aligned.
	Group facilitation procedures have been employed	0 1 2 3 4 5	Documentation would be particularly helpful for later use with the community or organization.
	Basis for moving toward action is clear	0 1 2 3 4 5	
	Documentation of group processes, if used	0 1 2 3 4 5	
	Documentation of decisions and how they are made	0 1 2 3 4 5	
	Action-Oriented Decision Total _____		
6. Developing a strategy for improvement	Movement from data to strategy	0 1 2 3 4 5	This is a key part of the hybrid framework since an improvement strategy is about to be implemented.
	Evidence that strategy comes from earlier work	0 1 2 3 4 5	Are plan details specified, is it accepted by the community or organization, is it incremental, and so on?
	Success map(s) prepared	0 1 2 3 4 5	
	Plan specifies details (schedules, responsibilities, etc.)	0 1 2 3 4 5	
	Plan is incremental in nature	0 1 2 3 4 5	
	Plan explored via MAUT, FTA, and so on.	0 1 2 3 4 5	
	Plan thoroughly discussed	0 1 2 3 4 5	

Framework Step	Items to Observe		Special Considerations
	Plan is feasible	0 1 2 3 4 5	Has some initial thinking about evaluation shown up in what has been done so far?
	Possible expansion of involved group	0 1 2 3 4 5	Cooperation and collaboration should be noticeable in the plan.
	Larger group input obtained	0 1 2 3 4 5	
	Broader community or organization included in implementation	0 1 2 3 4 5	
	Cooperation taken into account	0 1 2 3 4 5	
	Collaboration taken into account	0 1 2 3 4 5	
	Leadership being considered	0 1 2 3 4 5	
	Preliminary evaluation thinking in strategy	0 1 2 3 4 5	
	Improvement Strategy Total ___		
7. Implementing and evaluating the action plan	Activities taking place as planned	0 1 2 3 4 5	The improvement strategy is being implemented as planned.
	Formative evaluation data collected	0 1 2 3 4 5	Corrections are being made as necessary.
	Corrective actions taken when called for	0 1 2 3 4 5	Evaluation data are being obtained and used.
	Summative evaluation data collected	0 1 2 3 4 5	Think beyond the incremental tryout.
	Management of the effort	0 1 2 3 4 5	
	Discussion of expanding beyond pilot is there	0 1 2 3 4 5	
	Implementation/Evaluation Total ___		

(Continued)

Table 6.2 (Continued)

Framework Step	Items to Observe		Special Considerations
8. Recycling back to first steps for expanding the improvement package	Critical initiating group still there	0 1 2 3 4 5	For group chemistry, some of the initiating group should be active and participating.
	Internal drive still there	0 1 2 3 4 5	It is important that the assets and needs are key to thinking about where to go from here.
	External involvement but not control	0 1 2 3 4 5	
	Commitment continues	0 1 2 3 4 5	Review prior data collection and findings before any new data are obtained (avoid the latter if possible).
	Two-approach awareness continues	0 1 2 3 4 5	
	Review of earlier needs data	0 1 2 3 4 5	
	Review of earlier assets/resources data	0 1 2 3 4 5	What decisions are made, and why?
	Consideration of new data for collection if required	0 1 2 3 4 5	It is essential to widen the level of support and involvement.
	Mixed methods utilized if deemed necessary	0 1 2 3 4 5	
	Value of information collected	0 1 2 3 4 5	
	Arriving at decision for next steps	0 1 2 3 4 5	
	Building broader involvement in next steps	0 1 2 3 4 5	
	Cooperation is expanding	0 1 2 3 4 5	
	Collaboration is expanding	0 1 2 3 4 5	
	Recycling Back Through Total _____		

with the context to ascertain needs. This is analogous to the hybrid framework in this text. A structure has been proposed but not in a rigid way. So the total checklist, like the one for needs assessment, would have many empty entries.

Also pertinent here are the history of needs assessment, the criticisms of it, the observation that the two supposedly opposite positions have been steadily blending together, and the more recent mixing of approaches in evidence from about 2000 to the present time. They represent preliminary attempts to work across what were originally dramatically different approaches and underlying philosophies.

People using asset/capacity building and needs assessment are in the process of sorting out what would be the best ways to do so, what compromises have to be made, whether they can be used without bias, how community members and organizational staff should be involved in procedures and decision making, what might be cost-efficient and effective methods to employ, and so on. Given that status, it is no surprise that many parts of the checklist will not be occurring until we have more hands-on experience with the framework. It is in more of an exploratory mode for communities and organizations as they study where they are and what could be done to improve. The checklist should be viewed as tentative. It will change as more hybrid-type implementations are done and as we learn the "dos and don'ts" from them.

FEATURES OF THE CHECKLIST

Viewing the checklist as tentative is important for examining the real-world examples in Chapters 7 and 8. There, only one particularly critical part of the checklist will be used, with the understanding that the overall checklist has utility for thinking about the entire hybrid framework process. Before going to the next chapters, here are details about some of the specific items in it.

Totals per Section

Totals were built into the checklist in anticipation of more complete usage of the hybrid framework. Then there would be evidence of many of the steps, and it would be possible to give them scale values. (The scale provided is one option, but others may be utilized.) Sums across items for a step would be an indication of the degree to which that part of the framework was implemented. That is, does the framework have fidelity? Cutoff points could be established for no implementation and very low, medium, and high levels.

It would also be possible (and it may be desirable) to give differential weights to items so those of special importance would contribute more heavily to the totals. At some point in the future, we might go as far as to say that if there were 15 items in a section, a minimum number (12, 8, etc.) would have to be present to conclude that the step was operational. This would require consideration of what are the most important items. Only extended experience with the framework and checklist would lead to developing such numbers.

Step 1. Scoping the Context

Several things stand out in this section with the first being locus of control. If the endeavor does not include or start from a local and concerned group with visions of what might be, it seems deficient in regard to empowerment and a "can do" attitude. If that is not there, the whole process could easily slip into an externally driven model, which is antithetical to its intended purpose and usage. Observation that community members or organizational staff were involved from the beginning is important, but more critical to the process is that their voice was the impetus for improvement. If that doesn't happen, we simply cannot say that it is the hybrid framework that is being seen. In reviewing what has been done, look closely at how it was accomplished and for the input and direction of internal individuals.

Other items come from the premises of the hybrid framework—multiple, mixed methods are notable in how data were obtained, and multiple sources (people, groups) show up in data collection. Another concept is that needs and assets and resources are equal partners—openly looked at and valuable information has been generated for new understandings and insights in regard to what is missing and the strengths that are there.

These things would be judged via work products and inspections of minutes or other records of the group. (Hopefully they have been kept to permit judgments to be made.) In assessing the scoping activity the involvement of the initiating group in decision making might receive additional weight in arriving at a final value for the category of items.

Step 2. Deciding What Actions Should Be Taken

This step emerges from the prior one to guide the group into concrete, more in-depth action. An indicator here would be summaries and arrays of findings that help the group in its discussions. These would come from reports and documentation. Notes kept from the discussions of the group, as well as what decisions the group members made, affect ratings. How well did they value the exploration of both needs and assets and the results so obtained?

Step 3. Dividing the Working Committee Into Two Subcommittees

In the best of all possible worlds, the group would divide into two independent parts—one for needs and the other for collecting expanded lists of assets and resources. The minutes, notes, or other sources should reflect that this has occurred and that the two groups were given the appropriate responsibilities and charges. This may, or more than likely will, result in additional methods being used or some previously located information being probed more deeply. As more is collected, earlier summaries and data portrayals will grow, and if the new entries are dated, this will corroborate that progress is being made.

Steps 4 and 5. Conducting the Assessment in Greater Depth and Using What Has Been Learned to Make Decisions for Possible New Programs

This is a major nexus in the hybrid framework. Based on what is now known and understood, the group members begin major deliberations about what the information tells them and how they might think about actual programs leading to new developments. They seriously compare the needs and the assets to see if they align and, given that, what might be done next. It sort of becomes the make-or-break point in the overall framework. The process must move from fact finding to action planning. What did the group actually do; what did members see in the results; what solutions, even if in preliminary form, were talked about; what options were discussed; and are they pertinent to the key issues and opportunities in front of the community or organization?

What has arisen from the discourse? Are the group members utilizing the amalgam of data and information that has been generated? Do they see what the major needs are and what resources can be tapped into and brought to bear for improvement? Do they see ways to utilize resources in unanticipated ways? Are there unique combinations of them that they may employ to produce unforeseen yet positive outcomes? How well do the needs and assets/resources coincide, and should that be the direction to go? Again, notes, minutes, and documents would be the basis for ratings and judgments.

Step 6. Developing a Strategy for Improvement

In conjunction with the above activity, the action plan is critical, for it sets the tone for the future. A lot of the entries in this section of the checklist relate to the features of the plan. Is it in accord with what was found before, and how well is it thought through? Does it seem to be the best alternative, especially if MAUT and causal analysis were employed? Are concrete dimensions of the plan specified, such as who does what and when it will be done? What about the leadership for the new venture—is it clear, and what individual or group will be assuming these duties? Does the plan have provisions for evaluation and utilization of data? Cooperation and, in particular, collaboration will be vital for implementation. Does this come out in the plan specifications? Has consideration been given to an incremental start and then ratcheting up to more full-scale operation at a subsequent date?

Information for ratings would come from such things as the success map(s), responsibility sheets, and other planning devices. If there was any evaluation of the process at this time, the reflections of group members would prove excellent for assessing how considerations of solutions and new strategies had gone. Moreover, keep in mind that continuously updated and expanded summary tables are a key ingredient in the hybrid framework. They too constitute evidence about how the planning has proceeded.

Step 7. Implementing and Evaluating the Action Plan

Indeed, the improvement strategy is only as good as its implementation and what the evaluation shows has taken place. If the evaluation was designed appropriately and data were available, it would demonstrate how activities were carried out, their effectiveness, and if results were used. The outcomes also play a critical role in seeking support for further actions and involvement. What happened in actual use, what did the group learn, was change based on findings, and are there any outstanding events that would be helpful in more promotion of this activity or for other new ones not previously done?

Additionally, it may be reasonable and necessary to be thinking as the initial effort is under way of how to obtain more resources and ways of including others in the hybrid effort. Who might such people, groups, or organizations be? What might be the rationale for their participation? What could they bring to the table to enhance services and the numbers of those benefiting? Are there resources in terms of monetary funds, inter-agency collaboration, and other facets of what they do that would meaningfully contribute to the endeavor?

Step 8. Recycling Back to First Steps for Expanding the Improvement Package

Surprisingly, what at quick glance appears to be a perfunctory activity might be more crucial in the scheme of things. A way to approach new endeavors was given earlier—it was to start incrementally and then to build from a more humble beginning. The idea was that success reinforces success and morale will be more positive coming from this stance. There are other ways to think about change, but the incremental approach is recommended. It allows us to make mistakes on a small scale and to handle or avoid them when the level is increased. Based on that path for doing things, the group could consider going to a much fuller implementation of what was just done with modifications to avert snags and problems. This would be one facet of recycling back to the beginning.

In that vein, it would mean taking a fresh look at our summary Table 3.3 and other tables as relevant to what we are currently undertaking. Are there other features of the new program or project to which we should be attending? Are there parts to it that we did not have the funding or resources to put in place that could now be structured in fairly easily? What would the enhanced entity look like? Would it serve a larger audience in a positive manner than what has been offered before? These are logical questions, and recycling could be predicated in this way. It would be valuable, and it takes advantage of what we know a lot about.

Additionally, returning to the original work and the summaries might lead the group to now put needs and assets not focused on under a new microscope. They were important before but were not at the top of the list. Might they become more salient, if everyone agreed to deal with them in a creative light?

There is yet another way to approach the final step, although it should only be done after deliberation. The group may decide that it wants to explore other aspects of the community and/or organization. There were things group members missed or key areas that simply were not examined, and over time they became more important. What this means is that the hybrid framework should be looked at as though the group was starting over from the top. There is nothing wrong with this, but do it with open eyes. It is an expensive way to go; despite that, we know from our past work how to get and interpret data and have instruments and procedures that could be adopted. Only follow this course when the energies and morale of the group are taken into account.

Whichever of the possibilities is chosen, this activity is the last step of the framework and is similar to those conducted before. By now, documenting of activities and dating of tables and other products should be ingrained. They should be reviewed for guidance about recycling.

ONE LAST THOUGHT

With the checklist as the measuring stick, what are some examples that demonstrate hybrid work? What fields do they come from, and how well do they balance needs with assets and resources without compromising the two positions? What might they have done differently? This is the substance of Chapters 7 and 8.

The checklist is a useful tool, but there is one other source of information that offers much information and perspective about the hybrid process—it is the initiating and involved group itself. Many of its members have been a part of everything from the beginning. They have views and have seen procedures that worked and others that did not. Their opinions and views are too valuable to be overlooked.

There are several ways that they could become incorporated into the assessment. One would be via questionnaires. A version might be open-ended with five to eight questions that require written responses for valuable, personal input. Since the size of the group might be 10, pursuing the members' opinions should not be a great burden, or use a survey that is primarily scaled. It might follow a needs assessment structure of asking about the importance of and the extent to which items have been achieved. Discrepancies would be looked at and explored for insights.

Finally, a focus group interview could be conducted, led by an external person to lessen the possibility of bias. The small group is now comfortable in voicing its thoughts, and this might be an opportunity for all participants to express their opinions in way that they did not have before. The session with permission could be taped as a way to recruit others into future endeavors.

HIGHLIGHTS OF CHAPTER 6

1. There are varying degrees of implementing hybrid ideas. A procedure is needed for judging what is in the literature or reports.

2. The hybrid framework was examined in terms of variables important for doing it and for making value judgments about them. Questions about each step were raised, and highlights of activities were suggested.

3. Based on Point 2, an extensive checklist was developed. Each item per step was to be rated on a scale from no evidence of it to a very high level of occurrence. Items could be summed to indicate the extent to which the overall step was there.

4. Mention was made that at present there is no exemplar that contains all parts of the framework. One would only be able to rate selected features of what is there per step. Judgments are more preliminary.

5. Some items may be more important than others, and hence their ratings could carry more weight.

6. Items were discussed in an overview manner for more insight into how the checklist could be applied.

7. The initiating group itself was mentioned as a valuable evaluation asset. It could be surveyed via open-ended or scaled questions, or there could be an FGI of members.

DISCUSSION QUESTIONS

1. Does the evaluation checklist make sense, should other concerns have been posed, and so forth? Think about this and add to the discussion.

2. A quantitative checklist was provided, but a qualitative approach using a descriptive narrative could be informative. How could that be done, and what should guidelines for it be? Should there have been qualitative sections built into the checklist, and what should they require of the reviewer? Should there be reflective prompts for looking at completed efforts?

3. Fidelity of implementation is a consideration in evaluating if a hybrid stance was prominent as opposed to more of a needs assessment or an asset/capacity-building endeavor. Examine the checklist. At a minimum, what do you think should be there, and what are the reasons for your choices?

4. The draft checklist has many items in it, is lengthy, and perhaps is unwieldy. What would you do to shorten it, and in doing so what would you be willing to sacrifice?

5. On the other hand, the checklist may be missing key elements for the hybrid framework. What would you add to it, and what is your rationale for doing so?

7

Cases Exhibiting Hybrid Framework Characteristics

Examples From Public Health

W hy public health? Keeping a population healthy requires a considerable amount of involvement on the part of communities and providers of services. Consider what happened in the United States in getting its citizens to voluntarily be inoculated against polio.

When the author was in his 20s, Sabin and Salk developed vaccines to prevent polio. It is germane to note that almost everyone in my age range went to school with classmates who had minor to major crippling from the disease. Stopping it was a huge breakthrough. In earlier generations, its effects were devastating. B. R. Witkin, my first coauthor on needs assessment, passed away of complications from the disease that recycled years after childhood.

I did not receive my vaccination from a doctor or a minute clinic (now in retail pharmacies and other outlets), as the latter was a long time away. Rather, cities and metropolitan areas mounted vast public awareness campaigns and recruited different locations within them to offer shots or oral delivery of the vaccine. There were public service ads in the media that encouraged individuals to come in for treatment. Indeed, I went to a small Catholic church near where I lived for the vaccination.

Public health would be a fertile context for using the framework, and many examples should come from that field. The first step to locate cases was to conduct literature searches starting with broad terms, then narrowing them more to the concept of joint needs assessment and asset/capacity building. The strategy was modified as materials were found and reviewed. Community-based participatory research approaches, as well as community needs assessments, were explored when that phraseology came up. The time frame was mostly from the late 1990s until the present. That was based on the fact that the Kretzmann and McKnight book appeared in 1993, and hybrid usages would need a period to appear.

Articles and reports were examined in regard to characteristics fitting the criteria of hybrid thinking. How would one know if enough of needs assessment and asset/capacity building in a complementary fashion was truly there? The question is important because, as noted in Chapter 6, it was unlikely that much in the way of comprehensive or full implementation would be taking place.

With that proviso, here are some of the major considerations that governed selection:

- Assets and resources were investigated in the article or report.
- Needs were being determined, examined, or taken into account.
- The two approaches were there even when one may have predominated.
- Mixed methods were being used.
- Needs were identified usually but not entirely via existing quantitative data.
- The voice of the community or organization was in evidence, especially in the way that data were collected (often qualitative in nature) and in data interpretation and decision making.
- The needs and assets were played off of each other to a degree as a possible path for improvement.
- It was acknowledged, if only tacitly, that there were two ways to approach development or improvement, and there was a sense of the contrasting philosophies.

Judgment was exercised as to whether a situation satisfied enough of these criteria to warrant inclusion. Another factor was that community members or key personnel from an organization would be the driving force behind the endeavor. It was not to be controlled or driven by external individuals or consultants. That involvement was OK, but they were not to be the ones who determined directions in the focus of a study and the vision of where things might be going. This very important factor was sometimes not so apparent. The German Village example (Exhibit 3.1 in Chapter 3) is closer to the ideal on this dimension. As time passes and doing simultaneous needs assessments and asset/capacity-building efforts becomes more common, we may see more clarity on this point. Lastly, titles of articles or reports are not as informative as desired. What was termed *needs assessment* may actually be nearer to the hybrid. The picture was not always fully clear.

OVERVIEW OF PUBLIC HEALTH CASES

In Table 7.1 on page 158, three exemplars from public health are overviewed. It includes their authors, the year in which the study was conducted, and some of the aspects of hybrid work being demonstrated with a rating of their strength. For the latter, + would be that it was there minimally and +++ that it was an extremely strong part of what was done. It would be desirable to see many plusses. Comments are in the last column.

CASE 1. RAPID NEEDS APPRAISAL IN THE MODERN NATIONAL HEALTH SERVICE: POTENTIAL AND DILEMMAS—THE UK STUDY

With a needs assessment title, is this study appropriate? Ordinarily not, but it was more of a hybrid.

Structure of the Project

It was done in four localities in the West Cumbria area of the United Kingdom and had numerous activities that firmly embedded it in the book context. The purposes were to seek involvement across sectors in communities, have direct participation of community members in the investigation, use many different methods iteratively, and build upon what was learned to improve. The work was carried out by a team of external university researchers to see if services available through health service

Table 7.1 Overview of Cases From Public Health in Regard to the Hybrid Framework

Author(s) & Year	A/CB	NA	Mixed Methods	A/CB & NA	Joint Philosophy	Comments
Case 1. Balogh, Whitelaw, and Thompson (2008)	++	++	++	++	+++	An outstanding study done in the UK that parallels much of the thinking in this text
Case 2. Williams, Bray, Shapiro-Mendoza, Reisz, and Peranteau (2009)	++	+++	+++	++	++	Explanation of three models for doing this work, comparative application, and issues encountered
Case 3. Pepall, Earnest, and James (2006)	++	+	++	++	++	Emphasis on rapid participatory appraisal with needs assessment part of the process

organizations were based on identified needs in the local environment. This says needs assessment, not asset/capacity building, so why is it here?

Reading further, all of a sudden the authors veer into a perspective that a capacity-building approach was what they wanted to do—not to emphasize deficit or needs thinking. That revelation moves the study into the hybrid mode. And beyond that, needs were in the broader social and community sense—in other words they had a more encompassing understanding or perspective of needs. Exhibit 7.1 contains a description of what they did.

Exhibit 7.1 Activities Incorporated Into the Rapid Needs Appraisal (and Asset/Capacity Building)

Formation of a working group of health service providers

    Providers were in charge of meetings.

    Emphasis was on the providers being active in the process.

    One of the provider roles was in decision making and direction setting.

    Independent studies were to be done in four communities.

    The working group was to be involved continuously, not just one time.

Due to difficulties in convening, the group

    used a Delphi-type survey;

    worded questions in asset and action terms;

    avoided needs or deficit type of statements;

    provided Delphi feedback to the group; and

    conducted some interviews.

Finding out what was already known (needs)

    Public health studies

    Public health information

    Assembling local heath profiles

    Reports of various organizations

    Unemployment data

    Scanning of newspaper articles

    Demographics

    Epidemiology data

Collecting local data

    Neighborhood forum meetings

    Police/community liaison meeting

    School reports

(Continued)

(Continued)

From data collected, the research team created identities for the communities:

Tangible dimensions

Demographics

Levels of service

And so on

Symbolic dimensions

Networks

Social capacity

And so on

A list of specific assets and capacities for each of the communities was created mostly from information collected above (asset/capacity building).

Needs-type and asset/capacity data and information were provided to each community.

Some Delphi survey work in one of the communities was also used.

Mixed patterns of data collection occurred per locality.

Many of the principles and strategies in the hybrid framework were employed in this case, and it received high marks in Table 7.1 for the presence of asset/capacity building (A/CB) and needs assessment (NA), for the use of mixed methods, for seeing the A/CB and NA approaches as complementary, and most importantly for the joint philosophy category. In the words of the authors, it clearly reflects the hybrid wavelength.

Our own view was that a capacity building model rather than a deficit model of need would most closely reflect the aims of the Health Action Zone and we also recommend a broad definition of need encompassing social and community needs. (Balogh, Whitelaw, & Thompson, 2008, p. 234)

For What Aspects of the Checklist Was There Evidence?

Only Section 1 of the checklist will be used to assess what was done. This is based on the fact that in a 12-page journal article extensive summarization is required, and therefore not all details will be provided. In rating items in the checklist, reading between the lines and interpretation admittedly were there.

Other considerations from the study come into play. The authors often cite time pressures and unrealistic expectations of the working group, the decision makers. In hybrid activities, along with action plans for improvement and moving forward, it simply may not be meaningful to have goals for the short term or to assume that things will change in that time span. Throw in the complication that this is being carried out in four distinct communities, and complexity escalates like trying to turn around a huge oceangoing ship on a dime. It just doesn't happen. If the ocean has many high whitecaps, turning becomes even harder.

Table 7.2 on page 162 contains the first section of the checklist with a few items deleted, but most have been retained as they fit a case like this. Ratings are estimates about the presence of an item. The other sections of the checklist are not included due to article length, and not all items within them would occur in any local study. Even with full documentation, only a portion of them would likely be there, but still some comments (see discussion of the case) are possible. The study authors provided invaluable insights to explain the subtle features of working with communities and trying to involve all parties as much as they could.

Discussion of the Case

First, Balogh et al. (2008) pointed out that the policy makers expected too much to be done too fast. There is a human imperative to act, want to get going, and not waste time in identifying needs and assets and considering options for putting them to good use. Implementing the hybrid framework is like the adage in carpentry—measure twice and cut once. Be careful before you do something. The problem these policy makers encountered is one that needs assessors also face, the rush to judgment. In doing needs assessments, asset/capacity-building efforts, or combinations of them, it may be necessary to inform decision-making parties about the nature of the work. Given the amount of data collected, interpreted, and

Table 7.2 Application of the First Part of the Evaluative Checklist to Assess the Degree of Fit for Case 1 With the Hybrid Framework (ratings in **bold**)

Framework Step	Items to Observe		Special Considerations
Scoping the context	Critical initiating group	0 1 2 **3** 4 5	There should be some sense or vision of the future.
	Internally controlled more	0 1 2 **3** 4 5	
	External involvement but not control	0 1 2 **3** 4 5	Internal control or internal voice should be strong.
	Commitment to endeavor	0 1 2 **3** 4 5	
	Sense of vision	0 1 2 **3** 4 5	External involvement but not control should be in evidence.
	Prior experience in such ventures	0 1 2 3 **4** 5	
	Readiness for self-study	0 1 2 3 **4** 5	
	Awareness of two approaches	0 1 2 **3** 4 5	Multiple methods are apparent.
	Collection of starting information	0 1 2 3 **4** 5	Learning things about the organization or community expanded thinking and perspectives.
	Clear indications of need	0 1 2 3 **4** 5	
	Clear indications of assets/resources	0 1 2 3 4 **5**	
	Mixed methods utilized	0 1 2 3 4 **5**	
	Quantitative methods used	0 1 2 3 4 **5**	
	Qualitative methods used	0 1 2 3 4 **5**	
	Value to information collected	0 1 2 3 4 **5**	
	Scoping Total 63		63 out of 75 possible points awarded, with 10 of the 15 items being at 4 or higher

framed into a meaningful whole for informing choices, the scope is well beyond a short-term, quick fix—an assessment of this type is not a panacea.

Second, it was observed that the capacity for new initiatives was variable depending on the circumstances and experiences of each community.

Some had done more in the past and were better able to move to action. It was as though there were existing infrastructures and a community learning mien that were utilitarian and important. In fact, in one of the four locations a prior investigation had been good enough that the project team questioned whether the community would benefit from looking at needs or assets at all.

Third, the investigators suggested that engaging local providers in a fully functioning cohesive working group was difficult given the demands of their ongoing duties and responsibilities. That was underscored by the fact that they as outsiders were asked to do the study as opposed to greater involvement of the organizations that were participating. Despite the best intentions of the researchers to enhance capacity by leaving behind a base of community expertise, it just did not happen. The issue of locus of control and how to get and maintain a feeling of community and organizational investiture is a complex undertaking.

Fourth, two different types of needs emerged as the project progressed. There was a number-based, harder, quantitative one that was more absolute in appearance. It was the traditional deficit need. There was another coming from qualitative data and input that related more to solutions or thinking of ways to tie needs and assets together. This led to an interesting table in which the authors compared deficit needs to the other needs coming from the asset perspective. It was a unique way to present findings and one that could engender a spirited conversation about options to be pursued. As the authors stressed, it could even result in more innovative responses to the situation.

Fifth, the study probed a series of subtle issues. What might it take to get better commitment of the agencies that were part of this project? This becomes more complex when a range of groups and individuals are included in an investigation. It was noted that it takes a lot more time to sensitively dig into needs and assets and eventually arrive at a deep-seated understanding of capacity. Lastly, the authors stressed that each local community, while similar to others, has its own egocentric constitution.

Sixth, a conclusion that might be drawn from Table 7.2 is that the other sections of the checklist have no relevance and are more of an academic license. That view contains some truth but not entirely. In the article, there were brief mentions of meetings or taking data and findings to broader groups for interpretation and input. Also, from the start, the rapid needs appraisal was highly iterative, and although not all dimensions of this were described, they were alluded to as were repeated interactions and meetings with various parties.

The hybrid framework demands that kind of activity. The suspicion is that to a degree it was being implemented beyond the first section of the checklist, and if the members of the group conducting the study were not limited by journal requirements, other sections and items would have been observed as operational. Certainly, scoping was done in depth, and without it the framework does not have the legs it needs. This particular case was exceptionally strong in this regard.

CASE 2. MODELING THE PRINCIPLES OF COMMUNITY-BASED PARTICIPATORY RESEARCH IN A COMMUNITY HEALTH ASSESSMENT CONDUCTED BY A HEALTH FOUNDATION

Three models of community-based participatory research (CBPR) were studied in the context of community health mobilization. The emphasis was not stated as needs or asset/resource assessments, but features of both were apparent. Three related approaches (models) were examined as to which was best. In the write-up, the authors cover such events as local analysis of quantitative and qualitative data, the use of mixed methods, asset mapping, participatory approaches, and epidemiology—all aligned with the hybrid framework.

Structure of the Project

This endeavor was part of the Healthy Neighborhood Initiatives of the Episcopal Diocese of Texas. It was the culmination of associated studies implemented and modified over a 10-plus-year period. The three models have overlapping aspects with varying amounts of intensity. While one model stood out, the authors provide a clear and insightful discussion of issues in all three and the difficulties encountered in this kind of work. Their perceptions generalize to many different settings and environments.

Exhibit 7.2 is a summary of the key dimensions of the models and what it takes to put them into play. A significant difference between Models A and B in contrast to C is that when the latter was done, the initiator was the community collaborative as opposed to an external party for the first two. Table 7.3 on page 167 is an analysis of the case for the scoping section of the checklist.

Exhibit 7.2 Models and Activities Incorporated Into the Community-Based Participatory Research Case in Community Health

Premises

 Collaborative approach involving multiple partners

 All applications beginning with a topic of importance to the community (perhaps a need)

 Learning and empowering environment

 Inclusion of all partners

 Knowledge and information distributed to all of them

 Builds off of work done for urban research centers funded by the Centers for Disease Control and Prevention

 Partly comes from participatory rural appraisal

 Role reversal with the community becoming the teachers and the researchers, the learners

Model A—Pertinent Aspects

Get a numerical picture of local community-based statistics and an assortment of data-based sources and reports.

 Quantitative profiles developed

 Qualitative data from key informants and focus groups

 May include questions about strengths as well as needs

 Community asset mapping

Model B—Pertinent Aspects

Get more depth of understanding.

 Phase 1

 Conduct a deeper qualitative study using participatory rural appraisal techniques

 Train 10 community members

They then participated in all facets of the effort including data collection, discussions, and analysis.

 Led nine small community group discussions

 Examined health issues

(Continued)

(Continued)

  In groups, suggested root causes and consequences of health issues

  Developed visual trees of the above

  Presented results to the community in a community event

Phase 2

  Rapid epidemiological survey à la World Health Organization

  Rapid cluster sampling

  Determination of prevalence of health issues and verification of what was found in Phase 1

  Assisting local agencies to learn the above technique

Community members were trained to conduct relevant interviews and then employed as interviewers (218 interviews were done).

They developed a community health collaborative.

Model C—Pertinent Aspects

  Model B was seen as better than Model A.

  Costs were high, so that was a concern.

  Some of the aspects of Models A and B were incorporated.

  Quantitative data was used.

  Community asset mapping was done.

  Community-trained interviewers were used, but far less so.

  The community event was retained from one of the models.

  New activities were included.

  Reliance was on an existing community coalition.

  Community members were added to the collaborative cited under Model B.

Discussion of the Case

It is no surprise to anyone looking at this case that the costs were high, and the *first* issue the authors raise is what is required to do similar studies and that researchers should be alert to numerous unexpected

Table 7.3 Application of the First Part of the Evaluative Checklist to Assess the Degree of Fit of Case 2 With the Hybrid Framework (ratings in **bold**)

Framework Step	Items to Observe		Special Considerations
Scoping the context	Critical initiating group	0 1 2 3 **4** 5	Internal control occurred especially and more dramatically in Model C.
	Internally controlled more	0 1 2 **3** 4 5	
	External involvement but not control	0 1 2 **3** 4 5	
	Commitment to endeavor	0 1 2 **3** 4 5	Internal voice was there but especially in Model C, so the ratings could go to 5 for it.
	Sense of vision	0 1 2 **3** 4 5	
	Prior experience in such ventures	0 1 2 **3** 4 5	
	Readiness for self-study	0 1 2 3 **4** 5	External involvement, but not control, was somewhat dependent on the model.
	Awareness of two approaches	0 1 2 **3** 4 5	
	Collection of starting information	0 1 2 3 **4** 5	Multiple methods were in evidence.
	Clear indications of need	0 1 2 3 **4** 5	
	Clear indications of assets/resources	0 1 2 3 **4** 5	Learning things about the organization or community expanded thinking and perspective.
	Mixed methods utilized	0 1 2 3 **4** 5	
	Quantitative methods used	0 1 2 3 **4** 5	
	Qualitative methods used	0 1 2 3 **4** 5	
	Value to information collected	0 1 2 3 **4** 5	
	Scoping Total 63		63 out of 75 possible points awarded, with 10 of the 15 items being at 4 or higher
			Total points would vary depending on which of the three models was employed.

expenditures that arise. This is like the earlier example in the text about the "Westington" school project. Unless an effort is small, it goes without saying that more resources will be needed even when volunteers are included and community members are trained to stand in for expensive formal interviewers. The authors point to little nuances that eat at finances such as the costs for community members and maintaining communication with all players. They mention that the interviewers were invaluable and helpful but were not funded adequately.

Second, another concern was time, a precious commodity. The authors did not note this, but projects always take more than anticipated. This repeats what was cited for Case 1. Building trust across many partners and within communities is intensive not only to establish a program but also in the considerable energy devoted to keeping it alive and viable.

Third, communications were a problem since it was necessary to have Spanish speakers and translators. This may not pertain to other cases, but some aspects of communication they observed were problems that cut across settings. One was in getting on crowded schedules of administrators. Another was having clear channels for parents and communicating with different constituencies. By analogy, the author was part of a national study where different wording (vernacular, frame of reference) on surveys for principals and teachers had to be used to ensure that ideas and concepts were clear to all individuals and groups (Altschuld & White, 2010; Altschuld & Witkin, 2000). Communications necessitate diligence.

Fourth, the three models are very much along the lines of the hybrid framework. Indeed, Williams, Bray, Shapiro-Mendoza, Reisz, and Peranteau (2009) affirm the value of one of its tenets—the inclusion of a community or an organization firmly throughout the entire process. This was a serious message in the three models, particularly Model C.

Fifth, a rich set of methods was utilized, and the authors suggest that by combining tools, the community-based participatory research was greatly enhanced. Further, a neat feature related to community meetings (community celebration events). Visuals were employed to help facilitate sessions. Causal trees and consequences were displayed, as were photo collages. This, in conjunction with sizable community-generated information, proved to be wonderful input into local community deliberation and reflection.

Sixth, an outgrowth of Point 5 is that there was improved interpretation of quantitative data. This is the result of having many sources of data coming from multiple methods and having a lot of eyes (including community ones) reviewing and assigning meaning.

Seventh, communication has a very positive side. It led to better exchanges and understandings across agencies, community health providers, and community members. The celebratory events were an excellent way for people to get to know each other. Interestingly, photovoice is now being added to the toolbox of CBPR as a method that would fit well with community involvement, especially for interpreting findings and getting discussions going.

Eighth, noticeable in this case and others is the flexibility that is required. The pieces and parts in each of the three models, the collection and analysis of data, using what has been learned, and working with varied constituencies all point to the fact that everyone involved has to be adaptable and patient and accept progress as well as setbacks. Go back to the first point about when unanticipated costs and expenditures arose and had to be resolved. Whether it is a small group or an individual leading the effort, be ready for snags and difficulties.

Flexibility has advantages and disadvantages for the staff from providers of services that are involved. It enhances interactions with stakeholders, but at the same time it could underscore an imbalance of power favoring providers and may lead to the collection of distorted or biased data. The devil is in the details as to how CBPR is implemented and varies from context to context.

This brings to the fore the perplexing issue of whether CBPR is predicated on an asset/resource stance, a needs assessment one, or the hybrid framework. It cuts across them well except for one factor. Where is the impetus for it coming from—what is the major motivation? Is it under the aegis of the community or more the agencies and providers? In a purist sense and given the possible imbalance of power, the study may conflict with the idea that the community is in control of setting its own destiny via project decisions. If that is even partially accurate and if it generalizes to CBPR types of studies, it goes back to the dependency concern identified in arguments for the asset/resource side of the equation.

The world is not pure, pristine, or antiseptic, but septic, and just doesn't operate in an ideal fashion. The voice of the consumer (the community) was there, did affect what was done, and was valued, but is it as paramount as asset/capacity builders would want? Maybe yes, maybe no. Every circumstance has its own vagaries that affect implementation and that lead to a high or low community locus of direction. It is an ultimate goal that may be difficult to fully achieve.

Ninth, going beyond Table 7.3, what about the rest of the sections in the checklist? Other information supplied in the summarized article includes that over $400,000 of funding was gained for projects in the local area based on project efforts. Although not in full detail, the overview of the celebratory outreach event was helpful. Moreover, attention was directed to gaining and keeping meaningful (not superficial) community involvement. Comprehensive documentation of all events would have led to positive findings for other parts of hybrid framework usage.

CASE 3. UNDERSTANDING COMMUNITY PERCEPTION OF HEALTH AND SOCIAL NEEDS IN A RURAL BALINESE VILLAGE: RESULTS OF A RAPID PARTICIPATORY APPRAISAL

At initial glance, this case too may appear not to be suited for the book. However, its focus is on assets/resources and needs assessment with heavy community involvement.

Structure of the Project

The abstract for the project described it as implementing rapid participatory appraisal and community-based action research for asset-based community development (Pepall, Earnest, & James, 2006). It was done for a community radio station in Bali with a low literacy population.

Rapid participatory appraisal was viewed as a good way to collect community input and perspectives without excessive expenditures. It would not take much time and would provide valuable information. It was an iterative type of methodology, thus fitting with the hybrid framework. It would go through what is called an asset-focused rapid participatory appraisal (RPA) cycle, a process of collecting information, followed by analysis and planning/acting on what has been learned, and then going back through the cycle.

A model (the Health Information Pyramid) was the basis for generating interview questions. Data were obtained from key informant interviews, observations in the field, and review of existing documents. While the focus was on assets, the authors acknowledged needs and problems but stressed that this could not be the sole basis for moving forward. They felt that their approach enabled them to combine both problems and solutions. A summary of the project is given in Exhibit 7.3 and the checklist evaluation in Table 7.4 on page 171.

Exhibit 7.3 Activities Incorporated Into Case 3

Phase 1

    Communicating with stakeholders

    Planning, collecting, and analyzing information about assets

    Planning, collecting, and analyzing information about needs

    Data primarily from key informants

Phase 2

    Further discussions with community participants

    Verification of what has been collected and learned about assets

    Verification of what has been collected and learned about needs

    Sharing in the discussions about issues and possible improvement strategies

    Generally from key stakeholders

Other methodological features

    Field observations

    Informal individual and group discussions

    Collation of existing secondary data (needs information)

    Semistructured questionnaires that guided the interviews

    Questions reviewed for cultural sensitivity

    Questions revised as appropriate as the process was ongoing

Table 7.4 Application of the First Part of the Evaluative Checklist to Assess the Degree of Fit of Case 3 With the Hybrid Framework (ratings in **bold**)

Framework Step	Items to Observe		Special Considerations
Scoping the context	Critical initiating group	0 1 2 **3** 4 5	The study was a mixed bag on control and possibly more externally directed, but the voice of the community was solidly there.
	Internally controlled more	0 1 2 **3** 4 5	
	External involvement but not control	0 1 2 **3** 4 5	

(Continued)

(Continued)

Framework Step	Items to Observe		Special Considerations
	Commitment to endeavor	0 1 2 **3** 4 5	Awareness of the two approaches was evident.
	Sense of vision	0 1 2 **3** 4 5	
	Prior experience in such ventures	0 1 2 **3** 4 5	Multiple methods were used.
	Readiness for self-study	0 1 2 **3** 4 5	
	Awareness of two approaches	0 1 2 3 **4** 5	Much learning about the community expanded thinking and perspectives.
	Collection of starting information	0 1 2 **3** 4 5	
	Clear indications of need	0 1 2 **3** 4 5	
	Clear indications of assets/resources	0 1 2 **3** 4 5	
	Mixed methods utilized	0 1 2 **3** 4 5	
	Quantitative methods used	0 1 2 **3** 4 5	
	Qualitative methods used	0 1 2 3 4 **5**	
	Value to information collected	0 1 2 **3** 4 5	
	Scoping Total 60		60 out of 75 possible points awarded, with 8 of the 15 items being at 4 or higher

Discussion of the Case

First, the team that did this study commented on the need for a group representing multiple sectors to carry out the endeavor. Several individuals were included who knew the local customs and were fluent in Bahasa Indonesia (Indonesian language). They were instrumental in obtaining local leadership approval. In cultural efforts like this, that was absolutely essential. The researchers were from Australia, so sensitivity was imperative. (See Hung, Altschuld, & Lee, 2008, for a research study in Taiwan where cultural and language issues arose from a team consisting of two Taiwanese and an American with different perspectives that had to be attended to and resolved.)

A *second* feature was that despite the fact that the 57 key informants were not randomly sampled, the authors felt that they did obtain the views of the community without large expenditures. Triangulation of sources added to the validity of findings. In other words, a degree of rigor was realized. This would be a strong point of such endeavors where methods are implemented as best they can be in field settings. Procedures are not perfect, but when multiple methods complement each other, a corroborative strength emerges.

Third, the value of formal and informal discussions with individuals and groups was underscored in terms of what it produced for the locality. The investigators exercised care in sampling to ensure that poorer community members were included and their voice was heard. To enhance participation, small token gifts were provided.

Fourth, on the needs assessment side, the investigators found sources of census information from the local government. Regional health authorities provided more in the form of health service utilization statistics.

Fifth, the researchers conducted field observations of the community. This, in conjunction with the interviews and discussions, led to an asset map of the community.

Sixth, detailed notes for each day of the project were examined for recurring or interrelated themes. This took place across all sources. Where discrepancies were encountered as they normally would be, new or other data were sought for clarification.

Seventh, the study generated a lot of insightful results. They dealt with needs to work on the overall economic situation of the community, areas in which health service promotion and provision should be improved, concerns about child labor (the community was poor), causes of health problems, considerations for how the radio station could do a better job of benefiting its community, and local assets.

Three main strategies for changing and enhancing the community came from what was learned. Two of the strategies were not in the health emphasis of the project, and although not intended it was meaningful input for another area, should be duly noted, and should if important enough be pursued.

Eighth, there is great value in community involvement as it builds the base for action. Community members began to develop ownership in what came from the study and what could change because of it. Since a radio station was a key element, the idea arose that it might feature more local voices in broadcasts—something that could be implemented with little cost and with the potential of a big payoff, especially as it showed that the voice of the people was really being taken into account.

Ninth, how well did this effort match the hybrid framework? Like the two other cases, it fits the general parameters of the framework. Needs assessment and asset/capacity building were prominent, and one cannot overstate the concern for community participation and sensitivity to it. Reading into the article, mention comes up about multiple meetings with the community and how what was gathered through them and the other procedures contributed to in-depth perspectives of health issues and others affecting community life. If the full checklist had been applied, there would be ratings for other facets of the hybrid. The study led to concrete suggestions for new/enhanced activities for the community. It definitely is consistent with the tenets of hybrid thinking.

ACROSS THE THREE CASES

An analysis across the three studies in terms of features in the framework would be useful. Before offering it, note that there were several other publications considered for inclusion. One was a needs assessment but with a twist conducted by Iutcovich in 1993. The concept was to do the assessment with the heavy involvement of the community so that it would be empowered to change and be an integral part of improvement. It had components of the hybrid including a needs assessment committee (NAC) that went beyond an advisory role. The NAC did much work vital to the assessment such as determining what questions should be asked and designing a draft of the survey. This effort was not included due to its date and that it might be loading more on needs assessment. It also was not very specific on the concept of identifying assets and resources.

The second possibility was called common needs assessment, or CNA (Garfield, Blake, Chatainger, & Walton-Ellery, 2011) as prescribed for humanitarian action. It is a needs assessment that is carried out across multiple sectors and stakeholders to collect and analyze information about discrepancies and capabilities and subsequently inform decisions about needs (vulnerabilities) in communities. What results would inform decisions and early recovery responses? As the authors point out, "working together to design the assessment can foster collaboration, making possible a shared understanding of priorities and improving coordination across agencies" (Garfield et al., 2011, p. 3). Other reasons for CNA are efficiency, timeliness, shared learning, coordination across agencies that are working together, and efficiency. This process overlaps with needs assessment/asset capacity building, and it has numerous useful ideas and procedures. It is a good reference but was not included in this text because its focus leans more toward needs than the full balance of criteria employed for selection.

Another thing to mention is that many techniques have elements in them that relate well to the hybrid framework. Consider the description of community-based participatory research, rapid participatory appraisal, and what is in the synthesized needs assessment and asset/capacity-building framework in Chapter 2. This is positive, and implementers should be aware of such overlaps as they conduct investigations to promote positive change and growth.

All three of the cases in the chapter required a lot of work to collect volumes of data, write and interpret findings, establish and maintain com-

Table 7.5 Summary of Some Main Features of the Hybrid Framework in the Three Cases

Feature	Extent of Occurrence	Comments
Understanding of premises of needs assessment and assets and resources	Extensive, and all three cases directly expressed such understandings.	This finding shows evolution of thinking.
Implementing needs assessment and asset/capacity-building processes and procedures	A consistent feature of the three cases, and implementation was done in depth.	This is a central premise of the hybrid framework, and it can be done well.
Iterations of activities and procedures (actual cyclical activities or inferred ones)	To the extent possible, this was evident in every instance.	Sometimes it will be necessary for clarification or expansion of contradictory results. It generally increases time and costs.
Seeking the voice and input of the community for data and even interpretation	There is no question that this happened in all three investigations.	This wasn't perfunctory but was planned and implemented. Community input was a big factor.

(Continued)

Table 7.5 (Continued)

Feature	Extent of Occurrence	Comments
Value of the voice of the people and community	In all of the studies, the authors asserted the importance of this feature and adherence to it.	It makes a study more complex and will take more time, but everyone agrees on its salience.
Literature actively consulted for guidance	There are numerous citations in all three cases and use of what was found in the studies that were reviewed.	It could be an artifact of the descriptions coming from published articles where citations are important. The literature was genuinely consulted in regard to the design of the endeavors.
Mixed qualitative and quantitative methods used to corroborate each other	Abundantly clear every time, and data led to greater understanding.	It is an outstanding part of all three studies. There is sensitivity to the nuances of different types of data.
Careful deliberation of complex, multifaceted data	Each study refers to multiple meetings and sessions reflective of deliberation.	Mixed-methods data may be complex and automatically necessitate such deliberation.
Expectations of decision makers and stakeholders	Since time may be elongated, be aware of the sometimes unrealistic pressure to move to decisions.	This type of press is frequently encountered in needs assessments and was notable in one of the cases.
External involvement	It is evident from the beginning of the project through to its completion.	It is doubtful that these efforts could have been done without such involvement.
Community/ stakeholder involvement and community control	Community involvement was there to a great extent, but the aegis (impetus) for the	This feature is different from the focus of building communities from the inside.

Feature	Extent of Occurrence	Comments
	endeavor may be more external.	Community control wasn't precluded but may not be always realistic for getting things done.
Time horizons	As noted above, depending on the scope of the project, the time required to establish and maintain community and stakeholder involvement could be large.	These can be time-intensive activities. Time is needed to get going and to periodically keep on top of relationships.
Cost features and the need for flexibility	If the scope is large and even in small studies, costs will be a serious consideration. However large the project, be alert to snags and their implications, and keep communications active across numerous players.	Not all of the cases discussed the need for flexibility and cost aspects of what they did. It is safe to say that they will be an essential part of projects.
Other variables	All projects were summaries in the published literature, and numerous subtle details could not be covered. Thus there are many other aspects that might have been part of the table.	One interesting thing was what the investigators considered to be the salient ingredients that made for success or failure.

munity involvement, seek community insights into what the data mean, and so forth. By the same token, some features may not fully resonate with what a hybrid should have. Table 7.5 is a summary of main elements of the hybrid and how they present collectively for the cases.

HIGHLIGHTS OF CHAPTER 7

1. A rationale was provided as to why cases from health were chosen for the chapter.

2. General parameters for searching the literature were explained, as were features that influenced the interpretation of the findings.

3. An overview of three cases from health coming from the United Kingdom, the United States, and Bali was given, and each was looked at in depth followed by analysis and rating of its key aspects.

4. Before looking across the three cases, a somewhat older needs assessment study not chosen (date of publication, primary focus on needs) was briefly described. Common needs assessment (CNA) was similarly mentioned.

5. Table 7.5 contained an analysis across the three cases. As expected, because of selection, they were strong in terms of hybrid features (see Tables 7.1, 7.2, 7.3, and 7.4).

6. One aspect that did not present well was the locus of control. The voice of the community was noticeable in the cases, but it did not seem to be the driving force or the impetus, which is less than desirable from the asset/capacity-building side of the equation.

DISCUSSION QUESTIONS

1. In the three cases, a great deal of effort and time was expended. Qualitative and quantitative data were collected; sincere outreach to the community was commendable, well intentioned, and extended over time; needs and assets were major foci; and so forth. What are your perceptions about expenditures to do the work, who should the funders be, and could they introduce bias into the process?

2. In one investigation, the researchers noted that several communities had prior pertinent experience and therefore were more responsive to participation. Change could more readily take place in such settings. This variable may have major bearing on these types of ventures—what should we look for, and what kinds of

questions could be asked that would alert researchers to this characteristic?

3. Each case was evaluated on the first part (scoping) of the checklist. That may be due to published articles being examined instead of comprehensive reports, or it could be that the checklist is over the top. Go back to the checklist. What might be the main things to emphasize, and what could be deemphasized?

4. Time frames are not totally clear, but undoubtedly the cases required a fair investment of that commodity. The time in Bali was considerably shorter, but it had an intense period of activity guided by an external research team. What about time in such investigations? How long should they take, and if a lot of time is required, how would motivation and involvement be maintained?

5. The external impetus versus the internal one is a bone of contention—visibly or sitting under the surface. Consider and discuss the following questions:

   Could any of the three cases have been successful without external support, guidance, or even direction?

   What biases could be introduced?

   Can an endeavor of sizable scope be done without an external group being there and doing a majority of the activities?

   What are the roles of all parties, and what are the best ways of organizing?

   How do we keep the community meaningfully involved over time, and what might this take in terms of coordination and resources?

6. There are a myriad of issues and things to think about when conducting hybrid studies, and research done about such projects would be informative.

   Speculate about research questions that could be raised. What procedures could be used to learn about them?

   Have you read or seen any of these studies, and if so, what were their findings?

   The three cases cited were exceptionally good, but certainly there are others that did not work well. How could we investigate them in order to not repeat mistakes?

7. The examples were exemplary in using quantitative and qualitative

data and in obtaining information from many sources. In one case and probably in others the data did not always agree and necessitated additional fieldwork. What do we do when data and findings are not complementary, and how do we resolve such problems?

8. Lastly, what the three cases did is demanding. Deciding on direction, designing techniques for collecting data, utilizing many sources of data, involving multiple constituencies so that they have ownership in what has been learned and suggested for improvement, and interpreting from observations, surveys, interviews, and databases are complex entities by themselves, let alone occurring in consort in a comprehensive community-based investigation. With that in mind, think about concerns such as the following:

How could the investigations be streamlined in method or data collection while at the same time collecting enough data to move the community forward?

If some things were done to a lesser degree or not at all, what would be lost, and what would the disadvantages be?

8

Cases From Other Fields

F or hybrid implementation, it is not surprising that examples are found in public health given its importance and the local and national funding that flows into the field. These cases are complex, usually take an extended period of time, and require a lot of resources for identifying assets and resources (Chapter 7). It should be stressed that federal and state levels and even local ones maintain health care and disease statistics from routinely collected data that are entered into accessible databases. Information about needs is commonplace, and workers in relevant professions are attuned to it and readily take advantage of what is available. This is also in their formal training via epidemiology. Combinations of needs assessment and asset/capacity building à la a hybrid are appropriate for them.

Researchers, evaluators, and needs assessors in a number of other fields (education, social work, community affairs) do not have epidemiology in their training programs. Thus they may not have the understanding that lends itself almost naturally to working across approaches. Going further in these areas, the focus on a more traditional deficit position may be common. It may crowd out consideration of an alternative. Whatever the reason, fewer projects were found that cut across the two approaches, and those that did tended to load more on asset/capacity building than on needs assessment.

An overview of several cases is provided in Table 8.1. In their full explanations, there are similarities to those in the prior chapter. Contexts vary, but techniques for collecting and utilizing information aren't diametrically different.

Table 8.1 Overview of Cases From Fields Other Than Public Health That Were Moving Toward Implementation of the Hybrid Framework

Author(s) & Year	A/CB	NA	Mixed Methods	A/CB & NA	Joint Philosophy	Comments
Case 1. An investigation into community violence by Hausman, Siddons, and Becker (2000)	++	++	++	++	++	A study to reduce the rate of firearm violence in North Philadelphia
Case 2. The needs assessment and asset/capacity-building study of Minnesota's Agricultural Utilization Research Institute (Spaeth, Larson, & Wagner-Lahr, in process)	+++	+++	+++	++	+++	A case predicated on the three-phase model of needs assessment but with a heavy dose of asset/ capacity building and many involved groups and individuals
Case 3. Snippets from multiple cases embedded in four policy papers on the "CADISPA Trust" (2013) website (see text for papers from 2009 to 2012)	+++	+	++	++	++	Papers that focused on asset/ capacity building in communities but also included ascertaining needs

OVERVIEW OF CASES FROM FIELDS OTHER THAN PUBLIC HEALTH

The table entries include the author(s), when the work was conducted, key aspects of the hybrid framework it demonstrated, and a rating of its strength in that regard. For the latter, + would be a judgment that it was there, ++ that it was there in a major way, and +++ that it was extremely strong—plusses are desirable. Special aspects of what was done are in the Comments column.

CASE 1. USING COMMUNITY PERSPECTIVES ON YOUTH FIREARM VIOLENCE FOR PREVENTION PROGRAM PLANNING

The emphasis of this project, while stronger on assets, did have a needs assessment component. It was seen as appropriate for this text.

Structure of the Project

A coalition in North Philadelphia was concerned with youth firearm violence. It wanted to examine the problem and to resolve it or at least reduce the level of crimes committed with guns. Remember in Chapter 7, and relevant here, it was observed that some communities have been involved in looking at needs and resources in the past. This gives them a better chance of succeeding in a new endeavor. Having that experience may be significant, further reinforcing existing partnerships that could pay big dividends.

The community in Philadelphia wanted to understand the situation, frame solutions, identify assets that could be applied to resolve the situation, engage key members of the community and groups in solutions, and as suggested in the hybrid framework determine variables that would indicate progress and be useful for evaluating outcomes. This was a major undertaking.

The coalition was very much along the lines of what the hybrid framework recommends. It consisted of a youth outreach organization, public health and law departments of a university, and medical care providers. Numerous project directors, representatives of city agencies, the foundation that funded the effort, and others were involved. Community members who had a history of working on programs were part of the effort. The coalition had an evaluation team, subcommittees, a governing council, and a community advisory group. In Exhibit 8.1 and Table 8.2 on page 188, what they did and the application of the first part of the evaluation checklist to the case are described.

Exhibit 8.1 Activities Incorporated Into the Firearms Prevention Project

Formation of the project

    Determining actors and groups to be represented

    Developing committees and a governance mechanism

    Enhancing community member involvement by eventual inclusion on the governing council

Review of other similar projects conducted in other inner cities (use of the literature)

Description of the target neighborhoods and areas (needs orientation)

    Use of existing reports for the areas of the city in concern

    Trends in data over years

    Demographics

    Youth homicides

Description of a conceptual pyramid

    Foundation consisting of community composition, organization, and capacity for action

    Middle level consisting of the socioecological factors affecting health

    Top level consisting of existing services that have bearing for improvement

Rapid participatory appraisal (RPA)

    Follows tenets of RPA in general but more investigator led

    Community heavily included in analysis, interpretation, and use of information

    Semistructured individual interviews of key informants

    Questions about topics:

    Community composition

    Organizations

    Capacity

    Aspects of the environment (socio, economic, physical)

Health services

And so on

Sample initially consisted of key informants and then expanded by a "snowball" technique

Covered a wide spread of the community

Included youths

Interviewers recruited with experience applicable to the study

Three hired interviewers

Good listening and communication skills

Also participated in the analysis

Analysis

Key themes identified

Clustered into four main ones

Assets

Problems (needs)

Solutions

Indicators of successful programming

Interviewees meeting as a group to discuss themes

Reports from the interviews being fed back to interviewees

Results (positives)

PERCEPTIONS OF THE PROCESS

The above process was considered to be a needs assessment and asset/resource identification.

Interviewers felt that the results captured what had been said.

A strong community identity emerged, including a sense of pride and history.

(Continued)

(Continued)

Interest arose in new efforts to help the community:

Local groups were mentioned in this regard.

Local agencies did not arise in the interviews.

Aspects (positive and negative) of the physical community were noted.

Results (negatives)

Drugs and drug problems are the root cause of the problem (violence and guns).

The problem is increasing.

The youth community has changed and become more resistant to older solution ideas.

Drugs are affecting many facets of the community (education, housing, etc.).

Senior citizens seem leery of participating in new efforts (intimidation may be a factor).

Unemployment

Young men in particular are affected.

Training in job skills and readiness is needed.

Insufficient educational services are in existence across many segments of the community.

More activities for youth are needed.

Some services are there but not coordinated.

Even what churches do has to be better tied together.

Health concerns

Alcoholism in addition to drugs

Abandoned houses leading to trash and rat problems

Physical quality of streets

Solutions

Getting rid of drugs

Seeking help from outside the community in relation to eliminating drugs

Recognizing the issue and its severity

Strengthening the police presence

Increasing educational and vocational services

Increasing services for youth

Enhancing internal community groups and allowing them to pull together more

Recognizing the criticality of the internal community to long-term success

Strengthening cooperation and coordination

Engaging in better communication

What are the signs of successful improvement activities and programs?

Safer environment

Less drug abuse, violence, crime

Fixing up homes, more appealing neighborhoods

Organizations, people, and services (e.g., police) working together to improve the community

Visibly increased services

One thing to emphasize is that there was community input and insight into the evaluation of activities that would result from the study. If the full evaluation checklist had been used, this case would have rated fairly high on later aspects of it.

Discussion of the Case

First, the authors raised the question of what constitutes a neighborhood and noted that there are many subneighborhoods in a larger one. At this finer level of detail, people in them are less aware of resources available nearby. Staff observed that they did not fully understand the local communities in which the investigation was conducted. The subtle diversity was hard to comprehend.

Second, the authors observed fear in the interview responses. With it comes isolation, which may account for some of the lack of awareness of services available to residents. At the same time, the interviewees recognized that internal solutions were important to resolving problems and were equal to the idea that there must be external awareness of the issues.

Table 8.2 Application of the First Part of the Evaluative Checklist to Assess the Degree of Fit for Case 1 With the Hybrid Framework (ratings in **bold**)

Model Step	Items to Observe	Rating	Special Considerations
Scoping the context	Critical initiating group	0 1 2 3 4 **5**	Internal control should be there, or the internal voice should be strong—it was prominent here.
	Internally controlled more	0 1 2 3 **4** 5	
	External involvement but not control	0 1 2 3 **4** 5	External involvement, but not control, was in evidence.
	Commitment to endeavor	0 1 2 3 **4** 5	The group that developed seems to be into the self-study.
	Some sense of vision	0 1 2 **3** 4 5	Learning things about the organization or community expanded the group's thinking and perspectives.
	Prior experience in such ventures	0 1 2 **3** 4 5	
	Readiness for self-study	0 1 2 3 **4** 5	
	Awareness of two approaches	0 1 2 3 **4** 5	
	Collection of starting information	0 1 2 3 **4** 5	
	Clear indications of need	0 1 2 3 **4** 5	
	Clear indications of assets/resources	0 1 2 3 **4** 5	
	Mixed methods utilized	0 1 2 3 **4** 5	
	Quantitative methods used	0 1 2 3 **4** 5	
	Qualitative methods used	0 1 2 3 **4** 5	
	Value to information collected	0 1 2 3 4 **5**	
	Scoping Total 66		66 out of 75 possible points awarded, with 13 of the 15 items being at 4 or higher

Thus the "can do" attitude and feeling of empowerment was in the thinking of the community.

Third, solutions suggested in the interviews actually became the basis for action. To a high degree they loaded on the concepts of coordination and communication. The project led to the formation of three subcommittees charged with developing programs aimed at reducing firearm violence. Each had a cross section of the community in its membership. The procedures recommended drew heavily on linking organizations, agencies, and services together for improvement, and strategies went so far as to involve youth in their implementation, which was almost a centerpiece of what was to be done.

Fourth, a strength was that those who participated in the study became instrumental in subsequent new initiatives. In this text and previous writings, the author has stressed that this is crucial for ultimate success and change in needs assessment, asset/capacity building, or a combination of the two. It propels subsequent development and improvement.

Fifth, as noted above and in accord with the hybrid, evaluation was part of what the subcommittees were putting into place. Concerns focused on ensuring the quality of leadership, looking at the process of programs, keeping adequate records, prioritizing outcome indicators, and making observations of efforts. This part of the framework might not be realized in many circumstances. It demonstrates that the coalition was open to the citizenry and wove the citizens' perceptions into the process.

Sixth, while a timeline was not provided, a sizable period was needed for collecting input and for trust to develop. This was a cost but, in terms of what was achieved, a necessary and a worthwhile one.

CASE 2. THE AGRICULTURAL UTILIZATION RESEARCH INSTITUTE (AURI) OF MINNESOTA

Agriculture is a major driver of the U.S. economy, as attested to when Hurricane Katrina hit New Orleans in 2005 and disrupted huge shipments of farm goods from the Great Plains and upper Midwest. Recently, the state of Minnesota established the Agricultural Utilization Research Institute (AURI) to promote the transfer of technology and research to its large agricultural industry and nearby states in regard to basic areas—bioproducts, renewable energy, coproducts (coming from residues generated from corn in the manufacture of ethanol, from processing of raw materials into edible substances, etc.), and food. AURI is an outgrowth of extension as it enters a new era of service to the public.

Structure of the Project

Immediately, this calls for needs assessment and asset/capacity building. Needs must be addressed in relation to establishing new directions, enhancing productivity and profitability in agribusiness, changing practices in the field, developing career opportunities, and so forth (Altschuld & Hung, 2012). At the same time, there are vast assets in family and large farm enterprises, research centers and labs, and large and small commercial establishments. There is value in identifying and cataloging them and juxtaposing needs against them to establish policies and procedures for improvement and the betterment of the state and the region.

The activities (needs, resource identification) occur in a complex environment. Building consensus, empowerment, and ownership are essential to this kind of endeavor. Many individuals and groups are involved—farmers, businesspeople, university scientists and researchers in other venues, company staffs, service providers, food processors, educators, and others. Needs-related questions could be formulated:

What are the problems facing producers?

What information that AURI has or will develop will be attended to by potential users?

What information is most persuasive and utilitarian, and why?

What trends are occurring in areas of concern or interest?

How do practices align with what is known about the four foci of AURI?

What do farmers understand about market conditions?

What problems and issues are they encountering in delivering what they produce to middle and end users?

What is happening, and what should happen, in regard to alternative energy sources?

What is employment in all facets of agriculture at the present time?

What might it be in 10 years?

There is no shortage of what could be examined, and similar thinking could be applied to assets. Recognizing the nature of the situation, the director of AURI, in conjunction with staff, state government, and key groups, elected (in 2012 and continuing in 2013) to determine needs and assets and to see what the problems and resources are and how they could be looked at in a proactive manner. External contracting was employed to determine gaps, resources, and strengths, which will be carefully reviewed. A detailed description of the case is in Exhibit 8.2, and the application of the first part of the evaluation checklist is in Table 8.3 on page 194.

Exhibit 8.2 Activities Incorporated Into the AURI Needs Assessment/ Capacity-Building Project

Recognition of the situation

Actors to be involved

Extent of the issue on the needs and assets sides

Having the resources for expert involvement

Seeing the importance of investigating assets and needs independently

Recognition that funds would eventually become scarce

Independent local councils in operation—better coordination would be desirable

Stress on the potential of collaboration

Focus on capacities

Contracted with an external agency for assessment of capacities/ opportunities

Idea of targeting what AURI does to take advantage of capacity areas

Interdisciplinary strengths

Better alignment of assets with where the most good could be done

Interestingly, guiding this was the three-phase model of needs assessment.

Heavy reliance was placed on the Needs Assessment Kit (see Chapter 1).

A broad-based needs assessment committee (NAC) was formed with wide representation.

Local council buy-in and support of the endeavor was crucial and there.

Meetings were externally facilitated.

AURI considered itself to be a catalyst in the process, not a controller.

(Continued)

(Continued)

Initial get-together session

NAC Pre-Assessment meeting

Orientation

Focus on current status of individual organizations as related to the study

Looking for commonalities

Discussion of advantages of working together (establishing the base)

Meeting agenda supplied in the in-progress report

Outcomes

Local councils worked together on specific projects (positive history there).

There were crosscutting issues.

Notion of leveraging was part of the discussion.

Rich interaction occurred, but the full agenda could not be accomplished.

Loss of completing agenda was mitigated by buy-in.

For the future

Need for coordination to move forward

Work with external contractor to better define the tasks to be done

Focus on several of the key issues for in-depth exploration

How to capitalize on agricultural talent, especially for employment

Ways to leverage funding for research

Negotiation across entities

Subsequent meeting and activities

Maintaining attendance statewide requires attention, and AURI did focus on doing so.

AURI reviewed prior work to get everyone on the same page.

Discussion of an agricultural research capacity assessment and strategic road map to be done by consultant group looking at assets, strengths, and opportunities;

needs; and

possible outcomes from doing this.

Also, how could results be linked to markets and other facets of agriculture?

Breakout and discussion groups were incorporated into the sessions.

They created "what is" and "what should be" statements.

After the meeting, staff pulled together and summarized what was done.

They contacted those who could not attend for input.

They made contact with local councils.

They did interim steps pursuant to the next meeting.

Next steps (project is in process at the time of this writing)

Planning for next meetings

Considerations of instruments to use

Developing an instrument with multiple sections to look at needs

Administering same to involved statewide group

Going beyond Pre-assessment into Phases 2 and 3, Assessment and Post-assessment

Moving toward priorities and procedures for doing so

Meeting with the governor and key state administrators

Discussion of the Case

First, as with the previous cases, this is an extensive undertaking that could not be done without outside expertise, and sizable funding. To the credit of AURI staff, careful thought was given to what their role and stance should be and how external individuals would be integrated into the work. It was critical that the voice of stakeholders be there and that their buy-in be kept foremost. To date, this seems to have been accomplished.

Given that extensiveness, this venture will take a considerable period of time to produce fruitful results. Quick turnaround would not be expected. Stakeholders and decision makers should be made aware of this early on and not assume that immediate changes and new directions will occur as a result of initial activities. Unrealistic pressure for outcomes can occur and should be dealt with openly; otherwise, difficulties will be encountered.

Table 8.3 Application of the First Part of the Evaluative Checklist to Assess the Degree of Fit for Case 2 With the Hybrid Framework (ratings in **bold**)

Model Step	Items to Observe		Special Considerations
Scoping the context	Critical initiating group	0 1 2 3 **4** 5	Either internal control should be there, or the internal voice should be strong—it was notable here.
	Internally controlled more	0 1 2 3 **4** 5	External involvement, but not control, was evident.
	External involvement but not control	0 1 2 3 **4** 5	The group that developed seems to be into self-study.
	Commitment to endeavor	0 1 2 3 **4** 5	Learning things about the organization or community expanded the group's thinking and perspectives.
	Sense of vision	0 1 2 **3** 4 5	
	Prior experience in such ventures	0 1 2 **3** 4 5	
	Readiness for self-study	0 1 2 3 **4** 5	
	Awareness of two approaches	0 1 2 3 **4** 5	
	Collection of starting information	0 1 2 3 4 **5**	
	Clear indications of need	0 1 2 3 4 **5**	
	Clear indications of assets/resources	0 1 2 3 4 **5**	
	Mixed methods utilized	0 1 2 3 4 **5**	
	Quantitative methods used	0 1 2 3 4 **5**	
	Qualitative methods used	0 1 2 3 4 **5**	
	Value to information collected	0 1 2 3 4 **5**	
	Scoping Total 65		65 out of 75 possible points awarded, with 13 of the 15 items being at 4 or higher

Second, is this a needs assessment, asset/capacity building, or closer to the hybrid framework? Although it uses the three-phase model of needs assessment, a lot of its activities fit the hybrid (including the determination of assets and resources), and it is perceived to be an example of the process. One small difference is that assessing needs and assets is more sequential than simultaneous in the framework. Circumstances may dictate such an order.

Third, this investigation is for a state, and that complicates matters greatly. At the time of this writing, two meetings have been held of the NAC, and a third is in the plans. Keeping up attendance and participation of busy NAC participants from all parts of the state and in different areas related to agriculture will not come easily, and even with electronic meetings and connectivity it will be a difficult proposition. How are communications maintained, and how will AURI see to it that the buy-in and ownership persist over what might be a lengthy period? These are serious questions. There was a drop-off from the first to the second sessions as might be anticipated. AURI staff were sensitive to this possibility and made commendable attempts to contact those who could not be there for comments and views as well as to make sure that they were apprised of progress and potential next steps.

Doing so is necessary for the flow and pace of this project. Without it, there is likelihood of less success or even failure, but it comes with a price. Keeping involvement going does not take place by happenstance. It is a calculated investment with resources and time being required. This is an almost hidden cost that groups absorb but do not record or think about. This was also observed in other cases, and because of it there is difficulty in estimating the funding needed for investigations. Certainly, activities that tie things together are continuous throughout a study, as well as later for planned and undertaken actions. One thing that might be done is to have staff members keep logs of contacts they make by phone, e-mail, or other means. In this way, we could get a picture of the time to keep the hybrid running and functional.

Fourth, this was an interesting application and unanticipated twist on the three phases of needs assessment. AURI tweaked it so that its third phase was much more into asset/capacity building along with some aspects of that being embedded in initial work. This strategy may yield insights into alternative ways to do the hybrid framework. Or it could be argued that this project was emanating from a needs assessment base and therefore was more oriented that way. A case study here would be interesting as to how well the two parts of the hybrid approach were blended into a whole.

Fifth, the attention to the details of potential meetings was apparent. AURI staff in their facilitation role were diligent in letting all participants know about upcoming meetings, agendas, what had been accomplished to date, and other details. This created a positive and solid foundation, and it was assumed that people from across the state would notice and see the sincerity and seriousness with which a complex set of issues was being addressed. Perception of the endeavor could only be enhanced by this stance. This was built into project plans, and it was the right course to follow.

CASE 3. SNIPPETS FROM MULTIPLE CASES IN THE PAPERS ON THE CADISPA WEBSITE

When the author was looking for examples of hybrid work outside of public health, he had dinner with an old friend and mentioned the search for examples. The friend sat up and recalled that the CADISPA website from Scotland had entries that fit (R. Jurin, personal communication, September 18, 2012). He was on target.

Scotland was facing tight budgets that would affect communities, particularly rural ones. The need was there, and without looking at resources, serious consequences in human terms would appear. Many policy papers were on the website that dealt with "community resiliency," not needs assessment or asset/capacity building. The term was different, but the concept was not. Resiliency, which was not in the original literature query, refers to the ability of a community or a collective to handle adversities and be proactive for the well-being of its members. It implies communities working together to plan for programs that are preventative for health, financial strains, and other things that may arise. A resilient community or organization is capable of dealing with and resolving situations, whereas others may just hold steady or lose out when problems are encountered. This was a common theme throughout the website entries.

Four policy-oriented papers (APS Group, 2011; Boyle & Harris, 2009; Carnegie UK Trust, 2011; Woolvin, 2012) were selected for inclusion here. They did not contain complete cases but drew heavily from community-based endeavors exhibiting many of the principles in the framework. Descriptions of salient features were highlighted throughout the materials. In the papers, the starting point was the assets that a community had to offer (the bedrock strengths of Kretzmann and McKnight, 1993), but at the same time they were not oblivious to needs, and needs data were part of the equation.

Another feature throughout was the voluntary ethos of rural settings or other similar contexts. A spirit of working collectively to solve problems was almost ingrained in the people. This included involving community members in the delivery of services such as transportation of the elderly or being partners with professional personnel in aspects of health care provided to individuals. This is analogous to the example in Chapter 7 in which prior experience with needs and asset types of efforts was a type of learning that facilitated projects and new ventures.

What comes from the Scottish papers may not totally generalize, but there are valuable principles adaptable to our context. Exhibit 8.3 has an overview of key elements from snippets of the papers, and Table 8.4 on page 201 shows the first part of the evaluation checklist applied to them.

Exhibit 8.3 A Distillation of Premises and Activities Prominent in the Papers on the Website

Basic premises

> Clearly seeing the need due to funding limitations
>
> Recognizing assets that collectively reside in communities
>
> Focusing on assets and capacity but considering needs
>
> Thinking about communities and services required by them
>
> Discouraging dependency type of thinking
>
> Recognizing that a community must determine its own direction
>
> In some instances, the community must be an integral part of service delivery.
>
> Short-term efficiency (saving money and resources) thinking is not the way to go, especially at the expense of the long-term good.
>
> Government agencies must change to foster meaningful community involvement.
>
> The voice of the people must be there.

Models of what a well-functioning, resilient community means in terms of four features:

> Healthy engaged people
>
> Localized economy

(Continued)

198 ● Bridging the Gap Between Asset/Capacity Building

(Continued)

    Linkages in and across communities

    Inclusive and creative culture

Community involvement for long-term benefits

With such involvement, greater transparency

Improving performance/reducing costs

Avoidance of "top down" direction, more partnering

Humanism

Collaboration seen as critical

Engagement, empowerment, and enablement

Coordination and leadership

Long-term strategic planning

Dealing with rapid change

Break-through, break-even, and break-down communities

Activities (needs)

    Needs in the form of gaps, a consideration in the papers

    Examination of existing data in bases

    Looking at trends

    Reliance on health, employment, and utilization of services statistics

    Pressures on public services

    Public expenditures over time

    Demographic patterns and growth of an aging population

Observations from data about dealing with problems, not seeing proactive prevention

    Noting where discrepancies are located as well as overlaps in services

    Housing prices, crime rates, and so on

    Local and disaggregated data

    Studying climate and environmental changes in relation to needs

    Community engagement in research and self-study

Extent of vulnerability in the community and to persons in re to jobs, health, and so forth

Data from surveys and interviews

Household surveys on energy

Extracting needs from the data

Oral histories

Prioritization suggested based on needs but always with asset thinking being prime

Activities (asset/capacity building)

Seeking information from the community by a variety of mechanisms

Training for community meetings complete with forms for brainstorming

Forms focus on break-through communities, break-even communities, and those breaking down.

Extensively use scenarios with community groups.

Employ tools (instruments) to determine the extent to which the four features of a resilient community have been achieved.

Look for linkages to other communities.

Stress the concept that no community can do it alone.

Avoid use of resilience principles to promote politicized agendas.

Do surveys and assessments of the nature of community assets such as volunteering, physical facilities, and so forth.

Oral and cultural histories

Create a sense of local values.

Community members might collect and analyze data.

Visit local places of culture.

Encourage local events to reinforce culture.

Use summary tables to capture the nature of the culture (similar to devices proposed for the hybrid model in this text; see Table 3.3).

(Continued)

(Continued)

Tie assets and capacity building with needs.

Get away from a dependency mind-set.

Focus on public services.

One aspect is coproduction (service delivered by professionals and government but with large-scale and meaningful involvement of community members).

Heavy emphasis was placed on volunteers (in one of the papers this led to an in-depth study of volunteerism in the area).

Recognize that some services (police, justice) are not amenable to this approach, but aspects of them may be.

Results

Numerous examples of results are embedded in the papers.

The authors cited positive instances in Washington, DC, and Wisconsin regarding the juvenile court system and offenders with similar application and outcomes for a youth jury approach in the United Kingdom.

Fifty thousand individuals with long-term health conditions have received support from like individuals in the United Kingdom.

All of the papers have citations to success stories.

Other outcomes were noted such as broadening of social networks or fairly creative ways of service delivery (giving credits to local leisure services for volunteer effort) not considered previously.

Some stress was placed on longer-term outcomes.

To reiterate, the papers, which are for public services in Scotland, are in response to needs arising from budgets that are to be reduced or at best remain flat. Need is clearly there, but the main emphasis is asset/capacity building. Needs are a lesser part of the materials, and at times the author of this text inferred them from what he found on the website.

Using the checklist is problematic because detailed examples were not in the policy papers, yet excerpts from many efforts helped to capture a sense of what occurred. They led to the composite in Exhibit 8.3 and the ratings in Table 8.4. Without more information, the second item in the

Table 8.4 Application of the Part of the Evaluative Checklist to Assess the Degree of Fit for Case 3 With the Hybrid Framework (ratings in **bold**)

Model Step	Items to Observe		Special Considerations
Scoping the context	Critical initiating group	0 1 2 3 **4** 5	No rating is given for internal control since none of the materials reviewed contained a complete case.
	Internally controlled more	0 1 2 3 4 5	
	External involvement but not control	0 1 2 **3** 4 5	External involvement was obvious via the government emphasis.
	Commitment to endeavor	0 1 2 3 **4** 5	
	Sense of vision	0 1 2 3 **4** 5	Awareness of the two approaches was evident, but stress was placed on one.
	Prior experience in such ventures	0 1 2 3 **4** 5	
	Readiness for self-study	0 1 2 3 **4** 5	Certainly mixed methods were found in all of the papers, but the methods were not always extensively described.
	Awareness of two approaches	0 1 2 **3** 4 5	
	Collection of starting information	0 1 2 3 4 **5**	
	Clear indications of need	0 1 2 3 4 **5**	
	Clear indications of assets/resources	0 1 2 3 4 **5**	
	Mixed methods utilized	0 1 2 3 4 **5**	
	Quantitative methods used	0 1 2 3 4 **5**	
	Qualitative methods used	0 1 2 3 4 **5**	
	Value to information collected	0 1 2 3 4 **5**	
	Scoping Total 61		61 out of 75 possible points awarded, with 12 of the 15 items being at 4 or higher

201

table was not rated. Programs had been initiated based on determination of needs and assets and resources, as well as comparisons of them.

The snippets that were mentioned might have rated high on other sections of the checklist. Thought had been given to the evaluation of improvement endeavors and would have led to significant ratings on other items, and in one paper there was a summary table congruent with what was proposed for the hybrid framework in Chapter 3.

Discussion of the Composite

First, context is important—public service in Scotland, looming budgetary issues, and the recognition that there were resources (human, community) to attenuate the situation. There was a long-standing culture of volunteerism, and such history is important. How well approaches like these might generalize to education, business, or various state agencies is a question.

Second, there are concerns about resources and time frames. Studies like these cannot be carried out in an instant without diligence and a great deal of persistence. They include community groups and service delivery organizations and agencies, and entail costs for coordination. They necessitate that needs be assessed and that resources and assets be identified. Upfront capital must be there. Who will pay the bills and buy into what is to be done is not to be glossed over. More detail would have been desirable.

Third, in virtually every case, much information about assets and needs was collected, with more weighting on the former. How was the information amalgamated into coherent, valuable, and useful data sets for decision making and priority setting? The readings were insightful but need more specifics. What happened in the details, in coming to conclusions about what the data were indicating and what direction might be pursued? What was and wasn't done, and why were certain actions taken and others not? What might summary tables contain?

Fourth, are these internally or externally led projects or some combination of the two? The voice of the people and their eventual participation was obviously valued, but who made the choices about the data collected and what it led to were not so patent. Was the process top down, bottom up, or a mixture, and was one voice more prominent than another? Roles and responsibilities and how they factor in are important, and whether some patterns work better than others is a consideration for this type of work.

Fifth, politics come into play. Public organizations, agencies, service providers, and others like to control their turf. For example, in coproduction as done in Scotland, professionals may have to concede some of their territory to segments of the public in regard to service delivery. How does this sit with them, and are they willing to relinquish what they hold dear in their practice to others? Could this affect the quality of services? If done on a large scale, who handles the extended list of players? What are the hidden costs, and how would they compare to other mechanisms for delivering programs directed toward issues and problems?

Sixth, an aspect of the policies and projects was movement away from a short-term, narrow, efficiency focus to a longer perspective and broader outcomes. This departs from current thinking. At the same time, it calls for being accountable for in-depth results and achievement of impacts. It may be a challenge to more orthodox views of service delivery.

Seventh, the overall stance in the writings forces a reconsideration of how communities and public agencies join together for betterment. That was accomplished with an asset/capacity-building approach tempered against needs. The ideas are refreshing for employing a hybrid framework for improvement and development.

ACROSS THE CASES

Many of the entries in Table 7.5 would apply to the cases in this chapter, and repeating them would be redundant. Much of what was there fits here, although the degree would vary. What will be explained now are additional observations coming from the summaries of North Philadelphia, Minnesota, and Scotland. One of the cases was from an article, and the other two were from documentation (a report in progress and a website of many papers). The latter did not detail all aspects of what was done but provided enough for the author to make inferences.

In these cases and in the previous three, the problems being investigated were substantive, vast in scope, and of deep concern. Doing solely a needs assessment or the identification of resources and strengths would not suffice. Neither by itself would be up to the task. The situations required that assets be marshaled to resolve issues and develop programs to resolve them. Without fully understanding the area of concern, knowledge of assets and lists of the same would not be as meaningful as when each side of the equation has been explored.

The examples in the chapter necessitate long periods of time to delve into and come up with and install solutions across groups, service deliverers,

204 • Bridging the Gap Between Asset/Capacity Building

individuals, and agencies. Size does matter, and smaller entities may elect to assess needs or probe resources, but not to do both. The finances to support the use of a hybrid framework may not be at hand, and groups will opt for one approach or the other. Dollars will dictate what can be done. This is especially true when the subtle costs of communication and coordination are considered for hybrid efforts.

Another thing is that the six studies in Chapters 7 and 8 received high and similar scores on the first category in the rating schema. That is not surprising because they were selected as fitting the premise of the book, exemplifying the hybrid framework. If a broader spectrum had been chosen, the scoring would have varied more. Other investigations would still illustrate main principles but probably would not have enough resources to do work like this, and corners undoubtedly would have been cut.

Lastly, two of the cases in this chapter were unusual in their emphasis on evaluation. In one, the voice of the people in large part determined such content. That was striking. Ultimately, what outcomes are being achieved will have to be addressed in order to say that hybrid undertakings are worth the cost and investment of human capital, an obvious point begging for substantial evaluation data to buttress the argument in favor of the framework.

HIGHLIGHTS OF CHAPTER 8

1. Issues involved in searching the literature were raised, including the terms that were employed for seeking examples outside of public health.

2. An overview of three selected cases was provided, and the cases were presented in regard to what they did.

3. To avoid repeating the analysis in Chapter 7, only unique facets across these cases were offered in terms of scope, communication, coordination, time, and so forth.

4. Included in that discussion was the idea that the issues of concern were major and anything less than the hybrid framework would have been insufficient.

5. Lastly, the hybrid entails a strong and substantial base of support, which may not be there for smaller endeavors.

DISCUSSION QUESTIONS

1. Building from the above point, is size so prominent that the hybrid framework will not be used when dollar and human resources are more limited or perhaps there are shortcut ways it could be conducted? What are your thoughts?

2. What is an adequate time for major endeavors, and if it is more than a year or two how will organizations, agencies, or communities maintain commitment, motivation, and so forth? What are ways to ward off a maturation effect?

3. The assets part of things can get daunting, especially for a large community or for a state. How might it be conceptualized and then investigated? How would under-the-surface assets, such as contributions of family members to an individual's health when that person is confronted with a major illness, be assessed? The same idea applies to community programs where volunteerism could be key. What would you do to get an estimate of such assets and resources?

4. It was suggested that staff members involved in a hybrid study keep logs of time spent in facilitating the project. Can you think of other ways to collect this subtle and complex data?

5. All three cases indicated the inclusion of groups and organizations in the study and in solutions in a significant, not a lip-service, way. How is this to be carried out, who does it, and at what expense to them or their organizations? How is this sustained according to your perceptions?

9

Research and Utilization

Discussion questions at the end of Chapters 1–8 have been used to spur thoughts and ideas. The hybrid framework is a concept under construction, yet to be fully tested. It may never be employed in its entirety, but be adapted only in pieces as they fit situations. It is proposed as a way to assist communities and organizations in moving forward. With that in mind, considerations for research and utilization will be examined in Chapter 9.

For research, the hybrid is given in Table 9.1 as are questions about it. The columns include, with one exception, steps, concerns about them, areas to be explored, and additional observations. The exception is that the first row deals with the overall framework. Is it sensible, what about philosophical underpinnings, and so forth? What could be done to learn more about it? Then the row-by-row entries are reviewed in some depth. It is hoped that this will stimulate inquiry, development, refinement, and improvement of the framework.

THE OVERALL FRAMEWORK (TABLE 9.1, ROW 1)

The premise of the framework is that two oppositional positions can be blended together, eventually leading to programs and projects for change and development of organizations and communities. Is that reasonable? Judging by the cases in Chapters 7 and 8, the answer is yes, for it was implemented without many problems, but the response may be too superficial and quick.

In almost all instances, the investigators stated that they were aware of the assets and needs philosophies and considered both important.

Table 9.1 The Overall Framework, Steps in It, Issues, Research Possibilities, and Additional Observations

Framework or Steps	Issues	Research Possibilities	Additional Observations
Overall Framework	Is it reasonable to combine potentially opposing positions, and does that matter so much in practical situations? Are all of the steps necessary? How might implementation vary by size of the endeavor? How might it be viewed by initiating groups?	Qualitative studies could be done to attain general perceptions of users. What steps are actually done, and does that depend on the size of the enterprise? Some of the questions might get at underlying assumptions and conflicts that may have arisen.	It may be difficult to obtain funding for this research. Given that support might be tight, build some research seamlessly into the context. This research is likely to be more in the province of external individuals or consultants.
1. Scoping the context	Who was involved, and what were they like? What about organizations as initiators (see the cases in Chapters 7 and 8)? What was the locus of control? How about the impetus? What actually was done?	Detailed case studies of successful and unsuccessful efforts fit this method. Identifying and categorizing structures of implementation, as well as examining records and minutes and collecting qualitative information, would be key.	The probability is that different structures will be found that fall into classes. It may be hard to locate unsuccessful ventures and gain access for research. Aspects of initiators or initiating groups could be very informative.
2. Deciding what actions should be taken	How was a decision arrived at to move forward and continue the enterprise? What was learned that was most useful and informative?	Aside from methods for the first step, approaches might be employed such as having involved individuals keep short journals.	An insider perspective might be interesting and revealing. Insights gained may readily generalize.

208

Framework or Steps	Issues	Research Possibilities	Additional Observations
	Were needs and assets looked at equally? What was decided to do next, with a particular focus on the hybrid?	Periodic, almost informal, focus group interviews might be conducted. Perhaps have an embedded participant observer.	Perceptions as the process is under way could identify where problems are encountered and how to navigate rough waters.
3. Dividing the working committee into two subcommittees	Does this really happen? Do groups collect information regarding needs and assets jointly, not separately as suggested in the framework? What kinds of information are sought, and from what sources? How do they portray what has been located to facilitate decision making with an eye toward new projects and efforts?	What do the records, minutes, and work products of the group tell us about this step? Are there full reports of projects and programs employing the hybrid to help us understand how it is implemented? Would our study reveal how this work was done and who did it (internal, external, a mixture)? Can we learn about the partnership for needs assessment and asset identification?	As the process begins to go deeper, we don't know much about its nature. This would mean getting records, detailed reports and summaries, and doing in-depth analysis of them. It might help to see what activities are most necessary and thus streamline what is done in hybrid use.
4. Conducting the assessment in greater depth	An extension of the prior step but with attention paid to how what has been found is put into a useful and summarized format.	See entries directly above.	See entries directly above.

209

(Continued)

Table 9.1 (Continued)

Framework or Steps	Issues	Research Possibilities	Additional Observations
5. Using what has been learned to make decisions for possible new programs	What occurs here is crucial to the whole endeavor. How has the information been pulled together and collated? What conclusions were drawn from it? What seems to stand out in the group's choices and emerging options?	Records as before are important for comprehending the process. Embedded observers and minute takers could provide data for how the group came to decisions. Individual debriefings should give an intimate feel to what has transpired.	This is the step where the rubber begins to hit the road. It is where choices are made as to what should be done for improvement. How this occurs over numerous efforts leads to understanding of hybrid processes.
6. Developing a strategy for improvement	What is the strategy for improvement? Are concrete plans evident, and can we see how they came from earlier steps? Has the feasibility of the plans been examined? Is it clear who has what responsibilities for what? Does the plan have clear outcomes, and how would they be assessed?	The plans should be reviewed in terms of likelihood of success, short- and long-term dimensions, reaching the community, budgets, and other features. Are there provisions for the evaluation of the project and how evaluative data will be collected? Reviewing plans across different settings would be a solid contribution to the literature.	What plans look like in different situations would help others embarking on a hybrid process. How results from prior steps led to plans, if documented, would guide individuals in other organizations and communities.

Framework or Steps	Issues	Research Possibilities	Additional Observations
7. Implementing and evaluating the action plan	Has the plan been implemented? Has it been monitored (formative evaluation)? How well did it work, and what outcomes (intended and unintended) did it produce? How were snags in implementation handled, and what about their impact on outcomes?	Do reports contain implementation data and what has been realized from the new efforts and directions? Are well-kept accounts of implementation available? If possible, external observers could be used for qualitative types of studies of new efforts.	The best testimony for a hybrid process would be examples of its use that led to community or organization development and advancement. Problems that were encountered and how they were treated or how to avoid them would be utilitarian for others.
8. Recycling back to first steps for expanding the improvement package	Has what has been started become the basis for further development? Is a learning and growth culture becoming more established? Is there sustainability—has the community or organization become more self-directed to build from needs and assets?	Conduct follow-up studies of the participants, the communities, and/ or the organizations after the first go-round with the hybrid process. Use surveys, and do site visits across locations. Do formal and informal interviews of participants about what happened, its value, the impact, and so on.	The hybrid process is really a mechanism for learning. What has infiltrated the thinking of the community and organizational participants? Has longer-term sustainability been achieved, and if so, what is its essence?

211

They were more enthusiastic about the positive dimensions of resources with needs playing a part (a lesser one) in the drama. They did not want to emphasize a deficit approach even though it was going to be looked at and tied to assets. Needs were there, but assets and strengths were more pronounced. While this isn't an equal balance, it isn't negative, and as stressed in the first chapters, if you cannot achieve that stance, it is better to begin with assets.

Another observation is that this book was published somewhat after all of the located studies were completed. Therefore, they would not be expected to fit totally with the substance of a proposed framework. A more serious consideration is whether the two approaches can be included in one investigation without compromising basic tenets. Can an involved group (community members, staff from an organization, facilitators) be open to needs and assets and resources at the same time? That could be studied empirically. If access to a project could be gained as it was starting, involved individuals might be interviewed about their perceptions. Do they think that needs assessment and the identification of assets and resources are in opposition? Does it really matter or affect learning about their environment? As noted before, when beginning with assets, needs are there—a perception of discrepancy exists. It simply can't be avoided. Here is where we are now, and here is where we want to be or should be.

Other concerns about the overall framework are that it might be upsetting to those with strong needs assessment or asset orientations, that it may be better for some specialized areas, and how it came into existence. Taking these in order, the author was a strong adherent of needs assessment before diving into the literature. He still holds many of those values, but his views have broadened, and in a hybrid study it is important to heed the positive message coming from assets. Needs are deficits, and a heavy focus on them can be negative, affecting enthusiasm and motivation. Seeing things that way may not work well. It must be tempered by a "what do we have/what can we do/what are our strengths/what is under our control/what can we undertake," not "what do we expect others to do for us," type of attitude. Acting this way should be embraced and enhance motivation and enthusiasm for progress.

As for the field, the framework may be more apropos for some. Health and related areas appear frequently with regard to blends of methods and approaches. In health, part of one's training is epidemiology, which has elements of needs assessment, database studies looking at deficiencies. In several of the Chapter 7 cases, this is exactly what was implemented along with coming at issues from an assets base. Professionals with such training are attuned to using needs data and almost naturally gravitate toward linking such data to assets. Epidemiology also has a qualitative dimension for determining where a disease comes from and uses both types of data. In seeking causality, researchers go to the field to observe and conduct interviews. It is a natural combination of procedures, and the hybrid is right in line with that stance.

As for how the framework or structure originated, it was synthesized from the literature as a guess of how two distinct camps could be blended together. Admittedly, the synthesizer is into needs assessment, but that is now attenuated and muted with needs assessment and asset/capacity building housed in one structure. What resulted is a hybrid for examining what others have done to see if it would be reasonable. It was an ideal played out against the real world. It was never assumed that all of its eight steps could or should be implemented. Could communities and organizations actually put the whole shebang into operation or think about doing that with the activities and costs that might be required? Rather, here is a scaffolding in order to choose what has the most benefit and relevance for the local context and issues of concern. Conversely, without the framework, the process would be more haphazard.

Research would provide in-depth understandings about how to work across philosophies and methods and push the art of what we do forward via the findings of meaningful studies. Qualitative ones (interviews, document reviews, focus group interviews) immediately come to mind, complemented by surveys. Experimental studies are not too likely, but ex post facto (causal comparative) research would apply.

One last point is that since research will be highly dependent on records and documentation, it is imperative that local groups keep them when investigating their settings. If a committee is small and grassroots, it is much to assume that this will always be done. Still, groups should be encouraged to do so. For formal endeavors with external funding and professional staff, the likelihood of records increases. External funding usually requires that written reports be supplied to the sponsors.

In all instances, a good idea is that records and products be dated to keep track of what transpired. The dates help to show how ideas and discussions evolved and what outcomes were realized at what times. If there are summary tables (like Table 3.3), they will demonstrate what the group did, the kinds of information and sources tapped into, and what was produced. Documentation is an audit trail from inception to completion. It is invaluable for evaluation, going from Step 8 to Step 1, and for later groups to review when they use the hybrid framework.

STEP 1. SCOPING THE CONTEXT (TABLE 9.1, ROW 2)

There are many things to think about here. How do these enterprises begin, and how are they sustained? Do they come from an assets base or from needs (even if just a sense of needs)? Is there a guiding vision, and whose is it? What is the nature of those involved? What was done? What kinds of information gathering were undertaken? Did they get off on the right foot? How did they keep making progress? If they failed, what contributed to that outcome? How do internal and external actors work together? Is a one-sided relationship present? Is it internally led or externally directed? Have partnerships been created with mutual trust and shared input? A few of these questions will be discussed.

What Is the Impetus for Hybrid Work?

Impetus relates to a nebulous yet important concept called "vision." The coach (Nick Saban) of what is recognized as the most successful college football program in the country was interviewed and stated that

> you've got to have a vision . . . you've got to have a plan to implement it. Then you've got to set the example . . . , develop the principles and values that are important, and get people to buy into it. (O'Keefe, 2012)

This is how the improvement or development might begin. What is vision? Is it a need (a deficit, a deficiency)? Is it seeing assets and possibilities? Is it both? It is difficult to define, but it is a necessary *je ne sais quoi* condition for getting going (see Exhibit 9.1).

Exhibit 9.1 A Real-Life Example of Vision

Recently my wife and I were visiting our youngest son who lives in a major western U.S. city. He is minor partner in a just-opened neighborhood bar and grill business. We saw it and were impressed with the ambience that he and his partners created and with the fact that in just over four months it was doing well in patronage and becoming recognized in the locality. When we were at the establishment, we met one of the major partners, its guiding light. He has kept meticulous records.

He showed me a photographic, chronological catalog of what it originally looked like so that I could see what it was now and how far it had come. The difference was striking and a testament to his vision and the sweat equity invested by the partners. To put it bluntly, if putting capital into the original property was based on what was there, the author would not have offered any funds—the need was too large. The place was run-down (seedy) and required much refurbishing and renewal. I'm a needs assessor, not an asset/capacity builder. So what did he see?

He is both a visionary and a realistic person coming from a business program in a local university. He had been a successful marketer for a chain of similar establishments and wanted to branch out on his own. He saw what it would take to bring the building to a level where it would be a functioning, viable enterprise. The need was apparent, and he was cognizant of it as discerned from our conversation.

But a stronger factor was a view of "what could be," a usual part of needs assessment but one subsumed in a vision. It was an opportunity and something that I feel most others, particularly I, would not have seen. It consisted of location and visibility (on a main street), parking along the side of the building, room for two outdoor patios and activities for use when weather permitted, and some indications of how the inside of the building might be reconfigured so that a local neighborhood bar might be transformed into a meeting and fun place. There are numerous rooms, so if one wants to mingle with other patrons, it is easy to do.

It is now a reality, not a vision. Yes, there was a discrepancy (a deficit) that was tempered by a vision. Is this needs, assets, or a natural merging of the two? The last part of the sentence is an accurate depiction of the process.

One researchable aspect of the hybrid is how it begins. Who are the key players, and how do they perceive the local context? What brought them to the table, and what knowledge and understanding do they bring to the discourse? What do they consider, and what do they not know that they would like to find out? If we could understand these features, they would represent a kind of learning that would be transportable to similar circumstances.

Internal Versus External: Which One?

In the perfect world, an internal group would coalesce around a desire to improve or change in some way. The members of this group would become the hub around which initial activities occur. They make the key decisions about directions. They specify questions to ask and the information sources to be looked at, collect data, interpret what was obtained, and determine how what they found could be utilized. This is the core working group, which would tend to be small in number at the start and expand later as the steps in the framework unfold and are achieved.

External involvement is quite different from above. It is not to make decisions, although advice and guidance from consultants and others is acceptable so long as it does not usurp local decision making. In terms of the framework, decisions are the province of the bottom-up constituency and are not top down or directed by outsiders.

In the cases in Chapters 7 and 8, that did not take place. In the health examples, the investigations were outsider led, but the voice of the community was notably there. There was a partnership on this internal-external continuum between outsiders conducting the study and those who provided information, often interpreted data, and helped to make decisions. This represents a departure from traditional needs assessment and is halfway toward the empowerment philosophy of asset/capacity building. How to characterize what is seen in practice? We could see situations where heavy external control could go to the point of being resented by internal, local constituents. Like in Figure 9.1, it is a tug of war between the sides.

In Figure 9.2, a balanced relationship between external and internal participants is occurring. It isn't a competitive turf war; instead, they see each other as contributors to possible ways to improve. Each group values the other one.

What does this say in regard to bottom-up initiation and decision making? It is something to aspire to—self-determination is a pillar of our society and ethos. This may take place, and it is good when it does. Actual practice may not work like this. The demands of collecting and analyzing data, as well as the necessity of organizing to do so and eventually to take action, suggest that an alternative stance is what happens. An external group has leadership in hybrid work, but community constituencies and/or organization staff are involved. Usually the external consultants and facilitators are funded for data collection, the design of procedures and instruments, analysis, interpretation, and the generation of reports. The community or staff members are not, so this is a way to proceed and ensure that the project is completed.

But it should be approached from an asset perspective. In a number of the studies in the prior two chapters, the people from whom data

Figure 9.1 The External-Internal Tug of War

Source: Thinkstock/ Digital Vision

Figure 9.2 The External-Internal Positive Collaboration

Source: Can Stock Photo Inc. / 4774344sean

and information were obtained were not targets or subjects (a negative connotation if there ever was one); rather, they are integral to the hybrid framework. Their roles go way beyond just providing data. They are collaborators in the best sense of the word. This requires careful planning on how to get the community to buy into the process with decisions based on input from all involved parties. What an area for research!

How well does this work? What factors impede, and what factors facilitate? Have people been questioned about how decision making was handled and if their voices were heard? How much extra time does it take to foster interactions that include everyone? What are the drawbacks to doing this—can efforts require too much time with the subsequent loss of enthusiasm and motivation? Much should be done to expand knowledge in this area.

What Does Scoping Require in Terms of Information?

We live in a world with almost instantaneous access to information. To "Google" is now a verb.

With that understanding, what does the initiating group require in terms of data to have a feel for assets and needs? The answer varies. Some issues are complex and demand much information; others are straight-forward, so less will be sought. Doing retrospective surveys would provide keen insights. Respondents would reflect on when the project started, what kinds of information were available, what was most useful, what influenced decisions, what was not useful, and why. Data could be collected across an array of efforts of small and wide scope and of short- and long-term duration. Reports could be scrutinized for what was actually obtained and when. If dated tables and summaries were kept, they would be a treasure trove of what happened. Data sources could be sorted into classes in accord with different situations and settings. Descriptive results would be invaluable for groups deciding to start a hybrid process.

Finally, from the cases in Chapters 7 and 8, only a small set of methods were employed for Step 1, and they were implemented one time or once in a while with some follow-up. Surveys, individual interviews, focus group interviews, analyses of existing databases or reports emanating from same, observations, and identifying assets and resources were noted. Other methods were not so prominent. Combinations of these techniques seemed to afford sufficient depth for local investigations, and doing more would have been a waste of precious resources.

STEP 2. DECIDING WHAT ACTIONS SHOULD BE TAKEN (TABLE 9.1, ROW 3)

Decisions for action occur earlier in the literature than later as in the hybrid framework. Since most of the located studies were highly focused, supported by external funds from concerned organizations, and often carried out by consultants, the full framework may be too much. How do groups make their decisions, what information do they attend to, and how do they synthesize qualitative and quantitative data into meaningful understandings? How do they transform what has been learned into strategies for action and improvement? What are the procedures that guide deliberations? (See techniques for research suggested earlier.)

One interesting facet of the cases was who participated in the decision process. Those studied and for whom programs and projects would be developed were not bystanders to what was being considered. They were part of assigning meaning to collected data and were included meaningfully in the discussion of new directions. By survey or interview, it would be interesting to probe how the deliberations went. For facilitators, how well did discussions proceed, to what degree were all players involved, what were the issues that came up, what concerns were voiced, what problems were encountered, how were they resolved, how efficient was the process, what were the advantages and disadvantages of involving many in decision making, if they had to do this over what should be changed, and so forth? When decisions are made, what sort of follow-up should there be with participants?

For participants, how well did the discussion go, did they feel all parties were equally valued for input, did they feel welcomed at the session, did decisions reflect everyone's ideas, were reasonable choices made, how would they rate the quality of this part of their involvement, and so forth? What sort of continued involvement would be good for the community or organization? Who (what groups or individuals) should be responsible for new initiatives? Do they have any misgivings about what might happen in the future?

Since most of the cases were pursuing decision making this way, it would be a fruitful avenue for research into the heartbeat of the needs assessment and asset/capacity-building endeavor. It could demonstrate how to foster collaborative partnerships that enhance community or organizational endeavors for betterment.

STEPS 3–5. THE NEXT SEVERAL STEPS (TABLE 9.1, ROWS 4–6)

Step 3. Dividing the working committee into two subcommittees

Step 4. Conducting the assessment in greater depth

Step 5. Using what has been learned to make decisions for possible new programs

From what was reviewed, not much of these activities were done. That may be due to the restrictions that journals put on manuscript length or the resources that the local investigations could devote to documenting and reporting all activities. Only so much can be summarized given time constraints and the purpose for which reports are used and audiences for them. Whatever the reasons, it is assumed that the steps may only be part of a long effort for large organizations or a sizable entity (city, community). The rejuvenation of German Village is an example in contrast to the shorter one from Bali in Chapter 7. Doing all steps would take a lot of funding and personnel.

To study such activities would entail identifying large, ongoing project entities and obtaining their records; still, it could be difficult to discern the steps. They may be there in pieces or embedded in prior or subsequent events or not labeled. They may have occurred but be buried in older files. On the other hand, if researchers independently reviewing records came up with similar findings, it would tend to verify the framework's utility.

Another way to collect data could be from interviews of those who had been involved over time or quite a ways back. If they are of the latter condition, they might not recall, might inaccurately recall, or might attune their memories to mesh with current perceptions, resulting in conclusions that are less accurate, yet their perspectives would offer insights into what happened. If the time period is very long, there are worries about mortality as a source of invalidity as some may have moved, may no longer be accessible, or may have passed away. Researchers are always advised to corroborate findings from such interviews via archived sources.

STEP 6. DEVELOPING A STRATEGY FOR IMPROVEMENT (TABLE 9.1, ROW 7)

It was gratifying to find case studies of hybrids that led to positive changes in the local situation. If this doesn't occur, why do this work?

It takes energy and determination to carry it out, and patience is needed. In most of the cases, plans or strategies were developed and results achieved. It is not clear that all outcomes can be attributed to the hybrid framework. In one situation, what was learned helped local areas to compete and successfully get additional funds. In another, it began a mechanism for much more visible local involvement. Ultimately, the test of the framework is whether it produces results that might not be realized without its implementation. That implies a controlled experiment with a manipulated variable, which strains credibility. What is more likely is that plans would be obtained and examined in light of knowledge emanating from the local investigation. Then questions such as the following could be asked:

- What specifically was found about assets and needs?
- Is there evidence that it led to the strategy for improvement and change?
- Is the purpose of the plan directly related to the needs or problems identified?
- Is the voice of the community or organization staff prominent in the plans, and is it recognizable and notable?
- Does what has been planned link to what was learned, and does it grow from that base?
- Does it concretely take advantage of the identified assets and resources?
- Is the fabric of the community or organization strengthened by building bridges across groups and services?
- Does the plan include timelines and responsibilities for getting things accomplished?
- What is the nature of the leadership for the plan, and how do the leaders relate to the key partnering groups and actors and players within them?
- Are there enough resources to get the job done?
- Is there a slow incremental start followed by gradual expansion?
- If growth is considered, what will it take to ramp up to a larger scale?
- Is the community a solid, not a superficial, part of the project or program?
- Is collaboration across groups in the environment evident?
- Are there provisions for evaluation that include formatively monitoring activities and collecting data about outcomes?

- Do the evaluation data contain indicators from constituencies regarding what they think the project might produce?
- Overall, is the plan feasible, and will it function as designed?
- What are its weakest points?
- Do we sense where it might fail, and what we should pay special attention to?
- Has any causal analysis been undertaken so that focus can be directed toward possible failure spots?

Once the researchers selected questions, they would rate what communities and organizations had done along with any comments made about the plans. These could be collated across projects to see if patterns emerged. What are the characteristics of large-scale, long-term proposed efforts? Do they resemble or differ from smaller ones? What aspects of plans do not seem to be there? Do plans have evaluation activities that will help promote an understanding of their operations and how they might or might not be contributing to success?

Such information would be important to know, for almost everyone at some time has been part of a collective process to do something new. Some of these have gone well, and when they do not, it is a turnoff, making it more difficult to engage in such activities again. What happened that reduced effectiveness? Undoubtedly, some of this may be due to personalities, and there may not be much that could be done about that. Or we haven't taken into account contingencies, places where what should happen simply doesn't happen. Translating assets and needs into a change that empowers and energizes a group is a particularly good thing to do. Investigating what others have done should pay high dividends in that regard in the future.

STEPS 7 AND 8. THE LAST ONES (TABLE 9.1, ROWS 8 AND 9)

Step 7. Implementing and evaluating the action plan

Step 8. Recycling back to first steps for expanding the improvement package

Underlying these steps is the concept of sustainability. How well has our improvement strategy worked? What can evaluation data tell us?

Who benefited, and in what ways did they grow or change? Will the effort still be there after the initial use? Were unintended positive or negative results noted? Will the effort continue, who will fund it, and who will be the implementers? What improvements should be made? How can we leverage off of it, and what should the expanded program look like?

Has a foundation been established for going from our initial platform to an extended one? Is the community or organization now a learning organism that adapts to its context and changes happening around it?

Have we gone back to our beginning considerations of needs and assets? What has not been attended to, and why? The original fact-finding was done earlier—does it still apply to current conditions, or is the information too old? We uncovered a lot of resources and assets before—how can we capitalize on them? Could we leverage what was found earlier? How should we organize to keep up momentum? Are we in a position to secure other resources for doing more of the job? If our new project has been successful, how can we get the word out about it? Should the initiating group be expanded to help us proceed into the future?

Here is where we should look at contexts in which there is a long history of using needs and assets to change directions. What would be necessary to continue the hybrid framework beyond the current point? Here it might again be useful to interview those who have been involved over a lengthy period of time.

What was it like in the early days, and how has the group evolved?

What were the major events—things that set the tone for keeping things in motion?

What were successes, and what were the failures or less-than-stellar outcomes?

What records were kept, and what can be gleaned from them?

In terms of personalities, who were the driving forces?

Reflecting on what happened, what major events or points in the life of the collective were the high points, and why?

What were the low points, and were there moments when continuation was questionable?

What is generated would be a historical record. History is important since it informs the future. It also provides perspective and proportion. If the archives and files are available, they can be displayed in the community or organization in prominent locations. Assuredly, they will attract attention.

The author lives in a large city that is celebrating its 200th birthday. The local newspaper has run photo essays showing what was and what is now. These are fascinating to see and help us to think about what might lie ahead.

RESEARCH ACROSS ALL STEPS— ABOUT METHODS (THE WHOLE TABLE)

Research is done to describe phenomena, test propositions, seek causality, and develop new understandings. Methods are descriptive, relational, and for causality experimental. Even though experimentation could be embedded in some procedures, for the most part manipulating variables in the hybrid context is debatable. Surveys, interviews, and analysis of records and documentation would mainly be employed, and causal comparative studies would be seen much more than experimental ones. Thus assigning causality to variables is difficult, and subjective judgment would be in play. We cannot say that this variable or that one was a critical factor in success or failure. This viewpoint is too restrictive, for when multiple cases are studied, much can be learned.

If independent reviews came to the same conclusions, it would be suggestive of how collective activities function. This follows a canon of proof proposed by John Stuart Mill; that is, if you see events and the same pattern or sequence is there across them, then they are connected through some aspect of causality. Replication partially compensates for lack of experimental control. Support for research into uses of the hybrid framework should be sought—from the author's point of view it would pay off.

UTILIZATION, A RECURRING AND SUBTLE THEME

Throughout, utilization of hybrid results is woven into the fabric of the text. Does the process lead to betterment for people, communities, and organizations? Is there a direct link to action? That is one understanding of the term, and in many of the cases there is direct evidence that this occurred. In Philadelphia, Scotland, Houston, and others, improvements were being made, and the lives of people were being affected. We want to see this, and without it, it would be difficult to support the hybrid framework. We might conclude that it was a good idea in theory but in practice it did not amount to much that was worthwhile. It is rewarding that results were realized, but the above connotation of utilization is insufficient, too narrow, too confined.

What was observed was more in the way of one-time changes or short-term ones, even if the specific programs and efforts continued over time. A broader meaning was noted in the Scottish papers where resilient communities were described. They were ones who learned to cope with adversity and could bounce back from it and keep perspective. This point was buttressed by the case in the United Kingdom where some communities seemed to have a leg up in being experienced and organized to deal with troubling situations.

There is a kind of subtle community or organizational learning that plays a critical role in progress. It is a *sine qua non* that has to be there or be capable of being developed for optimum implementation of the hybrid approach. If it isn't, the process just doesn't come off well, and less-than-stellar results are obtained.

Indeed, in one of the cases the investigators expressed dismay that they did not leave in place a strong enough infrastructure for the community to continue and expand upon what was begun.

This is an alternative way to think about utilization. Have the communities and groups grown in how they plan and contemplate moving forward now that they have investigated assets and needs? Are they different in this regard? Have they matured in the manner in which they capitalize on strengths and apply them to gaps or to new, unanticipated ventures? Will this mind-set generalize to future efforts? This is more difficult to measure, yet seems to be of greater importance than the outcome at the beginning of this section. There are almost covert indications in some of the cases that this is really what needs to take place. Success is to be judged not just in the short run but later as the group moves to new endeavors and should be a focus for research. A gestalt has been established in the collective, and it has been enabled to deal with problems and become adaptive. It has a mechanism (the hybrid) for building better communities and organizations. That is the ultimate goal and the one for which we should strive.

HIGHLIGHTS OF CHAPTER 9

1. The chapter began by noting that questions have been embedded in the text, with many related to research that could be conducted on the hybrid framework.

2. Table 9.1 was offered to raise issues about the framework and its steps. It contained some methods that could be used to study hybrid usage and comments about the potential value of findings that might be produced.

3. Each table entry was discussed with ideas as to studies that might be conducted. These were teasers to pique the interest of others, and to foster a conversation about learning more about the hybrid.

4. A few comments were made about methods for conducting studies.

5. The chapter closed with a note about utilization.

DISCUSSION QUESTIONS

Since the goal is to foster probing the hybrid framework, it would be redundant to pose any more questions except for the following point. The hybrid is a formulation, an educated guess of what might take place when doing a combined approach. It is hoped that the framework will engender more examples of its use, which in turn will inform and improve practice. If the text has sparked further interest in a restructured or different schema, that would be a most positive result. The reader is encouraged to think about alternatives and then to push understandings further along.

Please join in the journey!

References

Agricultural Utilization Research Institute (with Spaeth, T., Larson, N., & Wagner-Lahr, J.). (in press). *Overview: Research & promotion council forum* (AURI's approach to convene Minnesota's research and promotion councils to prioritize the agricultural industry's research needs). Minnesota.

Altschuld, J. W. (2004). Emerging dimensions of needs assessment. *Performance Improvement, 43*(1), 10–15.

Altschuld, J. W. (2010a). *Needs assessment: Collecting data.* Thousand Oaks, CA: Sage.

Altschuld, J. W. (Ed.). (2010b). *The needs assessment kit.* Thousand Oaks, CA: Sage.

Altschuld, J. W., & Eastmond, J. N., Jr. (2010). *Needs assessment: Getting the process started.* Thousand Oaks, CA: Sage.

Altschuld, J. W., & Hamann, M. S. (2012, October). *Overlooked dimensions in needs assessment surveys.* Demonstration session at the Annual Conference of the American Evaluation Association, Minneapolis, MN.

Altschuld, J. W., & Hung, H.-L. (2012). *Handouts for North Dakota Needs Assessment Workshop.* Grand Forks: College of Education, University of North Dakota.

Altschuld, J. W., & Kumar, D. D. (2010). *Needs assessment: An overview.* Thousand Oaks, CA: Sage.

Altschuld, J. W., & Lepicki, T. L. (2010a). Needs assessment and education. In P. Peterson & E. Baker (Eds.), *The international encyclopedia of education* (3rd ed., pp. 786–791). Oxford, England: Elsevier.

Altschuld, J. W., & Lepicki, T. L. (2010b). Needs assessment in human performance interventions. In R. Watkins & D. Leigh (Eds.), *The handbook for the selection and implementation of human performance interventions* (Chapter 32). San Francisco, CA: Jossey-Bass.

Altschuld, J. W., & White, J. L. (2010). *Needs assessment: Analysis and prioritization.* Thousand Oaks, CA: Sage.

Altschuld, J. W., & Witkin, B. R. (2000). *From needs assessment to action: Transforming needs into solution strategies.* Thousand Oaks, CA: Sage.

APS Group. (2011). *Commission on the future delivery of public services.* Edinburgh, Scotland: Author.

Baizerman, M., Compton, D. W., & Stockdill, S. H. (2005). Capacity building. In S. Mathison (Ed.), *Encyclopedia of evaluation* (pp. 38–39). Thousand Oaks, CA: Sage.

Balogh, R., Whitelaw, S., & Thompson, J. (2008). Rapid needs appraisal in the modern NHS: Potential and dilemmas. *Critical Public Health, 18*(2), 233–244.

Boyle, D., & Harris, M. (2009). *The challenges of co-production.* Discussion paper, NESTA, London.

Bradshaw, J. (1972). The concept of social need. *New Society, 30*(1), 640–643.

British Museum. (2011). *Journey through the afterlife: Ancient Egyptian Book of the Dead.* Retrieved from http://www.britishmuseum.org/channel/exhibitions/2011/book_of_the_dead.aspx

Brooks, D. (2012, May 2). Candidates should hang up the gloves, focus on strengths. *The Columbus Dispatch,* p. A11.

Bush, B. (2012, December 23). Schools' grad-rate increase in doubt. *The Columbus Dispatch,* pp. A1, A6.

Bush, B., & Ferenchik, M. (2012, December 22). Audit stirs reaction, but school board not up in arms. *The Columbus Dispatch,* pp. A1, A5.

Bush, B., & Smith-Richards, J. (2012, June 15). Schools probe attendance figures. *The Columbus Dispatch,* pp. A1, A8.

The CADISPA Trust. (2013). *About us.* Retrieved from http://www.cadispa.org/

Carnegie UK Trust. (2011). *Exploring community resilience in times of rapid change.* Dunfermline, Scotland: Fiery Spirits Community of Practice.

Centers for Disease Control and Prevention. (2013a, June 26). *National Health and Nutrition Examination Survey 2001–2002.* Retrieved from http://wwwn.cdc.gov/nchs/nhanes/search/nhanes01_02.aspx

Centers for Disease Control and Prevention. (2013b, June 26). *National Health and Nutrition Examination Survey 2003–2004.* Retrieved from http://wwwn.cdc.gov/nchs/nhanes/search/nhanes03_04.aspx

Centers for Disease Control and Prevention/National Center for Health Statistics. (2013). *About the National Health and Nutrition Examination Survey.* Retrieved from http://www.cdc.gov/nchs/nhanes/about_nhanes.htm

Chiasera, J. M. (2005). *Examination of the determinants of overweight and diabetes mellitus in U.S. children from the 1999–2002.* Unpublished dissertation, The Ohio State University, Columbus.

Chiasera, J. M., Taylor, C. A., Wolf, K. N., & Altschuld, J. W. (2008). *Correlates of diabetes in U.S. children from the 1999–2002 National Health and Nutrition Survey.* Unpublished manuscript.

Coleman, M. B. (2013, May). City has taken its first steps toward fixing schools. *The Columbus Dispatch,* p. E9.

Donnermeyer, J. V., Plested, B. A., Edwards, R. W., Oetting, G., & Littlethunder, L. (1997). Community readiness and prevention programs. *Journal of the Community Development Society, 28*(1), 65–83.

Downey, L., & Anyaegbunam, C. (2010). Your lives through your eyes: Rural Appalachian youth identify community needs and assets through the use of photovoice. *Journal of Appalachian Studies, 16*(1&2), 42–61.

Edwards, R. W., Thurman, P. J., Plested, B. A., Oetting, E. R., & Swanson, L. (2000). *Journal of Community Psychology, 28*(3), 291–307.

Ferenchik, M. (2012, December 22). Preserving more. *The Columbus Dispatch,* pp. B1–B2.

Fetterman, D. (2005). Empowerment evaluation. In S. Mathison (Ed.), *Encyclopedia of evaluation* (pp. 38–39). Thousand Oaks, CA: Sage.

Friedman, T. (2013, January). Collaboration is the key to success. *The Columbus Dispatch,* p. A9.

Garfield, R., Blake, C., Chatainger, P., & Walton-Ellery, S. (2011). Common needs assessment and humanitarian action. Network Paper, *Humanitarian Practice Network, Overseas Development Institute,* London, England.

Gupta, K., Sleezer, C. M., & Russ-Eft, D. F. (2007). *A practical guide to needs assessment.* San Francisco, CA: Pfeiffer.

Hamann, M. S. (1997). *The effects of instrument design and respondent characteristics on perceived needs.* Unpublished doctoral dissertation, The Ohio State University, Columbus.

Hansen, D. J. (1991). *An empirical study of the structure of needs assessment.* Unpublished doctoral dissertation, The Ohio State University, Columbus.

Harvard Family Research Project. (2013). *Out-of-school time.* Retrieved from http://www.hfrp.org/out-of-school-time

Hausman, A. J., Siddons, K., & Becker, J. (2000). Using community perspectives on youth firearm violence for prevention programming. *Journal of Community Psychology, 28*(6), 643–654.

Hung, H.-L., Altschuld, J. W., & Lee, Y.-F. (2008). Methodological and conceptual issues confronting a cross-country Delphi study of educational program evaluation. *Evaluation and Program Planning, 31*(2), 191–198.

Hunt, M. H., Meyers, J., Davies, O., Meyers, B., Rogers, K. G., & Neel, J. (2001). A comprehensive needs assessment to facilitate prevention of school drop-out and violence. *Psychology in the Schools, 39*(4), 399–416.

Iutcovich, J. M. (1993). Assessing the needs of rural elderly: An empowerment model. *Evaluation and Program Planning, 16,* 95–107.

Kamis, E. (1979). A witness for the defense of need assessment. *Evaluation and Program Planning, 2*(1), 7–12.

Kaufman, R. (1987). A needs assessment primer: A ten-step approach to help even beginners with this necessary, yet often dreaded task. *Performance and Instructional Journal,* October, 78–83.

Kaufman, R. (1992). *Strategic planning plus: An organizational guide.* Thousand Oaks, CA: Sage.

Kaufman, R., & Guerra-Lopez, I. (2013). *Needs assessment.* Alexandria, VA: ASTD.

Kretzmann, J. P., & McKnight, J. L. (1993). *Building communities from the inside out.* Chicago, IL: ACTA Publications.

Lauffer, A. (1982). *Assessment tools: For practitioners, managers, and trainers.* Beverly Hills, CA: Sage.

Lee, J. (2013). Heart study to enroll 1 million smartphone users worldwide. *The Week in Healthcare,* Technology. Retrieved from http://www.modernhealth care.com/

Lee, Y.-F. (2005). *Effects of multiple groups' involvement on identifying and interpreting perceived needs.* Unpublished doctoral dissertation, The Ohio State University, Columbus.

Lee, Y.-F., Altschuld, J. W., & White, J. L. (2007). Effects of the participation of multiple stakeholders in identifying and interpreting perceived needs. *Evaluation and Program Planning, 30*(1), 1–9.

Lepicki, T., Glandon, A., & Mullins, D. (2013). *ABLE Partnership Evaluation Model.* The Ohio State University, College of Education and Human Ecology, The Center on Education and Training for Employment. Retrieved from http://www.cete.org/projects/able/partnership-evaluation-model.php

Man, L., & Mandel, L. (2012). *Through the eyes of older adults: Using photovoice to understand volunteers.* Poster presentation at the Annual Conference of the American Evaluation Association, Minneapolis, MN.

McDavid, J. C., Huse, I., & Hawthorn, L. R. L. (2012). *Program evaluation and performance measurement: An introduction to practice.* Thousand Oaks, CA: Sage.

McKillip, J. (1987). *Needs analysis: Tools for the human services and education.* Thousand Oaks, CA: Sage.

Neuber, K. A., & Associates. (1980). Needs assessment: A model for community planning. *Human Services Guide, 14,* Beverly Hills, CA: Sage.

Neves, A. V. (2011, July 19). *Spaces and behavior: The CPTED approach.* Workshop presented to the professionals of city council via the initiative of the municipal police, Lisbon, Portugal.

Neves, A. V. (2013, January 30). *Collaboration in my research.* Informal e-mail survey sent to colleagues for rating components of crime prevention through environmental design.

Norton, R. E. (2011, Summer). DACUM International Training Center at CETE/OSU. *Centergram,* pp. 1, 4.

Nutt, P. C., & Backoff, R. W. (1992). *Strategic management of public and third sector organizations: A handbook for leaders.* San Francisco, CA: Jossey-Bass.

O'Keefe, B. (2012, September 24). Leadership lessons from Nick Saban. *Fortune.* Retrieved from http://money.cnn.com/

Pepall, E., Earnest, J., & James, R. (2006). Understanding community perceptions of health and social needs in a rural Balinese village: Results of a rapid participatory appraisal. *Health Promotion International, 22*(1), 44–52.

Siegel, J. (2012, June). Collaboration gets innovation loan. *The Columbus Dispatch,* p. B7.

Smith-Richards, J. (2013, January). Grades were changes, too. *The Columbus Dispatch,* pp. A1, A5.

Sork, T. J. (1998). Program priorities, purposes, and objectives. In P. S. Cookson (Ed.), *Program planning for training and continuing education of adults: North American perspectives* (pp. 273–300). Malabar, FL: Krieger.

Stevahn, L., & King, J. A. (2010). *Needs assessment: Taking action for change.* Thousand Oaks, CA: Sage.

Stevens, A. B., & Ortega, S. (2011). *Empowerment evaluation toolkit: Determining needs, resources, and capacity.* Columbus: Ohio Domestic Violence Network.

Warheit, G. J., Bell, R. A., & Schwab, J. J. (1979). *Needs assessment approaches: Concepts and methods.* Rockville, MD: National Institute of Mental Health, U.S. Department of Health, Education, and Welfare.

Watkins, R., & Guerra, I. (2002). How do you determine whether assessment or evaluation is required? *ASTD T&D Sourcebook,* pp. 131–139.

Watkins, R., West Meiers, M., & Visser, Y. L. (2012). *A guide to assessing needs.* Washington, DC: International Bank for Reconstruction and Development/International Development Association or the World Bank.

Weintraub, L. S. (1988). "We don't need no ejikayshun": Needs assessment reassessed. *Educational Planning, 6*(4), 24–38.

Weintraub, L. S. (1989). Planning and the cult of positivism: A needs assessment rejoinder. *Educational Planning, 7*(3), 4–12.

Williams, K. J., Bray, P. G., Shapiro-Mendoza, C. K., Reisz, I., & Peranteau, J. (2009). Modeling the principles of community-based participatory research in a community health assessment conducted by a health foundation. *Health Promotion Practice, 10*(1), 67–75.

Witkin, B. R. (1984). *Assessing needs in educational and social programs: Using information to make decisions, set priorities, and allocate resources.* San Francisco, CA: Jossey-Bass.

Witkin, B. R. (1988). To the editor. *Educational Planning, 7*(2), 3–4.

Witkin, B. R. (1992). Is this trip necessary? Needs assessment: A personal memoir and reappraisal. *Educational Planning, 8*(2), 13–33.

Witkin, B. R., & Altschuld, J. W. (1995). *Planning and conducting needs assessments: A practical guide.* Thousand Oaks, CA: Sage.

Woolvin, M. (2012). Mapping the third sector in rural Scotland: An initial review of the literature. *Voluntary Issues: The Scottish Government Social Research Series.* Kew, London, England: The National Archives.

Index

⑤SAGE research**methods**

The essential online tool for researchers from the
world's leading methods publisher

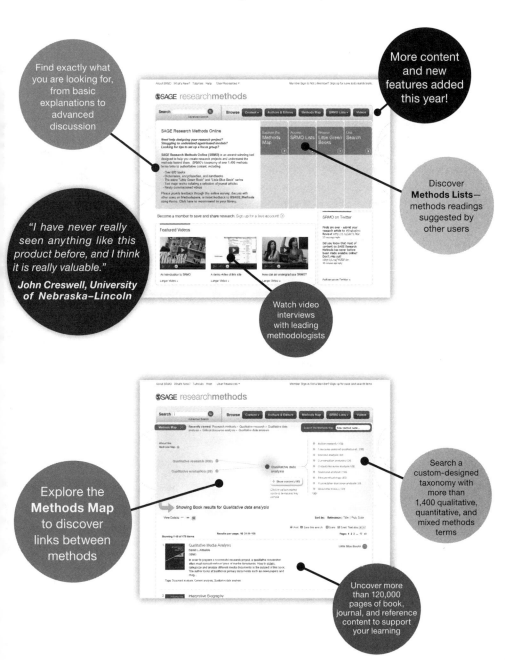

Find exactly what
you are looking for,
from basic
explanations to
advanced
discussion

More content
and new
features added
this year!

"*I have never really
seen anything like this
product before, and I think
it is really valuable.*"
**John Creswell, University
of Nebraska–Lincoln**

Discover
Methods Lists—
methods readings
suggested by
other users

Watch video
interviews
with leading
methodologists

Explore the
Methods Map
to discover
links between
methods

Search a
custom-designed
taxonomy with
more than
1,400 qualitative,
quantitative, and
mixed methods
terms

Uncover more
than 120,000
pages of book,
journal, and reference
content to support
your learning

Find out more at
www.sageresearchmethods.com